The E_____ace:
Rimbaud _____ ___is Commune

Theory and History of Literature
Edited by Wlad Godzich and Jochen Schulte-Sasse

For other books in the series, see p. 171.

The Emergence of

Social Space:

Rimbaud and

the Paris Commune

Kristin Ross

Foreword by Terry Eagleton

Theory and History of Literature, Volume 60

University of Minnesota Press, Minneapolis

Published by the University of Minnesota Press
2037 University Avenue Southeast, Minneapolis MN 55414.
Published simultaneously in Canada
by Fitzhenry & Whiteside Limited, Markham.
Printed in the United States of America.

Library of Congress Cataloging-in-Publication Data

Ross, Kristin.
  The emergence of social space: Rimbaud and the Paris
Commune/Kristin Ross.
      p.   cm. —(Theory and history of literature: v. 60)
  Bibliography: p.
  Includes index.
  ISBN 0-8166-1686-8
  ISBN 0-8166-1687-6 (pbk.)
  1. Rimbaud, Arthur, 1854-1891—Political and social views.
2. Social problems in literature. 3. Space and time in literature.
4. Paris (France)—History—Commune, 1871. 5. Literature and
society—France—History—19th century. 6. City and town life in
literature. I. Title. II. Series.
PQ2387.R5784 1988
821'.8—dc19   88-4205
                                                          CIP

Contents

Foreword
Terry Eagleton

Socialist revolution would seem to demand the impossible not only of the power system it confronts but also of those who carry it through. To execute any profound social transformation calls for a resoluteness of purpose far beyond our customary dim, sporadic perception of ourselves as effective human agents. The revolutionary virtues are those of efficiency and sobriety, organizational capacity, and a readiness for self-sacrifice. Anyone who has taken a realistic measure of the power of the bourgeois state, and believes that such power could be significantly dented without the utmost self-discipline and determination on the part of its antagonists, reveals an enviably sanguine turn of mind.

Yet such revolutionary virtues are, of course, part of the problem as much as of the solution. For it is not difficult to see how they mirror the very system they are supposed to subvert. Resoluteness, efficiency, sobriety, self-sacrifice: if we learn these values at all, we learn them by and large from those whose pockets they help to line. If this is the case, we can turn to a different kind of revolutionary rhetoric entirely and speak not of the resolute, integrated political agent but of the disheveled, decentered one. Revolutions are about the shattering of identities as much as the construction of them, the generation of fantasy and disorder as well as of political constitutions. If they are not, then we probably know just about enough, historically speaking, to predict with some confidence that they will fail—fail, at least, in all the most fundamental ways. *The 18th Brumaire of Louis Bonaparte* finds something inherently theatrical and melodramatic in the great bourgeois revolutions, traced as they are by the play of fantasy, rhetoric and fiction, masking, posturing, and unmasking, a costumed staging and grandiose inflation of the signifier that is always already symbolic, and so easily translated into poetic idiom. *The 18th Brumaire*, one might say, is Marx's major *semiotic* text, all to do with the fissuring of historical signifiers and signifieds, parody and political cross-dressing, the merging of fantasy and reality in the crucible of intensive social change. Revolutions blow the lid off the unconscious in ways no revolutionary program could hope to foresee, releasing a libidinal charge whose relation to determinate social goals will always be ambiguous and uneasy. While the cadres worry about the food supplies, the people shoot at the clocks.

Not all the time, of course. Revolutions, by definition, are made not by the cadres but by the masses; and for this to come about requires on their part just those austere virtues that stand in deeply ambivalent relationship to the aesthetic, somatic, self-pleasuring dimensions of revolutionary insurrection. There seems to me as yet no adequate political model to articulate these two vital moments in some persuasive way. Nobody is greatly enamored these days of the notion of a pure class subject, whole and affirmative in its unitary identity, that has merely to materialize itself in historical practice to come into its own. Such subjects are usually little more than some suitably collectivized version of our old friend the bourgeois humanist subject, who has a stubborn enough history not to yield ground simply by being, so to speak, taken into public ownership. The idealized class subject would always seem to know already exactly what it needed, to be intuitively present to itself in its demands and desires; the political problem is then reduced to the question of its self-objectification, as though such objectification were not the condition of its self-discovery as much as the consequence. This well-bounded, essentialized, self-transparent subject is commonly thought to be the privileged revolutionary candidate of Marxism, though it might be rather more accurate to speak of it as the privileged candidate of a certain early phase of the work of Georg Lucács. The Marxist-Leninist tradition, perhaps these days the most ignorantly travestied of all socialist lineages among so-called radicals, was never quite as conveniently simpleminded as that. Marxist political theory has been all about blocs, alliances, class fractions, cross-class solidarities; what else was the concept of hegemony, widespread in the Second International but known to most only through the writings of Antonio Gramsci, than an attempt to think through the awesome complexity and contradictoriness of a revolutionary process that could never turn on a single isolated agent? As for Leninism, it would have been a little imprudent of the Bolshevik leaders to imagine some pure proletarian essence going it alone, in a society where the proletariat was not only a small minority marooned in an ocean of potentially revolutionary peasants, but disaffection was rife throughout sections of the intelligentsia and the petty bourgeoisie.

No doubt, however, the convenient caricatures of Marxism will continue to be offered; and no doubt too the proper dismissal of a now thoroughly discredited pure class subject will continue to obscure the kernel of truth in this doctrine. If it is politically and epistemologically dubious to dream of some self-composed agent who can already, this side of social change, state precisely what its interior needs and desires are, it is surely equally dubious to ignore the fact that a group of people courageous enough to take on the hardships of profound social disruption, not to speak of the organized brutality of the bourgeois state, must be in some sense self-affirmative. The paradox of revolutionary change is that it provides oppressed peoples with the opportunity to construct an identity for themselves, but that without some such identity already in place that process could never be initiated. Contemporary revolutionary nationalism is surely a case in point. The most sterile brand of such nationalism wishes to throw off imperialist rule in order to assert an already established national identity, whose only flaw is to have been contaminated and repressed by the presence of the colonialists. In an expression/blockage model dear to most Romantic thought, the colonized know already who they are; it is just that the colonialist refuses to listen. A more promising paradigm of revolutionary nationalism appreciates that the antiimperalist question turns on constructing the conditions in which it would be in principle possible for the colonized to find out what they might become, a dilemma over which the imperialists have never lost much sleep. Yet how is a people entirely bereft of culture, identity, and indigenous will to achieve anything as formidable as that?

If the untainted class subject is to be rejected, then, it should perhaps be with a modicum of caution. The alternative revolutionary paradigm to which we can then turn, that of the fractured, libidinal, disordered subject, involves equivalent gains and losses. Few oversights have more drastically impoverished Marxism than its deafness to the libertarian tradition. It is not so much, perhaps, that Marxism has denied the important truths of this heritage, as that it has perilously deferred them. Pleasure, desire, anarchic revolt, the illegible, unincorporable, and inarticulable: these things will have their moment, after the main business of the day has been concluded—except, of course, that such business will then never be concluded, or even substantially advanced. Marxism has long been aware that there is an infantile disorder known as instant gratification, which constitutes a living insult to those men and women throughout the annals of socialist struggle who were heroically prepared to sacrifice their own happiness for the sake of others. A readiness to defer gratification, to look with suspicion on those who convert revolution to their own private consumptional ends, is surely not in itself to be upbraided. To characterize revolution, as Raymond Williams has done, as an essentially *tragic* process is to recall the sober truth that there will always be those, more dedicated and selfless than oneself, who refuse to endorse the values of pleasure and bodily well-being until the conditions have been created in which these values may be available for all. It is quite another thing, however, to turn this admirable stance into the scelerotic dogmatism that would see nothing in the richness of libertarianism but irresponsible self-indulgence.

Perhaps, then, the revolutionary subject we are searching for is the delirious subject-in-process of the early *Tel Quel*, fragmented into ecstatic nonidentity by revolutionary desire. This will certainly safeguard us from the alarmingly replete subject of a certain Marxist theory; the only problem is that such an agent, in some of its versions at least, would hadly seem self-collected enough to topple a bottle off a wall, let alone bring down the state. It is necessary for us to "aestheticize" the revolutionary process, and it is equally essential for us to do nothing of the sort. On the one hand, revolution is for the fulfillment of the men and women who make it; on the other hand, the hypostasizing of revolutionary action as some magnificent end in itself, with all the self-generative, self-validating nature of the work of art, returns us to the dangerous mythologizing of Georges Sorel and the early Walter Benjamin.

How is the revolutionary subject to be tensed and spaced out, centered and decentered, sober and drunk, German and French, at one and the same time? What is the ratio within revolutionary action of ego and id, prose and poetry? It is on these questions that Kristin Ross's coruscating study of Arthur Rimbaud and the Paris Commune may shed some light.

The Commune, as Kristin Ross reminds us, was certainly no carnival. Some twenty-five thousand insurgents were dead on the streets of Paris in May 1871, more than in any of the battles of the Franco-Prussian war. Yet if it was not a carnival, it shared certain carnivalesque features, as this study brilliantly demonstrates. More than most classical revolutions, the Commune was a question of the rapid, dizzying transformation of everyday life, a dramatic upheaval in commonplace understandings of time and space, identity and language, work and leisure. The material preconditions for this lay in the nature of the insurrection itself. For the Commune, if one may risk the tautology, was a peculiarly *political* revolution, in a highly political society. Its base lay not in heavy industry and an organized large-scale proletariat, but in the seizing, defense, and transformation of a *place*, a city, a sector of "civil society" where men and women lived and congregated, traveled and talked. It was a revolt not so much within the means of production, rooted in factory soviets and a revolutionary working-class party, as one within the means of life themselves. It was a revolution out on the streets from the start, an uprising for which the bone of revolutionary contention was the streets themselves, rather than the streets as a front-line defense of a proletarian seizure of capital. It was thus a peculiarly *mobile*, multiple affair, in which what mattered was the citizen rather than the producer, the political issue of control over everyday culture as a whole rather than the protection and promotion of a more narrowly conceived class identity. What the various subordinate groups, classes, and class fractions had in common was precisely the besieged bastion of Paris, of a space that belonged to them all; and there could consequently be a constant traffic across the class lines between worker and artisan, revolutionary women and disaffected literati.

It is precisely this constant movement of transgression, of the dismantling and remapping of social and physical space, that lies near the heart of Ross's account. The Commune raises its fist against conventional spatial hierarchies—between distinct Parisian *quartiers*, country and city, and, by implication, that global carve-up of terrain between France the imperial metropolis and its client colonies. But this confounding and ''horizontalizing'' of hierarchies, for which Ross's symbolic index is the Communards' demolition of the Vendôme Column, forces its way into the sphere of cultural production too, interrogating the assumed distinctions between worker, artist, and artisan, and collapsing received oppositions within discourse between high art and popular *reportage*, poetic and political, the venerable and the vernacular. The event of the Commune emerges in this light as an early theatrical instance of what we now know as the avant-garde, as the mantle of an Arthur Rimbaud passes to Mayakovski and on to Bertolt Brecht.

Rimbaud, for Ross, is the poet of the Commune, which is no doubt one reason why a hermetically textual avant-garde in our own time has managed by some curious oversight to edit him out of their canon. To view him as the poet of the Commune is not, however, to engage in empirical scholarly debate about whether he actually leaned on a barricade on some particular Wednesday morning. The Commune forms the substance of much of Rimbaud's work, not as content or explicit reference, but as tumult, transgression, mobility, hyperbole, leveling, hypersensoriness, iconoclasm. Political history inscribes itself in the very force fields of his texts, between the lines and within the rhythms, in the whole kind of astonishing practice they are, rather than as some empirical background against which they can be measured. And to say this is to claim that this remarkable study does for Arthur Rimbaud what Walter Benjamin, in his great *Passagenarbeit*, did for Charles Baudelaire.

It is not clear that the author would entirely appreciate the compliment, since there is scant reference to Benjamin in her text, and the work on Baudelaire is absent from the bibliography. One detects a touch of the anxiety of influence here, of a silence evident enough to be eloquent; but there are surely some notable methodological parallels between the two studies, which extend well beyond the fact that both concern the city of Paris. To suggest that it does not matter whether the Commune makes a referential appearance in Rimbaud is to recall Benjamin's comment on Baudelaire and the crowd: the urban masses are so pervasively evident in his poetry that they never actually put in an appearance. Benjamin's hermeneutic is not ''symbolic,'' grasping the poetry of Baudelaire as an expressive emanation of a particular social history, but allegorical, treating the ''signifier'' of the texts as a material reality in its own right but then, by the allegorist's devious, ingenious sleight of hand, veering them impudently on their axis until they come to speak obliquely, in the very materiality of their letter, of more than themselves. The relation between text and history here is a question of form and force, of finding the very language of the poems alive with electric currents and shocking conjunctures that spring from a more-than-literary source.

It is surely some such allegorical method that Kristin Ross is practicing here too, even if her text never pauses to speak of it. What characterizes the allegorist is a certain interpretative wrenching and daring, an alchemical reading of arcane connections, allowing a sudden idiosyncratic correspondence to flash through in a moment of what Benjamin would have called profane illumination. It is a protomaterialist method against which Theodor Adorno sternly inveighed, involving as it does a boldly intimate juxtaposition of an item of the "base" with one of the "superstructure"; but for all its heterodoxy it can be a fertile, original approach, and much of the power of Ross's analysis can be seen to flow from it.

A number of examples can be given. There is the moment, fairly early on in the book, when Ross suggests a casually brilliant homology between the fashioning of barricades in the Commune and a radical form of writing. Barricades involve a kind of *bricolage*, a provisional cobbling together of whatever bits and pieces come usefully to hand; they are the antithesis of the monumental, recycling quotidian objects for startling new purposes. That this may also serve as a perceptive account of the poetic techniques of a Rimbaud, indeed of the revolutionary avant-garde in general, is then the "literary" point to be made, although the point is already, by definition, a good deal more than that. Again, there is the absorbing excursus of vagabondage, which manages to move all the way from how Rimbaud poetically experienced his own body to the vital political issues of labor, laziness, freedom, and leisure, in a striking political somatics for which some fascinating sociological evidence on vagabondae in nineteenth-century France is deftly marshaled. The point here, as in the book's other illuminating allegorical ploys, is that the eclecticism and *bricolage* of the object under study, its disdain for conventional generic categorizations, is being constantly mirrored by the author's own hermeneutical transgressions, her freewheeling, rag-picking range over a plethora of disparate forms of writing. As a final example from a work prodigal in original insights, one might mention the concept of Rimbaud's verse as somehow a "swarm," a capillary network of agitated, repetitive vibrations with something of the busy multiplicity of the urban crowd. Like the crowd, the prose poem is straggling, indeterminately bounded, equivalencing, paratactic, replete with a density and dizziness that mark the point where language is about to take off beyond language, where a veritable welter of linguistic modes jostle and collide.

Like language, every revolution tends to travel beyond its own bounds. It is hard to dismantle particular social institutions without dreaming for a moment of what it might be like to be liberated from institutionality altogether. At its finest, the anarchist tradition has always signified the "revolution within the revolution,'' marking out what remains to be done, what fantasies and desires still go hungry, when certain urgently necessary political changes have been installed. It has been left, on the whole, to the poets of revolutions to remind the politicians that the only finally adequate transformation would be one of the flesh itself. Kristin Ross is accordingly acute to see that Rimbaud's ''associality,'' his tramp-ish, adolescent, plague-on-you-all bohemianism, is no standard part of the *poète maudit* identikit but the sign of his profoundest social engagement. As in the work of that English Arthur Rimbaud, William Blake, the function of these apparently callow antisocial gestures is to draw attention to the limits of the polit-ical, for the sake of those who would fetishize that whole dimension. ''I am sorry to see my fellow countrymen bothering themselves with politics,'' Blake wrote. ''House of Commons and House of Lords seem to me to be fools. They seem to me to be something other than human life.'' But that, of course, was just the kind of political proclamation for which, in Blake's time, you might find yourself arrested. Blake, like Rimbaud, springs from the artisanal petty bourgeoisie and carries something of that into his similarly electic, bizarre, vernacular poetic forms, viewing poetry (as did the literary Communards) as a kind of political disruption and intervention. If one thinks of that finest and wisest of English social revolutionaries, William Morris, the historical necessity of a Blake or a Rimbaud is surely not in doubt. Neither of them would have been comforably at home in Morris's beautiful, generous-minded, intolerably staid, decent, and civ-ilized utopia. It is against the grain of this, as Ross reminds us, that we must recall Rimbaud's (and for that matter Blake's) ''transformed Utopian body of infinite sensation and libidinal possibility.'' As long, of course, as we also recall William Morris's tireless grass-roots political activity on behalf of the Social Democratic Federation and the Socialist League, and ask ourselves just how effi-ciently a Blake or a Rimbaud would have contributed to all that tedious, urgent committee work.

The concept of space forms the thematic keystone of this book, as its title sug-gests; and Ross is surely right to claim that this idea has proved of far less glam-orous appeal to radical theorists than the apparently more dynamic, exhilarating notions of narrative and history. This is ironic, because for Marxism, at least, it is that eminently spatial object, the human body, with which everything begins and ends. Marxism tells a story that tracks the body all the way up from the opposing thumb to the military-industrial complex. Bodies of a certain kind — prematurely born, communicative, needing to labor — must inevitably generate, unlike other animal bodies, a history; and for Marxism that history is a matter of the way this body extends itself into nature only to find that it has been plundered of its sensuous wealth. The goal of Marxism is the restoring to the body of its plundered sensuality; when this has taken place, Marxism may wither away.

It was Marx himself who, in a rebuke to the drafters of the Gotha Program, insisted that nature, not only labor power, was the source of value. The human body produces value only insofar as it inhabits a space, an environment whose stuff it shares. It is hard for us now to imagine that revolution in the perception of social space that accompanied the transition from feudalism to capitalism. Space in feudalism is parcelized, regionalized, particular; and it is precisely this, as Perry Anderson has argued in his *Lineages of the Absolutist State*, that helped to enable the rise of capitalism. What traumatic unheaval of perception is involved in thinking of the political no longer as a question of local sovereignty, of something interwoven with the labor and kinship relations of a specific place, but as an abstract *national* formation? John Barrell has reminded us in his study of the English peasant-poet John Clare that there is not even a word in English for a tract of land that is perceived visually but not necessarily pictorially. The term we have, of course, is "landscape"; our very terminology of place is an aesthetic one. Kristin Ross's book is nowhere more instructive than when it seeks to redeem the idea of space from such aesthetic reifications, showing us how the very construction of the discipline of geography in nineteenth-century France was an ideological arm of imperial rule. Her study thus joins the English school of Marxist geographers, of David Harvey and his colleagues, who seek to remind us that nothing could be more political than just the way objects are spatially distributed. The finest Irish play of the last decade, Brian Friel's *Translations*, displays the British rewriting of Gaelic place-names as an intolerable act of violence.

Kristin Ross has rescued Arthur Rimbaud for a left that is in dire need of him; and her book, with its lucid, companionable style, will surely stand as a major, permanent contribution to the socialist history of modern culture. It is churlish, in that light, to end on a rather more qualifying note. Ross's book shares a now fashionable suspicion of the "scientific" or "mature" Marx, and the term "mature" in her text is unfailingly shown in those ironic quotation marks. It is perhaps worth remembering that the "mature" Marx includes not only *Capital*, but what is probably the finest study of modern French politics ever written, *The 18th Brumaire*. Notions of "maturity" and "immaturity" indeed smack of the thought police; it would be an eccentric commentator who could categorize the young Marx's Paris manuscripts as adolescent. On the contrary, we have yet to catch up with them. In a splendid passage, Kristin Ross speaks of how the Commune was, like an adolescent, moving at once too fast and too slow, feeling the earth shift under its feet at the very moment it idled out its symbolic games in insouciant disregard of the terrors that threatened it. Such reflections recall Franco Moretti's comments on the centrality of the idea of youth for revolutionary Romanticism, in his exhilarating *The Way of the World*. Yet if there is a good immaturity, there is also a good maturity. Marxism cares for maturity because it does not wish to see men and women needlessly slaughtered. If you try on socialist revolution in chronically backward conditions, with scattered forces and an insufficient development of the means of life, then all you will succeed in doing, in Marx's own phrase, is generalizing scarcity. The official name for this generalization of scarcity is Stalinism. It is highly unlikely that men and women, in a situation in which the production forces have not been "maturely" developed, will voluntarily submit themselves to the draconian discipline involved in the primitive accumulation of socialist capital. If they will not, then it is probable that the bureaucratic state will do it for them. The dire consequences of that are on record, and are one good reason why socialism has stunk in the nostrils of the Western working class. There is a word in the classical Marxist lexicon for those who would throw men and women irresponsibly before the armed might of the state, before the time is ripe, and the word is adventurism. Something of that political irresponsibility characterized the otherwise stirring events of May 1968: it is, one might venture, a peculiarly French vise. No revolutionary cadre has the right to ask men and women to risk their lives without a reasonable chance of political success; and the reasonableness of that chance will depend upon the "maturity" or otherwise of given social conditions. There are those who overlook one of the most significant points about the Paris Commune, the fact that it failed. Perhaps failure is not important; perhaps that, too, belongs to the dreary teleology, the success ethic, of classical Marxism. As I write, 15 percent of French men and women have just voted for a fascist presidential candidate, many of these men and women being working class. Had the Commune not failed, that might not be the case. Words like "mature" and "scientific" have a prosaic ring, in contrast with the pullulating discourse of every leftist's favorite hippie, Arthur Rimbaud. Given the current intractability of class struggle in the United States, it is not surprising that many Americans have turned to rather more promising, less class-bound notions. The booming success of Mikhail Bakhtin Inc. is a case in point. The Paris Commune, as Kristin Ross demonstrates, represented a break with economism in the name of the cultural and political. This was its enduring triumph; it was also its downfall. For no political revolution, whatever libidinal attractions it offers to contemporary Western critics, will ever succeed unless it manages to penetrate to the very heart of capital, and overthrow its long-superseded sway.

Acknowledgments

I would like to thank Page Dubois, Franco Moretti, and my teacher and colleague, Norman O. Brown, for the encouragement and support they gave on reading substantial portions of the manuscript of this book. Thanks also to Mitchell Breitwieser, Joel Fineman, Stephen Heath, Denis Hollier, Fredric Jameson, Andrew Ross, and Ann Smock for various critical suggestions and help of many kinds. I am grateful, too, to my students at the University of California, Santa Cruz, with whom I first began to think about Rimbaud and history.

Terry Cochran's editorial assistance and Joanna Stericker's technical expertise in preparing the manuscript have been invaluable. Faculty research funds provided by the University of California, Santa Cruz, allowed me the necessary periods of study in France.

A special thanks to Adrian Rifkin for rewalking with me in Paris many of my early ideas about Commune culture. And finally, for their continuous encouragement and friendship, my gratitude and much more to Janice Bonora, Rachel Brokken, Roberto Crespi, and Alice Kaplan. Without the support of the latter's conversation, careful reading, and advice at every stage of its progress, I could not have completed this book.

An earlier version of Chapter 1 was published in *Yale French Studies* 73 (Fall 1987). An earlier version of Chapter 2 appeared as ''Rimbaud and the Resistance to Work'' in *Representations* 19 (Summer 1987).

Note on Translations

All quotations from Rimbaud are from *Oeuvres complètes*, ed. Rolland de Réné-ville and Jules Mouquet (Paris: Gallimard, 1967). The translations provided are taken whenever possible from Paul Schmidt's *Arthur Rimbaud: Complete Works* (New York: Harper and Row, 1976), and, to a lesser extent, Louise Varèse's *Rimbaud: Illuminations and Other Prose Poems* (New York: New Directions, 1957) and *Rimbaud: A Season in Hell* (New York: New Directions, 1961), and have been modified as necessary for my purposes. For "Le Bateau ivre" I refer throughout to the translation by Samuel Beckett. Translations from writers other than Rimbaud are drawn from the available English versions when these exist; full details are given in the Bibliography.

The Emergence of Social Space:
Rimbaud and the Paris Commune

Introduction

In this book I have pursued the structures common to everyday life — the social imagination of space and time — and the most condensed of fictions: poetry. To do so I have gathered the voices of an oppositional culture of the 1870s in France, and arranged them into a series of dialogues on common questions of values, methods, strategies, and postures — thus the particular problems that resulted in each of my chapters: urban space, laziness, geography, atomization and collectivity, and slogans. This has meant first of all establishing the semianarchist culture of the Commune and the decade that followed it: its discourses, its verbal and visual forms, its orchestrations of social relations, orientations, directions; its relations to the city; its associations and mass migrations; its fellow travelers, its displacements, entrances, and exits. If most of these terms bring into play the "horizontal" or geographic experience of human life, this is because that perspective was itself, as I came to realize, a product of the period in question.

That period, the 1870s in France, is but hastily dealt with, if not skipped over entirely, in most standard, traditional histories of France. Neither has it received the attention of more recent cultural historians intent on charting the demimonde culture of the Second Empire, the rise of the department store and modern bourgeois consumer habits, or the faded glimmer of fin-de-siècle decadence: the whole forward march of late nineteenth-century bourgeois culture that translates so well into narrative prose. The decade of the 1870s, according to one American historian, "lacks drama . . . it suffers by contrast with the somewhat more meretricious glitter of the empire just before it and with the generation of political turmoil, crisis, and scandal that immediately followed."[1] But for whom does it lack drama? Certainly not for those who would focus on the event (both its exist-ence and its bloody repression) that inaugurated the decade: the Paris Commune. For what could be more dramatic than the seizing of the government by Parisian workers on March 18, 1871? And what could be more dramatic than the massa-cre, two months later, of some twenty-five thousand, mostly working-class, Pari-sians at the hands of the Versaillais in a week-long battle in the streets of Paris? More people died in the final week of May 1871 than in any of the battles of the Franco-Prussian War, or than in any of the previous "massacres" (for example, the Terror) in French history.[2] If anything I have found the drama of that event to be a terrible lure, for it is difficult not to grant the Commune the status of excep-tional event—an accident, as many have called it; it is difficult to perceive in its glow the workers' movement and culture that preceded it and survived it.[3] An analogous problem confronted me as well in the field of literature: the legendary status of Arthur Rimbaud as magnificent exception.

But if drama, as we traditionally understand it, entails the verticality of peak moments, the crescendo of event, the rise and fall of stellar individuals, then the 1870s, taken as a whole, might indeed be found lacking. Or perhaps they propose a new understanding of drama. For in France the 1870s were a decade that com-prised two very significant *spatial* movements or events. It was the decade that saw the formation of a consciousness conducive to producing a colonialist, expe-ditionary class. The speed and mathematical directness with which the railroad proceeds through space, joining together previously inaccessible places as coor-dinates in a systematized grid, had already begun, within Europe, to make space *geographic*. Throughout the 1870s France prepared to accelerate that movement into a geopolitical one, to expand and project onto a global scale Haussmann's intraurban "fantasy of the straight line." France strengthened what would be-come its major role in the European transformation of space into colonial space, and in the establishment of an international division of labor. And second, on another but no less important scale, there occurred the spatial event of the Paris Commune, what in the 1960s was proclaimed by many to be the first realization of urban space as revolutionary space.

Why view the Commune as a primarily spatial event? To mention just a few of the spatial problems posed by the Commune, consider, for example, the relation-ship of Paris to the provinces, the Commune as immense "rent strike," the post-Haussmann social division of the city and the question of who, among its citi-zens, has a "right to the city"—the phrase is Henri Lefebvre's—or the military and tactical use of city space during the street fighting. These are some of the specific spatial issues of the book; here I want to consider a more general "hor-izontal" effect of the Commune: the way hierarchy came to be contested in the realm of the social imagination of the Communards before it was attacked on the political and economic level. To do so we must review briefly the events of the Commune.

When the dubious bourgeois republicans who had claimed power on September 4, 1870, capitulated to the Prussians, they announced a "peace" to end Napoléon III's disastrous war for which the working people in Paris would be made to pay. Class antagonism that had smoldered under the authoritarian social measures of the Second Empire intensified; on March 18, 1871, workers, many of them women who had borne the brunt of the hardships of the long Prussian siege of Paris, revolted. For seventy-three days a largely leaderless revolutionary government declared Paris an autonomous Commune and set about the free organization of its social life—free, that is, except for the constant threat of military reprisal from the "official" army at Versailles, which was to come, in the form of unprecedented carnage, in the final week of May.

But the Commune was not just an uprising against the political practices of the Second Empire; it was also, and perhaps above all, a revolt against deep forms of social regimentation. In the realm of cultural production, for instance, divisions solidly in place under the rigid censorship of the Empire and the constraints of the bourgeois market—between genres, between aesthetic and political discourses, between artistic and artisanal work, between high art and *reportage*—such hierarchical divisions under the Commune were fiercely debated and, in certain instances, simply withered away. It is these antihierarchical gestures and improvisations, what was entailed in extending principles of association and cooperation into the workings of everyday life, that make the Commune a predominantly "horizontal" moment.

We can take as an obvious and graphic example of the attack on verticality the Communards' demolition of the Vendôme Column, built to glorify the exploits of Napoléon's Grand Army. The strength of the gesture as antihierarchical act can be gauged by the hysteria registered in Parnassian poet and anti-Communard Catulle Mendès's account of the impending event. Mendès reads the destruction of the column as a leveling of history itself, an attack on genealogy and heredity designed to produce a timeless present. (Mendès includes in his journal the Commune decree he has just seen in the streets pronouncing the column's imminent demise):

> The Commune of Paris:
>   Considering that the imperial column at the Place Vendôme is a monument to barbarism, a symbol of brute force and glory, an affirmation of militarism, a negation of international law, a permanent insult to the vanquished by the victors, a perpetual assault on one of the three great principles of the French Republic, Fraternity, it is thereby decreed:
>   Article One: The column at the Place Vendôme will be abolished.

> It wasn't enough for you [writes Mendès], in a word, to have destroyed the present and compromised the future, you still want to annihilate the past! An ominous youthful prank. But the Vendôme Column is France,

Figure 1. The Vendôme Column, five minutes before its fall. Courtesy Bibliothèque Nationale.

yes, the France of yesteryear, the France that we no longer are, alas! It's really about Napoléon, all this, it's about our victorious, superb fathers moving across the world, planting the tricolored flag whose staff is made of a branch of the tree of liberty! . . . Don't think that demolishing the Vendôme Column is just toppling over a bronze column with an emperor's statue on top; it's unearthing your fathers in order to slap the fleshless cheeks of their skeletons and to say to them: You were wrong to be brave, to be proud, to be grand! You were wrong to conquer cities, to win battles. You were wrong to make the world marvel at the vision of a dazzling France.[4]

La Colonne Vendôme.

Figure 2. The Vendôme Column, after its fall. Courtesy Bibliothèque Nationale.

For Mendès the destruction of the column abolishes history—makes for a timeless present, an annihilated past, and an uncertain future. Alone in his room where he spends most of the Commune, wondering why he didn't have the sense to flee to Versailles along with the other "friends of order," Mendès perceives time to be at a standstill. For the Communards, the *existence* of the column freezes time: "a *permanent* insult," "a *perpetual* assault." Whose time is it? In Communard Louis Barron's description of the toppling, the column is just as much a symbol of the State, but the State is a whitened sepulchre:

> Tuesday, May 16. I saw the Vendôme Column fall, it collapsed all in one piece like a stage décor on a nice bed of trash when the machinist's whistle blew. Immediately a huge cloud of dust rose up, while a quantity of tiny fragments rolled and scattered about, white on one side, gray on the other, similar to little morsels of bronzed plaster. This colossal symbol of the Grand Army—how it was fragile, empty, miserable! It seemed to have been eaten out from the middle by a multitude of rats, like France itself, like its old tarnished glory, and we were surprised not to see any [rats] run out along the drainpipes. The

music played fanfares, some old greybeard declaimed a speech on the vanity of conquests, the villainy of conquerors, and the fraternity of the people, we danced in a circle around the debris, and then we went off, very content with the little party.[5]

Time, said Feuerbach, is the privileged category of the dialectician, because it excludes and subordinates where space tolerates and coordinates. Our tendency is to think of space as an abstract, metaphysical context, as the container for our lives rather than the structures we help create. The difficulty is also one of vocabulary, for while words like "historical" and "political" convey a dynamic of intentionality, vitality, and human motivation, "spatial," on the other hand, connotes stasis, neutrality, and passivity. But the analysis of social space, far from being reactionary or technocratic, is rather a symptom of a strategic thought and of what Tristan Tzara, speaking of Rimbaud, called an "ethics of combat," one that poses space as the terrain of political practice. An awareness of social space, as the example of the Vendôme Column makes clear, always entails an encounter with history—or better, a choice of histories.

"Social space," then, became my way of mediating between the discursive and the event. I came to an understanding of the concept through my work on a project about Marxist philosopher Henri Lefebvre and the social thought and movements surrounding that other supremely antihierarchical event: May 1968 in Paris. It is tempting, but of course historically inaccurate, to analogize the events of May 1968 with those of May 1871. Much has been made of the migration of Commune slogans and iconography across a century where they erupted again in many of the same streets. It is true, however, that the events of May 1968 bore a complex relation to the history of the interpretation of the 1871 insurrection. And in this sense my own encounter with Lefebvre was perhaps theoretically overdetermined. For while Lefebvre first raised the notion of everyday life (or its synonym, "social space") to the status of a concept in a book he wrote immediately after World War II, his most substantial rethinking of theories of everyday life and social space took place in the late sixties.[6] At that time he was engaged simultaneously in completing a prolonged and controversial meditation on the Paris Commune, in associating with members of the anarcho-syndicalist group, the Situationists (who themselves produced a provocative interpretation of the Commune), and in participating in the movements that led to the events of May 1968. Perhaps my own experience—as well as that of Alice Kaplan, Adrian Rifkin, and others with whom I worked on the everyday life project—of being socialized during the late 1960s and its aftermath, played a role in producing my fascination with the experience of a generation of writers, political thinkers, geographers, and poets whose political imaginations were formed by the event of the Commune. And that experience also, I think, drew me to certain contemporary theoretical voices, to wayward or renegade Marxists such as Lefebvre, or

Jacques Rancière and the circle of writers around the journal *Révoltes logiques*, which took its name from a poem of Rimbaud's—writers whose intellectual and political development, like that of Lafargue, Rimbaud, Reclus, and other Communards a hundred years earlier, was profoundly altered by their contact with a version of historical agency.

The analysis of space, like the analysis of poetry, has been, until recently, neglected within traditional Marxism. The exceptions to this tendency are Lefebvre and the primarily French and American Marxist geographers writing in journals like *Hérodote* and *Antipode* who in the 1960s elaborated their theoretical position mostly through unearthing and reexamining the long-repressed figure of Communard geographer Elisée Reclus, inventor of social geography. Within traditional Marxism, however, a preoccupation with spatial categories was taken as the mark of "spatial fetishism," a wrong-thinking conceptualizing of space as an autonomous determinant, separate from the structure of social relations and class conflict—a theoretical confusion deemed somewhat akin to technological determinism. But space, as a social fact, as a social factor and as an instance of society, is always political and strategic. And because it is characterized, among other things, by the difference in age of the elements that form it—the sum of the action of successive modernizations—social space cannot be understood according to an old and facile "history versus structure or logic" opposition.

Social space, for Lefebvre, can be understood as a kind of recoding of his initial concept of everyday life. Another way of saying this is that everyday life—what remains when all specialized activities have been eliminated—is primarily (but not entirely) a spatial concept. Like the state for Marx, everyday life for Lefebvre is only *modern* everyday life: the product of the great nineteenth-century European migration to urban centers and the waning of unifying styles disseminated by church and monarch. Everyday life is born in nineteenth-century Europe in the same gap or rift that separates a private, domesticated world from a public, institutional one. Alice Kaplan and I have argued elsewhere that the importance of Lefebvre's concept of everyday life lies in its introduction of a third term into the most important philosophical opposition of the twentieth century: the opposition between the phenomenological and the structural.[7] Everyday life is neither the realm of the intentional, monadic subject dear to phenomenology; nor does it dwell in the objective structures—the language, institutions, kinship structures—that are perceptible only by bracketing the experience of the individual subject. Neither the subjective (the biographical) nor the objective (the discursive), but both: literally and *dans tous les sens*.

In some sense my study of Commune culture could be said to begin with that well-known injunction from Rimbaud: that he be read or understood, as he put it, both literally and *dans tous les sens* (in all directions, according to all five senses, according to all possible meanings). The second part of his call, for an azimuthal, polysemic understanding as opposed to a literal one, was for me somewhat less problematic to think about than the first. For my own training in literary criticism was largely about being attentive to the lure of the polysemic; it was about producing the sophisticated reading, whose value far outweighed the merely and unanalyzed literal, or what we were taught to call, "naive" reading. In fact, the literal or naive reading was presented to me in my graduate studies as but the necessary step (a menial task, preferably performed by others) in the developmental move to a sophisticated, formalist, and polysemic reading. It was that which was to be surpassed, a vestigial, evolutionary relic. And according to some vast and unquestioned intellectual division of labor, the work of the literal or the naive—what dirties the hands of archivists—was always to be performed offstage, and not by theorists.

But if I were to read both literally and *dans tous les sens*, I would have to develop a new perspective on both the biographical (historical) material and the information to be gleaned from close textual interpretation. For that kind of reading would entail a balancing act: neither did I wish to mobilize formalist skills for the reading of historical data—a practice that has come to be called, in recent years, the "new historicism"—nor could I allow the weight of psychosexual, biographical fact to determine, in the sense of explain, textual intricacy. On the one hand I was faced with the historically acknowledged, and I think, unquestionable, particularity and force of Rimbaud's oppositional, iconoclastic, annihilatory voice. And, on the other, as I came to see more and more, with that voice as one that speaks within and by means of a vast cultural system, a system that should be conceived *not* within the limits of some purely literary history but rather as made up of elements and languages that are not distinctly literary. A centrifugal reading of Rimbaud, which he himself invites, in fact leads very far afield. For it opens out onto a whole synchronic history, onto the web of social and political discourses and representations that simultaneously *place a limitation on* and *enable* meaning to take place.

As I began to consider my subject under the rubric of synchronic history, my own theoretical distance from much of the current social or "contextual" analysis of art became clearer. My concern was to establish oppositional or "vernacular" culture, voices that are for the most part conspicuously absent from or repressed in much of the recent attempt to rethink the relation between history and art that comes under the heading of the "new historicism."[8] In such critical narratives, the critic, adopting the point of view of some more advanced stage of capitalism's development, inevitably reinstills or rereads into the event in question the values or "bitter wisdom" of his or her own critical vantage point. Oppositional voices or moments in this critical paradigm become the "always already co-opted" of the forward movement of capital. A striking example of this depoliticizing strain in cultural criticism can be found in the recent French rewriting of the events of May 1968.[9] Certainly one reason for the use I make of a kind of phenomenological perception—my attempt to imagine social constructions of space and time — is that it helps avoid the metaleptic "it couldn't have been otherwise" dead end of such analyses. By imagining the lived experience of actors in particular oppositional moments, in other words, one can avoid an analytic structure that insists on starting from the (predetermined) result.

When I turned to Marxist aesthetic theory, my problem became one of genre. For not only has Marxist theory neglected to develop a theory of space, but Marxist literary critics from Lukács through Sartre and on up to the current generation — Eagleton, Macherey, and even an occasional critic of poetry and provocative thinker of space like Fredric Jameson ("*narrative*, which I take to be . . . the central function or *instance* of the human mind")[10] — have continued to reassert the traditionally dominant concern with narrative and the novel genre. Walter Benjamin's massive study of Baudelaire and Paris under the Second Empire stands out in the marked neglect shown by Marxist critics for poetry. Bertolt Brecht — whose favorite poet was Rimbaud — was certainly aware of that neglect when he debated it in the 1930s with Lukács. Brecht's question — "What about the realism of lyric poetry?"[11] — is no less pressing today. This hesitation on the part of Marxist critics to concern themselves with poetry can be traced back to all too traditional assumptions, themselves a development of the late nineteenth century, that regard prose as the privileged vehicle for objective or political themes, and verse for subjective or individual ones — or, put another way, to the assumption that there exists a social production of reality on the one hand, and a desiring production that is mere fantasy or wish fulfillment on the other. Despite extensive feminist critiques of such divisions between the "personal" and the "political," these assumptions remain largely intact and are reinscribed in Marxism as generic omission.

Many of the best readings of nineteenth-century bourgeois cultural production, analyses that resist treating art as a miracle of poetic creativity independent of economic or social developments, still seem to flounder in their theoretical attitude to the "masterpiece." A single masterpiece might, for example, be decoded by a literary critic in such a way that it is made to reveal or offer up all of the social relations of the Second Empire. A reading like this certifies not only the analytic acumen of the critic — the master decoder who takes on the subtle riches and multivalent significations of the masterpiece — but the masterpiece's enshrined position in museum or canon as well. The wealth of social history "revealed" by the masterpiece forms a kind of landscape or ornamental drapery that reinforces canonical status and thus, paradoxically perhaps, the masterpiece's inertia. For my own purposes, an unquestioned cult of the masterpiece seemed singularly at odds with both Rimbaud and the people who pulled down the Vendôme Column. Another problem with such "contextual" analyses of art — analyses that leave untroubled the distinction between "text" and "context" — is that the "social history" that emerges full blown from the interpretation of the masterwork tends itself to be left unanalyzed — as if the formal analysis of a text or painting offered up a social context that did not in turn have to be analyzed! Again social history remains merely decorative. But another analysis, particularly an analysis by a historian, might easily err in the opposite direction: by refusing culture its role in the articulation of social conflict, by limiting its role to that of providing décor for the "real" social conflict taking place.

In the course of writing this book I have come to see the kind of division of labor that has defined literary studies for some time—between the historical and the theoretical, or the historical and the linguistic, the contextual and the textual, the literal and the *dans tous les sens*—as politically counterproductive. And I have begun to recognize versions of that division of labor, often in dimly recognizable shapes, as that which formed the primary subject of debate and conflict during the Commune. Much of the formalist sterility of our own critical tendencies, in other words, bears the trace of nineteenth-century doctrines that proclaim the superiority of intellectual work over manual work, and the natural destiny that ordains some to perform one task, and others another. During the Commune these issues were fiercely debated as poets, cartoonists, musicians, and writers took sides for or against the insurgent government. One form the debate took was a radical questioning of the respective identities of worker and artist.

Workers and Artists

I would like to expand at some length on this debate by returning to the exemplary figure of Mallarmé's friend and fellow Parnassian, Catulle Mendès. Mendès, as I mentioned, lived out the Commune for the most part alone in his room; this rather furtive existence was interrupted by occasional and equally furtive forays out into the streets, forays he performed and then recorded faithfully in his journal. Mendès's journal, *Les 73 journées de la Commune*, is itself exemplary of a genre that sprang up immediately after the demise of the Commune: the hurriedly written eyewitness account or diary documenting everyday life under the Commune. Active Communards like Elisée Reclus's brother, Elie, who during the Commune served as the director of the Bibliothèque Nationale (a fact that the official history of the Bibliothèque Nationale neglects to mention!),[12] published an account many years later; so did Louise Michel and Jean-Baptiste Clément, composer of one of the better known Commune songs, "Le Temps des cérises."[13] Pro-Commune accounts like these tended to appear much later unless they were published in Switzerland or England; by contrast, the rapid publication and distribution of anti-Commune texts like Mendès's in the early summer of 1871 coincided with and helped justify the violence of the repression of the Commune, a violence with which Edmond de Goncourt, writing in his journal in May, heartily concurs: "The bloodletting is a bleeding white. Such a purge, by killing off the combative part of the population, defers the next revolution by a whole generation.''[14] By the end of 1871 a rigid censorship again prevailed. The onslaught of anti-Commune memoirs during the summer and fall was followed by a complete prohibition as the year ended, of any mention, pro or con, of the Commune.

In his journal Mendès describes how he is given to hallucinating late-night imaginary conversations with Gustave Courbet, president of the Fédération des Artistes under the Commune. The Fédération des Artistes, responsible for the organization of various concerts and cultural affairs, was mainly concerned with education and organization and hardly at all with artistic questions.[15] Mendès finds Courbet's position ridiculous. Doing a little bit of everything, even politics, is comprehensible, if not excusable, if you are good for nothing else. But what is unacceptable to Mendès is that kind of varied activity on the part of someone "who can make excellent boots like Napoléon Gaillard, or paintings as good as Gustave Courbet's"(166). Art for art's sake, of which Mendès is one of the most vocal, if not the most adept, spokespersons of his time, seems, as Franco Moretti has suggested, to be in a dialectical relation to production for production's sake, i.e., to booming late capitalism.[16] Mendès's concern is for the *bel ouvrage*—or rather, its loss—the loss of Napoléon Gaillard's excellent boots, the sacrifice of the masterpieces Courbet would have painted were he not so busy organizing artists or sitting on Commune committees. But can a lapse in production in itself produce such anxiety? Mendès's fantasy continues. Were Courbet or any other poet or artist actually to appear at his doorstep and try to get him to "federate," he announces, he would reply, "Leave me in peace, Monsieur de la Fédération, je suis un reveur, un travailleur." A dreamer, a worker. He concludes with his version of a call to action:

> Let us return home, messieurs the artists, close the doors, let's say to our servant—if we have a servant—that we're not at home to anyone, and after having prepared our best pen or taken up our best paintbrush, let us work in solitude, without stopping, with no other worry than that of doing the best we can. (167)

"I am a worker." To describe his own position, Mendès appropriates the term *travailleur* and inflects it with the full logic of the *métier*: the specialization that alone defines one's being. For workers or artisans, of course, that specialization, dating back to the justification of the division of labor in Plato's *Republic*, is simply the prohibition against doing anything else: "the *métier* for which nature made him and at which he must work all his life, to the exclusion of any other . . . in order to make the *bel ouvrage*."[17] In Plato's well-constituted state, a unique *métier* is attributed to each person; a shoemaker is first of all someone who cannot also be a warrior. What is at first a simple functional or structural division of labor—to each person one task—is rapidly transformed into a hierarchy of "natures": to each person the task that nature destined him or her to perform. In the late nineteenth century little has changed; in fact, in the world of generalized production, in the interest of progress, one can less than ever do two things at the same time. A shoemaker like Napoléon Gaillard is still he who cannot do anything other than make shoes (excellent ones, it appears). "Nature," according to an 1845 article in the journal *L' Artiste*, "has not allowed everyone to possess genius; she has said to one, 'make poems,' and to the other, 'make shoes.' "[18] Author Charles Nodier, writing in midcentury, has become unnerved by the quantity of shoemakers who have transgressed the rules fixing their status and have taken to writing tragedies in the style of Corneille. The democracy of writing, he warns, is transforming "useful workers and artisans" into "thieves, impostors, and forgers."[19]

Forging and falsifying: In Plato the prohibition against artisans doing something other than their proper task has its roots in barring their access to the realm open to (and "proper to") artists and poets, namely, the realm of imitation, of appearances and role-playing.[20] "Je est un autre." The artist, as imitator of an imitation, is inferior to the worthy artisan. The artisan is defined by his prohibition from games, falsehood, appearance, imitation, fiction, lying. Gaillard makes shoes; Courbet counterfeits reality. But during the Commune Courbet and Gaillard are not in their proper places. Art for art's sake may have its roots in production for production's sake, but a deeper anxiety fuels Mendès: the anxiety of displacement, of a shift or confusion in the hierarchy of tasks. Displacement, after all, hurts. I am a worker, Mendès writes. The rights of the inspired are retained by invoking the myth of the artisan and of labor as redemptive agency. The rights of the inspired are retained by Mendès's "borrowing" or imitating a role—by his asserting the right to precisely the activity (imitation) that is the privilege of the writer but forbidden the honest artisan, the good worker. "Je est un autre." The worker becomes the exemplum, the bearer of truth in order to be all the better excluded from the science reserved for scholars and the inspiration reserved for poets. The rights of the inspired conspire without violence in the reign of order.

What happens to a state if the shoemakers and the artists are not in their proper place? Production—*le bel ouvrage*—is not the real concern. A drop in production can be withstood. Mendès is not really mourning the unmade boots of Napoléon Gaillard or even the unpainted paintings of Gustave Courbet. His anxiety stems from the experience of displacement, from the attack on identity. "Je est un autre." Not being able to *identify* a shoemaker—and thus, perhaps, not being able to identify himself, an artist—makes Mendès nervous. In his "call to action" to artists everywhere, he advises them to grasp their "best pen" or their "best paintbrush": the tools of the trade. Tools as fetishized anticipation of the gestures and disciplines of the *métier*, but above all as identification devices: the brand, the badge, the heraldic emblem. During the Commune, however, shoemakers—and artists—have laid down their tools. And shoemakers and artists are not in their place. How can they be recognized?

How to Identify a Worker

The problem of how to identify a worker absorbed the attention and energy of a considerable number of people and was addressed in a variety of ways toward the end of the Second Empire. Here are three examples. Frédéric Le Play, the conservative, Catholic sociologist who sought to reform society by shoring up the authority of property owners, managers, and fathers, was placed in charge of the 1867 International Exposition held in Paris, an exposition whose ostensible goal was to display "objects for the improvement of the physical and moral conditions of the masses."[21] In fact, only one-third of the space allotted to this purpose was used. Much more space was taken up by a display of *objets d'art* to be used by the rich, and by a second display—not of objects created by workers but of workers themselves! In a section of the exposition entitled "Petits Métiers," model workers, male and female, could be seen plying their craft: lace makers, artificial flower makers, chocolate makers.

> The visitors to the exhibition could see them at work and could come to the enjoyment of two illusions at least. One was the appearance of the relative independence and self-motivation of the workers. The appearance, that is, because in the case of the lacemakers, they belonged to home based industries controlled by a single large capitalist. Nevertheless, the small unit or family unit could be seen as operative. Another illusion was the absence of industrial disease. In this display, none of the flower-makers would have torn or bleeding fingers.[22]

Such a display can in some sense be taken as a three-dimensional realization of the vast taxonomic project to which Le Play had devoted most of his life.[23] His aim was that of producing the image of the perfect worker for a newly industrializing, Catholic society, and he did so by grafting what he took to be the familial and moral values of rural workers onto the skills and energy of the industrious urban worker.[24] The conservative moralism of Le Play's construction of the "good worker" is perhaps most important in its implication of the consequences for workers—and in this, the exposition's zoolike display is all the more emblematic—of transgression, of escape to other worlds, or other conditions.

Denis Poulot's *Le Sublime, ou le travailleur comme il est en 1870, et ce qu'il peut être* (1870), written on the eve of the Commune, resonates with the fear of workers' transgression. As such, it reveals the same degree of bourgeois anxiety as Le Play's work, and the same will to construct, and thus wishfully "realize," the image type of the good worker. But Poulot's focus is the inverse of Le Play's. A bourgeois, Parisian industrialist with no pretense toward being a writer or an

PETITS MÉTIERS. — Les Fleurs artificielles. — Dessin de M. Gaildrau.

Figure 3. Petits métiers. Artificial flower making. Courtesy Bibliothèque Nationale, from
L'Exposition illustrée, 1867.

economist, Poulot sees himself more as a diagnostician. His concern is with
identifying the *bad* worker, with being able to recognize one when you see one.[25]
His position as *patron* allows him the opportunity to observe closely workers'
habits; from such scientific observation he establishes a ''pathological diagnostic'' designed to ferret out *sublimisme*: the illness affecting those workers most
insubordinate inside the *atelier* and those most oblivious to familial morals outside the *atelier*. *Sublime* (along with other slang expressions denoting superla-
tives: *chouette, rupin, d'attaque*)[26] was the word insubordinate workers used to
refer to themselves; Poulot designates such workers rather as *ivrognes* or *pares-
seux*. The standards Poulot uses to establish a scale ranging from the good worker
to the *sublime*—with many intermediate categories of moderate or incipient
sublimisme—emphasize drunkenness and laziness: the degree of drunkenness or
sobriety, the degree of laziness or ardor for work, the degree of conformity to the
bourgeois family model, the degree of violence between companions. Something
like a composite image of these four categories—the bloodthirsty, slothful,
drunken prostitute—would be used after the Commune to construct the image of
the Communard woman worker as *pétroleuse*.

It might seem peculiar to discuss my third example, that of Karl Marx, in the
reactionary climate of Poulot, Le Play, and the anxiety of identity. I should make

clear that my concern here is with a particular Marx, the Marx of the 1850s and 1860s, the "mature" Marx, architect of scientific socialism. That Marx might be said to have provided the best-known and most sustained attempt to ascertain the identity of the worker. In Jacques Rancière's reading of Marx, the Platonic myth of the artisan as he who can do nothing other than his *métier* is displaced, but essentially operative, in the Marx of "mature" scientific socialism. "The impossibility of [the artisan doing] 'something else' becomes that general law of history that resounds like an obsession in *The German Ideology* or *The Communist Manifesto*: we know 'only one science,' the science of history."[27] The worker is still destined to do his unique "proper affair." For Marx, the unique task of the worker is to suppress property; workers must transform their own condition into the general condition of society, because of the identity provided them by the positive principle that makes the unity of the historic process: production. To find out what the worker is, is to find out what he will be obliged to perform historically, in conformity with his being. The proletarian, for mature, scientific Marx, the Marx of the 1850s and 1860s, is the worker who still has only one thing to do, the revolution, and who still has only one identity: that of the lone historical agent who will destroy capital.

Je Est un Autre

Gustave Courbet's activities and everyday life during the Commune are well known. A member of the Commune, delegate to the *mairie*, member of the Commission on Education, and president of the Fédération des Artistes, he is, in his own words, "up to my neck in political affairs." "I get up, I eat breakfast, I sit down and preside twelve hours a day. My head begins to feel like a cooked apple. But despite all this turmoil of the head and of my understanding which I'm not used to, I'm in a state of enchantment. Paris is a true Paradise."[28]

Shoemaker Napoléon Gaillard's activities are less well known. In the months immediately following the Commune, a full half of the shoemakers in Paris were missing—massacred, arrested, in exile. "Shoemaking is the last of the *métiers*. If we find shoemakers in the first row everywhere where workers shouldn't be, it's because they are the most numerous, the least occupied, and the least mystified by the glory of the artisan."[29] Gaillard was a famous shoemaker, a member of the International, the author of a treatise on the foot, and an orator who had been imprisoned in 1869 for speaking at public meetings, a flamboyant figure and heavy drinker—a *sublime* according to Poulot's diagnostic categories. Fifty-six years old in 1871, he was the director of barricade construction during the Commune. But more significant, perhaps, than his shoemaking, and more significant, perhaps, than the fact that he stopped making shoes during the Commune in order to build barricades, is the fact that he insisted on being photo-

Figure 4. Napoléon Gaillard in front of his barricade at the place de la Concorde. Courtesy Adrian Rifkin from *Paris sous la Commune, par un témoin fidèle: La Photographie*, 1871(?).

graphed posing in front of the barricade he made—thus, as Adrian Rifkin suggests, ''authoring'' it, demanding and appropriating for himself the status of author that was denied him.

> Gaillard père, the head of barricade construction, appeared so proud of his creation that on the morning of May 20, we saw him in full commandant's uniform, four gold braids on the sleeve and cap, red lapels on his tunic, great riding boots, long, flowing hair, a steady gaze, ordering the staging of a spectacle that was immediately carried out. While national guards prevented the public from walking about on one side of the square, the barricade maker posed proudly some twenty feet in front of his creation, and, with his hand on his hip, had himself photographed.[30]

Gaillard does not choose to celebrate his status as worker. Instead he transgresses what is perhaps the most time honored and inflexible of barriers: the one separating those who carry out useful labor from those who ponder aesthetics.

In his claim to ''author'' his own work, Gaillard launches an attack on the good worker, on the very identity, as it was understood, of *l'être ouvrier*—an attack whose counterpart can be found in Rimbaud's own resistance to the identity he playfully accused Verlaine of embracing: that of a "bon Parnassien." These two flights from the idiotism of the *métier* form a single dialectical image. And it is this gesture—one that resonates with a nineteenth-century critique of specialization and of the division of labor—that I have attempted to trace in Reclus, Lafargue, and the other figures that move within and on the periphery of the Commune. My study began with Rimbaud and with what I took to be Rimbaud's flight from *l'être poète*: a flight that took shape, as I came to realize not with his famous silence, his departure for Africa, but in 1870 when he wrote his first poem. Rimbaud left literature before he even got there.

"Bosses and workers," Rimbaud writes in "Bad Blood," "all of them peasants, and common." And, "I have a horror of all *métiers*." Communard and anarchist Elisée Reclus, whose "invention" of the field of social geography, as I argue in Chapter 3, had to be repressed for the field of academic geography to take institutional shape, unknowingly echoes "Bad Blood":

> He who commands becomes depraved, he who obeys becomes smaller. Either way, as a tyrant or a slave, as an officer or as an underling, man is diminished. The morality which is born out of the present conception of the state and the social hierarchy is necessarily corrupt. Religions have taught us that the fear of God is the beginning of wisdom, whereas history tells us that it is the beginning of all servitude and all depravity.[31]

Reclus, like many of his generation, was a maker of slogans, and one of his slogans, "Travaillons à nous rendre inutile" (Work to Make Ourselves Useless), could be said to have been expanded into manifesto form by Paul Lafargue, the Communard to whom his father-in-law Karl Marx in an 1882 letter to Engels referred as "the last Bakuninist." Lafargue wrote *Le Droit à la paresse* eight years after the Commune, at a moment when the left, responding to the scurrilous right-wing histories of the Commune that portrayed prostitutes, drunkards, and vagabonds setting Paris aflame, had reclaimed as its own the task of constructing the Communard as good or model worker. In leftist hagiographies of the period and after, the Communard was a good family man who never beat his wife, never touched *eau-de-vie*, and wanted nothing more than to devote himself fifteen hours a day to his *métier*. At a moment when labor was being deified by both left and right, Lafargue advocated laziness.

The threat of Lafargue, Reclus, and Rimbaud, all exiles or figures of displacement, lies in the "bastard" nature of their thought. Reclus's geography, written for the most part in Switzerland where he was exiled after the Commune, is as he proclaims, nothing but "history in space." Rimbaud's poetry mixes the useful with the luxurious, the artistic with the artisanal, precious metals with trash. And Lafargue, in *Le Droit à la paresse*, suggests that revolutionary praxis, the attack on the existing order, comes not from some untainted and virtuous working class in the full flower of its maturity, but from a challenge to the boundaries *between* work and leisure, producer and consumer, worker and bourgeois, worker and intellectual.

"(What a century for hands!),'' writes Rimbaud. "I'll never learn to use my hands." Emancipation, in Roman and civil law, means to be freed from control; from the Latin *mancipare*, to seize with the hand (*manus*): emancipation, literally, to be unhanded. Emancipation, for Rancière, writing in the 1970s, takes as its point of departure not workers' solidarity or community, but rather their atomization under capitalism: the alienated seriality of workers dependent on competing with each other for work. Rancière has shown how the usefulness that gains the worker a place in the city is what prevents him or her from doing anything other than his or her task—from being a citizen, for instance: "Work is not, in and of itself, a principle of liberty and equality; the defense of its interest may be the politics of a new slavery."[32] Emancipation—the transformation of a servile identity into a free identity—must be based on a principle other than work, since the exercise and defense of work are what constitute the servile identity. Emancipation follows from dispensing with the positivities of workers' community, and from *radicalizing* that atomization instead:

> It is about making oneself a citizen-atom: an atom whose movement,
> free from that point on, must produce a molecular energy able to
> decompose into free atoms the mass of "fanatics of the corporation."
> The people, free and citizens, can only be the reunion of incandescent
> atoms. It is not masses but atoms that enter into fusion.[33]

The greatest danger to the "friends of order," in other words, is not in the masses; it is in their decomposition—what I call, in Chapter 4, the swarm.

"I'm not against the asocial," Bertolt Brecht says in conversation with Walter Benjamin. "I'm against the nonsocial."[34] Such a vision as Rancière's, by downplaying the emancipatory value of workers' culture or community, risks appearing nonsocial; in fact it is anything but. Mendès, the poet who is not at home to anyone, is nonsocial; Rimbaud, indifferent to conforming to conventional standards of behavior—be they moral, sexual, national, artistic, or lexical—is asocial. And nothing is more social than Rimbaud's asociability. Consider his experience, as he himself was wont to do, geographically. To do so means focusing on his intersection with collectivities and movements that have been traditionally deemed irrelevant to his development *as a poet*. Rimbaud's trajectory is part of the massive displacement of populations from the provinces to the city, that vagabondage whereby thousands of peasants, workers, and middle-class people learned of exile for the first time—a migration preparatory to that even greater geographic displacement, from the metropoles to the colonies. Rimbaud moves from the countryside—the "occidental forests"—through the capitals, to the desert. In his *Illuminations*, the fantastic city and the barren desert (or its equivalent, the polar regions), often in uneasy proximity, form the most prevalent landscapes. Worker-philosopher Louis Gauny suggests a reason for this:

> It is in the desert that seditious thought ferments, but it is in the city that such thought erupts. Liberty likes extreme crowds or absolute solitude. . . . But the unhappy inhabitants of the countryside, brutalized by taxes, are rarely visited by rebellion.[35]

If the peasant population in France forms an obstacle to rebellion, it is not because it is atomized (for this, in fact, is the reality of the social, what makes us human, the distance between us), but rather because of its character of being an indivisible mass—what Rimbaud calls *les assis* of Charleville, the seated ones, or *les accroupissements*, the squattings. Rimbaud's later works stage the dialectic of the city and the desert (or the city and the sea in "The Drunken Boat")—the crowd and an absolute, vertiginous, nonhuman or more-than-human solitude: the Drunken Boat as incandescent atom. These works reveal a thinker whose primary concern is that of emancipation.

Marx and the Commune

"The inventions of the unknown," Rimbaud wrote in May 1871, "demand new forms." Later that summer, Rimbaud composed a "communist constitution" (now lost) inspired by the form, the organization of the Commune. His friend Delahaye recalls it as follows:

> In the little states that made up ancient Greece, it was the agora that directed everything; the agora, that is to say, the public place, the assembled citizens deliberating, voting, with equal rights, on what had to be done. He then began by abolishing the representative government and by replacing it by a system of permanent referendum.[36]

For Marx too, the Commune's abolition of representative (parliamentary) government was entirely unforeseen, a true "invention of the unknown." Marx's writings about the Commune could arguably mark the beginning of a "third phase" in his thinking—one that is distinct from what is thought to be his mature "scientific" phase, and one that is involved in rethinking some of the themes of his early "immature" writings of the 1840s. Confronted in 1871 with the unexpected event of the Commune, Marx is led to focus on what he saw to be the Communards' unprecedented discovery of the "political form . . . under which to work out the economical emancipation of labor."[37] The economic emancipation of labor, in other words, presupposes political forms that are *themselves* emancipatory;[38] this is the lesson Marx takes from the Commune:

> The working class cannot simply lay hold of the ready-made state-

machinery and wield it for their own purpose. The political instrument of their enslavement cannot serve as the political instrument of their emancipation. (196)

Far more important than any of the measures or laws the Commune managed to pass was simply "its own working existence": the expansive, thoroughly democratic nature of its social organization. Its discovery of a "thoroughly expansive political form," a "completely new historical creation," was for Marx what made the Commune "the greatest revolution of the century."

Who were the agents of this decisive event? Who were the Communards? Although primarily manual workers, the Communards were by no means the new, industrialized proletariat that Marx, the architect of scientific socialism, had predicted. A significant percentage were the semiskilled day laborers (*journaliers*) who had migrated from the provinces to work on Haussmann's massive and fantastic urban-renewal projects; another significant group were traditional artisans.[39] A decisive role in the revolution was played by women, a population that had borne more than its share of the everyday hardships of the Siege: "Women started first, as they did during the revolution. Those of March 18, hardened by the war in which they had a double share of misery, did not wait for their men."[40] The Communards' self-definition, if not their origins, was decidedly Parisian, and their most immediate concerns had less to do with gaining control over the means of production than with avoiding eviction. (On March 13, a decree had been approved that required the forceful payment of all rents due and commercial debts unpaid during the siege.) The chosen targets of Communard violence, as Manuel Castells points out, were less the industrial capitalist than those emblematic figures charged with social classification and the policing of everyday life: the *curé*, the *gendarme*, and the *concierge*.

The event of the Commune caused Marx to return to some of the themes that had already emerged in what are called his early or "immature" writings of the 1840s. Manifest property relations recede into the background of his analysis of the Commune. Instead, a stronger focus on emancipatory political form and a new attention to the social and political forms that fetter that emancipation begin to emerge. Chief among these latter are the State and the division of labor.

The revolutions of 1830 and 1848, according to Marx, had succeeded only in transferring power from one faction of the ruling class to another. In each case, "the repressive character of the state power was more fully developed and more mercilessly used" (197). State power under the Second Empire reached unprecedented and grotesque dimensions; the Second Empire was "the last triumph of a State separate of and independent from society" (151). And the Commune, for Marx, was "the direct antithesis to the Empire" (151): "The Commune . . . was a revolution against the State itself . . . a resumption by the people for the people of its own social life" (150). The Commune's form, in other words, was emancipatory because and to the extent that it did not form a state; because and to the extent that it proclaimed its historical capacity to organize all aspects of social life freely.

For Marx the "State" as such is only the modern state. It is only in modern times that the state becomes detached from society and forms a "parasitic excrescence," existing over and above society all the while dominating it. The abstraction of the state belongs to modernity, because the abstraction of private life—an apolitical, civil sphere organized around particular, individual interests—belongs only to modernity.

Already in his 1843 *Critique of Hegel's Doctrine of the State*, Marx had argued that the political state disappears in a true democracy. In that essay he presents an important critique of parliamentarism and of the modern representative principle itself that is worth reviewing here. Representation for Hegel (in the *Philosophy of Right*) demands *either* the use of deputies (representatives) *or* the participation of "all individuals as single individuals" in the decision making of all public affairs.[41] The terms of Hegel's choice—either the representative or each and every one—are interesting in that they recall the terms of Rimbaud's version of literary representation: "literally" and "*dans tous les sens*" (according to all possible meanings). *Either* a literal, straightforward notion of representation, where the representative—be it political deputy or poetic signifier— "stands in for" the represented (offstage, in the depths) *or* a kind of chaotic polysemia: in all possible ways, according to all possible significations, all individuals as individuals participating in all public affairs. (This, in fact, is how Rimbaud historically has been read: *either* literally [biographically] *or* as the exemplum of a Tel Quelian polysemic modernism.) Marx, however, proves Hegel's choice to be a false one, just as Rimbaud will insist that he be understood both literally *and* in all possible ways.

Marx, writing in 1843, undoes Hegel by emphasizing the modern state's detachment from civil society. It is that very detachment that makes "representatives" necessary:

> Either the political state is separated from civil society; in that event it
> is not possible for all as individuals to take part in the legislature. The
> political state leads an existence *divorced* from civil society . . . the fact
> that civil society takes part in the political state through its deputies is
> the expression of the separation.[42]

If the state is separated from civil society, then representatives are divided from those they represent. But what if such a separation, because historical, is not inevitable? What if politics were not a specialized set of activities, institutions, and occasions? What if the proper task of the poet were not, as Rimbaud's contemporary Mallarmé was to proclaim, to "render more pure the words of the masses [le tribu]''? What if there were no distinct political sphere, no distinctly poetic perception or language? Marx's critique of Hegel continues:

> Alternatively, civil society is the *real* political society. If so, it would be senseless to insist on a requirement which stems from the conception of the political state as something existing apart from civil society [for here] the *legislature* entirely ceases to be important as a *representative* body. The legislature is representative only in the sense that *every* function is representative. For example, a shoemaker is representative in so far as he satisfies a social need. . . . In this sense he is representative not by virtue of another thing which he represents but by virtue of what he *is* and *does*.[43]

If the separation between state and civil society does not exist, then politics becomes just another branch of social production. Political emancipation means emancipation from politics as a specialized activity. Marx concludes his critique of Hegel with the suppression of politics and the extinction of the state. Thirty years later the Commune, which was both the thing and the rallying cry, put an end to the separation between event and sign, and an end to labor and politics as class attributes.

The Commune, then, reawakened in Marx a critique of the state he had already, to some extent, formulated in his "immaturity." In 1872 he added a new preface to one of his "mature" texts, the 1848 *Communist Manifesto*, writing now against the "revolutionary measures" that had, in the 1848 version, hinged on "centralization . . . in the hands of the state":

> The practical applications of the principles will depend everywhere and at all times upon extant historical conditions. We therefore do not lay any special stress upon the revolutionary measures suggested at the close of the second section. In many respects the passage would have to be differently worded today . . . in view of the practical knowledge acquired during the two months' existence of the Paris Commune when the proletariat held political power for the first time . . . the program has, to a certain extent, become out of date. Above all the Commune of Paris has taught us that "the working class cannot simply lay hold of the ready-made state machinery, and wield it for its own purposes."[44]

The stronger focus on the division of labor that emerges in Marx's writing after the Commune is, on the other hand, new. The state is not merely an instrument of the bourgeoisie; its detachment from civil society, its status as a distinct organism, is attained only *through and by means of* the social division of labor. The organs of centralized state power—the standing army, the bureaucracy, the police, the clergy, the judiciary—are "organs wrought after the plan of a systematic and hierarchic division of labor" (197). The *means* through which the Commune was possible was simply its sustained attack on the divisions of labor that render administrations and government "mysteries, transcendent functions only to be trusted to the hands of a trained caste."[45]

Marx's return to the themes of his "immaturity," and to the consideration of the actual natures of political and social organization, shows a departure from and critique of the evolutionist, progressivist view of what is taken to be his middle, scientific, and "mature" phase: one that proclaims the inexorable march of history toward capitalist centralization.[46] The principal tenet of scientific socialism is well known: only at an objectively defined stage of socioeconomic development (that of "mature" capitalist mode of production) and only as a result of the class struggle of the proletariat (workers performing their sole historical task) can the socialist transformation take place. By the standards of scientific socialism, the Commune, that "unplanned, unguided, formless revolution,"[47] can only be seen as an evolutionary accident. The Communards are "out of sync" with the timetable of the inexorable march of history. They are not the industrialized proletariat they are supposed to be. Like adolescents they are moving at once too fast in their unplanned seizure of power and too slowly. They are caught up in what was by all accounts an unusually mild and festive spring, unaware of or ignoring the massive Versaillais threat being mobilized against them, playing at symbolic games: demolishing the Vendôme Column while leaving the Bank of France untouched. When Marx takes the Commune seriously, he must confront the possibility of a multiplicity of roads replacing the unique Highway of History; he must give new significance to the decentralization of sociopolitical power. The country that is more developed industrially might still not be destined to show to the less developed, as he had written in *Capital*, "the image of its own future."[48]

The developmental model of Marx's own theoretical evolution is troubled by this autocritique: one that puts into question the very notion of "maturity." Late Marx bends back and touches young Marx in a recognition of the inadequacy of unilinear, "progressive" models of historical analysis. "Science, the new nobility! Progress. The world is on the march. Why shouldn't it turn around?" (*Une Saison en enfer*). And Lautréamont: "Plagiarism is necessary. Progress implies it" (*Poésies II*).

Poetry and Prose

That Rimbaud turned his back on the late nineteenth-century narrative of "formation" is apparent upon reading his "autobiography," *Une Saison en enfer*. But then Rimbaud himself has always been coded as an immature or adolescent taste. As a poet he has been relegated to a realm of subjectivism entirely lacking in social reflexivity. Within the canon of French poetry he is prescribed, both in France and America, as adolescent reading—what one reads before acquiring the mature, sophisticated taste for Mallarmé or Valéry. His unwritten masterpieces of maturity, lost to the African desert, are mourned like the lost boots of Napoléon Gaillard.

The traditional, teleological narrative of nineteenth-century bourgeois French culture recounts an inevitable movement: the redirection of what were previously, in the early part of the century, *social* energies, toward a complacent, late-century textual irony. But where do Lautréamont and Rimbaud, not to mention less canonical figures, fit in this narrative? Rimbaud, as I read him, alters the balance away from the textual toward lived practices. Lautréamont, whom I will consider only briefly here, and Rimbaud are the authors of the great poetic epics of the nineteenth century, *Les Chants de Maldoror* and *Une Saison en enfer*, the adolescents who with one voice call for an end to what they deem individual or "personal poetry":

> Personal poetry has had its moment of juggling with the relative and contorting with the contingent. Let us take up again the indestructible thread of impersonal poetry. (Lautréamont, 1870)

> Basically, you see in your principle only a kind of subjective poetry; your obstinacy in getting back to the University trough — sorry — proves it. But you'll always wind up satisfied without having done anything, since you don't want to do anything. Which is not to mention the fact that your subjective poetry will always be horribly wishy-washy. One day, I hope — many others hope the same thing — I will see objective poetry in your principle, and see it more sincerely than you. (Rimbaud to Izambard, May 1871)

Although Lautréamont died in 1870 at the age of twenty-four, a few months before the victorious insurrection of March 18, his *Poésies* (I and II, 1870) nevertheless anticipates Commune forms, the sloganeering and invective I discuss in Chapter 5. And his *Chants de Maldoror* (1869) has yet to receive the materialist and historical interpretation called for by Aimé Césaire that would show in that "mad epic an aspect ignored by many, that of an implacable denunciation of a very precise form of society, such as it could only appear to one of its sharpest observers around the year 1865."[49] Maldoror, according to Césaire, is a Vautrin surrounded by a swarm of Uruguayan vampires.

Rimbaud and Lautréamont are poets; the novel, for Lautréamont, is a "false genre": "How the turpitudes of the novel squat (*s'accroupissent* — a Rimbaldian word) on display!" (*Poésies II*). At the same time Rimbaud and Lautréamont perform the iconoclastic gesture that annihilates the French poetic tradition. They see the poetry of the last two hundred years as personal, "subjective" poetry: "Since Racine poetry has not progressed one millimeter" (Lautréamont); "Racine alone is pure, strong, and great. . . . After Racine, the game gets moldy. It's been going on for two hundred years" (Rimbaud).

The problem with the poetry of the preceding two hundred years is not just its prosody or its subject matter; personal poetry is symptomatic of a crisis in the poet's role as citizen. Both Rimbaud and Lautréamont frame their future programs in terms of the Platonic division of labor: "A poet must be more *useful* than any citizen in his tribe" (Lautréamont). In Rimbaud's words:

> The future will be materialist, as you will see. . . . Essentially it will be Greek poetry again, in a way. This eternal art will be *functional*, since poets are citizens. Poetry will no longer give rhythm to action; *it will be in advance.*

Poetry then must exist as critique, as evaluation: the active expression of an active mode of existence. To produce poetry that would be an agent as well as an effect of cultural and political change, Lautréamont and the late Rimbaud choose a hybrid, poetic prose—the bastard mix of poetry and prose. Their choice is an oppositional one. Their adolescent, iconoclastic gesture stands out like an evolutionary accident, a different and startlingly abrupt rhythm in the critics' narrative of waning social energies. Could it be that the seamlessness of that narrative has something to do with its uncritical, unanalyzed, and finally unhistorical embrace of the phenomenon then transpiring during the very period under analysis: the universalization of prose, the cultural dominance of the novel genre?

Of course, one side of late nineteenth-century poetic production, that of Mallarmé, has had an extensive and subtle twentieth-century critical legacy. It can be traced in the stylistic allegiance owed him by a figure like Lacan, and in his status as master or Urtext for the branches of literary criticism that have developed in the last twenty years out of structural linguistics. How much of poststructural theory—Kristéva, de Man, and particularly Derrida—can be traced, directly or indirectly, to a meditation on Mallarmé?

In the light of the dominant narrative of nineteenth-century French culture, Rimbaud, Vermersch, Reclus and the others emerge as nineteenth-century instances of what might be called the "vernacular."[50] The vernacular is the equivalent of a language that is naive or inferior, somehow incomplete: a particular speech, a dialect. "I have always belonged to the inferior race," Rimbaud writes in "Bad Blood," and "not knowing how to express myself except in pagan words, I would rather keep silent." As against the streamlined, the mass-produced, and the mechanized, the vernacular stands out as something unique and handmade, "a product or situation which the mass-market, price-accounting and bureaucratic administration cannot handle to full effect."[51] The vernacular is that which must be uplifted, swept up into the universal language and the forward momentum of progress. But it resists. Prose, for instance, the medium of explication and exposition had, by the midcentury, become the tool of the great pedagogical movement of the century of progress—a century that would bring methodical, step-by-step enlightenment to the uneducated masses:

These are the conquerors of the world,
Seeking their personal chemical fortune;
Sport and comfort accompany them;
They bring education for races, for classes, for animals
Within this vessel, rest and vertigo
In diluvian light,
In terrible evenings of study.

("Mouvement")

Rimbaud's and Lautréamont's production of a nonexpository, nondidactic prose puts them on the side of emancipation rather than pedagogy. We must understand their resistance to progress as distinct from the antiprogressivist clamor that could be heard throughout the nineteenth century: the clamor of bourgeois intellectuals who feared progress because they thought it meant equality. Rimbaud and Lautréamont resist the institutionalization and representation of progress because they know it has nothing to do with equality.

In various forms the vernacular can be seen serving as conceptual banner for the feminist or environmental or black movements: the alternative, particularized, new revolutionary subjectivities of our own time. By "vernacular" I do not mean a self-satisfied regionalism, a separate preserve of popular wisdom or class purity. Rimbaud's work is more anxious than that. And its anxiety is the anxiety of frequent displacement—frequent movement in the cultural space where contagion and meeting places are allowed to spring up *between* one class and another, or even between one species and another. Rimbaud, in other words, does not set out to create a savage, adolescent, or Communard culture. He participates instead in the articulation of a savage, adolescent, or Communard relation *to* culture.

Notes

1. Gordon Wright, *France in Modern Times* (New York: Norton, 1981), 221.

2. See Stewart Edwards, *The Paris Commune: 1871* (Devon: Newton Abbot, 1972), 313-50, and Jacques Rougerie, *Procès des Communards* (Paris: Gallimard, 1978), for accounts of the repression of the Commune.

3. See Alain Dalotel, Alain Faure, and Jean-Claude Freiermuth, *Aux origines de la Commune: Le mouvement des réunions publiques à Paris 1868-1870* (Paris, 1980), for an analysis of the movement of *réunions publiques* in Paris between 1868 and 1870. Based on these documents the authors argue convincingly against one prevalent view of the Commune as having been born of the unusual circumstances brought on by the Franco-Prussian War; they trace its origins rather to the strikes and public meetings, the revolutionary movement that followed the law passed in June 1868 legalizing public meetings.

4. Catulle Mendès, *Les 73 journées de la Commune* (Paris: E. Lachaud, 1871), 149-50.

5. Louis Barron, *Sous le drapeau rouge* (Paris: Albert Savine, 1889), 167.

6. See especially Lefebvre's three-volume *Critique de la vie quotidienne* (Paris: L'Arche, 1958-81); see also his important works on urbanism and space: *Le Droit à la ville* (Paris: Anthropos, 1968),

La Révolution urbaine (Paris: Gallimard, 1970), and *La Production de l'espace* (Paris: Anthropos, 1974).

7. See Alice Kaplan and Kristin Ross, introduction to *Everyday Life*, *Yale French Studies* 73 (Fall 1987): 1-4.

8. For a thorough examination of the ideological underpinnings of the "new historicism," see Carolyn Porter, "Are We Being Historical Yet?" Proceedings of the "States of Theory" conference, University of California at Irvine, April 1987.

9. For an outline of this position, in which the events of May become the first sign of what has since developed into the rampant "individualism" of the 1980s, see *Pouvoirs* 39 (1986). This volume also contains an excellent refutation by Cornélius Castoriadis of this attempt to eclipse the events of the 1960s: "Les Mouvements des années soixantes," l07-16. For a more extended version of the right's position, see Gilles Lipovetsky, *L'Ere du vide: Essai sur l'individualisme contemporain* (Paris: Gallimard, 1983), and Luc Ferry and Alain Renaut, *La Pensée '68: Essai sur l'anti-humanisme contemporain* (Paris: Gallimard, 1985).

10. Fredric Jameson, *The Political Unconscious: Narrative as a Socially Symbolic Act* (Ithaca, N.Y.: Cornell University Press, 1981), 13.

11. See the Brecht/Lukács debates, reedited as Brecht, "Against Georg Lukács," trans. Stuart Hood in *Aesthetics and Politics* (London: New Left Books, 1977), 68-85.

12. Paul Reclus, *Les Frères Elie et Elisée Reclus* (Paris: Les Amis d'Elisée Reclus, 1964), 182. One interesting decree passed under the Commune concerning the Bibliothèque Nationale forbade the lending out of books — this privilege having been abused during the Second Empire by readers building up their private libraries out of the national collections (Edwards, *The Paris Commune 1871*, 307).

13. See Elie Reclus, *La Commune de Paris: au jour le jour; 19 mars-28 mai, 1871* (Paris: Schleicher Frères, 1908); Jean-Baptiste Clément, *1871: La Revanche des Communeux* (Paris: Jean Marie, 1886-87); Louise Michel, *La Commune* (Paris: Editions Stock, 1898).

14. George J. Becker (ed.), *Paris under Siege, 1870-1871: From the Goncourt Journal* (Ithaca, N.Y.: Cornell University Press, 1969), 312. Goncourt's sentiments were echoed by other bourgeois writers and artists, most notably, perhaps, by Leconte de Lisle, who in a letter dated May 29, 1871, to fellow Parnassian José Maria de Hérédia, writes: "I hope that the repression will be such that nothing will ever move again and for my part I hope that it will be total."

15. For an account of the activities and significance of the Fédération des Artistes, see Adrian Rifkin, "Cultural Movement and the Commune," in *Art History* 2 (June 1979): 201-20, esp. 214-15.

16. Franco Moretti, *Signs Taken for Wonders: Essays in the Sociology of Literary Forms*, trans. Susan Fischer (London: Verso, 1983), 143.

17. Plato, *Republic*, II, cited in Jacques Rancière, *Le Philosophe et ses pauvres* (Paris, 1983), 30. The following discussion about the status of the artisan and the Platonic division of labor is indebted to Rancière's very provocative discussion of these questions, 17-88.

18. *L'Artiste*, April 1845, cited in Rancière, *Le Philosophe et ses pauvres*, 94.

19. Charles Nodier, "De l'utilité morale de l'instruction pour le peuple," *Rêveries* (Paris: Plasma, 1979), 182-83. Nodier recounts with satisfaction the example of a shoemaker who had the "admirable good sense" to "stay in his place": "three of my friends, Benjamin Constant, Jouy and Montègre, introduced me to a shoemaker named M. François, whose tragedies in the style of Corneille had dismayed the police of the Empire. This excursion off the paths of his natural destiny by a man whom I had begun to like worried me. He was aware of this. 'Don't worry,' he said to me, laughing. 'To have fun I make tragedies, to gain a living, I make boots.' "

20. See Rancière, *Le Philosophe et ses pauvres*, 26-36.

21. Jules Mesnard, *Les Merveilles de l'Exposition de 1867* (Paris: Imp. de l'Ahure, 1867), 6.

22. Adrian Rifkin, "Well-formed Phrases: Some Limits of Meaning in Political Print at the End of the Second Empire," *Oxford Art Journal* 8 (1985): 24.

23. See his *Les Ouvriers Européens* [orig. ed. 1864] (Tours: A. Maine, 1877-79), and *La Réforme sociale en France, déduite de l'observation comparée des peuples Européens* (Paris: Plon, 1864).

24. See Rifkin, "Well-formed Phrases," esp. 22-25.

25. Denis Poulot, *Le Sublime, ou le travailleur comme il est en 1870, et ce qu'il peut être* (Paris: Maspero, 1980). See especially the brilliant introduction to this edition by Alain Cottereau, "Vie quotidienne et résistance ouvrière à Paris en 1870," 7-102. Cottereau reinterprets Poulot's condemnation of the worker in *Le Sublime* as an encyclopedia of the ruses developed by workers to resist efforts to control their work and home life.

26. Alfred Delvau's *Dictionnaire de le langue verte* (Paris: Marpon & Flammarion, 1883), indispensable for reading Rimbaud, defines these workers' slang terms: *chouette*, a superlative of good; *rupin*, superlative of noble or elegant; *d'attaque*, to be solid or resolute. The first edition of Delvau's dictionary appeared in 1865.

27. Rancière, *Le Philosophe et ses pauvres*, 108.

28. Courbet, cited in Robert Boudry, "Courbet et la Fédération des artistes," *Europe*, April-May 1951, 125.

29. Rancière, *Le Philosophe et ses pauvres*, 92.

30. Le Comte d'Hérisson, *Nouveau journal d'un Officier d'ordonnance: La Commune* (Paris: Ollendorff, 1889), 295-96. Rifkin's discussion of Gaillard is part of his forthcoming book; see what are undoubtedly the most useful and provocative analyses of cultural movement (particularly visual and musical) at the end of the Second Empire and during the Commune in the articles cited in notes 15 and 22, and in "No Particular Thing to Mean," *Block* 8 (1983): 36-45.

31. Elisée Reclus, cited in Gary Dunbar, "Elisée Reclus, Geographer and Anarchist," *Antipode* 10 and 11 (1979): 16.

32. Jacques Rancière, "La Représentation de l'ouvrier ou la classe impossible," in Phillipe Lacoue-Lebarthe and Jean-Luc Nancy (eds.), *Le Retrait du politique*, (Paris: Galilée, 1983), 96.

33. Rancière, "La Représentation de l'ouvrier," 103.

34. Walter Benjamin, "Conversations with Brecht," in *Understanding Brecht*, trans. Anya Bostock (London: New Left Books, 1973), 116.

35. Louis Gabriel Gauny, *Le Philosophe plébien*, ed. Jacques Rancière (Paris: Le Découverte, 1983), 115-16.

36. Ernest Delahaye, *Rimbaud: L'Artiste et l'être moral* (Paris: Albert Messein, 1923), 38.

37. Karl Marx and Friedrich Engels, *Writings on the Paris Commune*, ed. H. Draper (New York: Monthly Review Press, 1971), 76.

38. See Derek Sayer and Philip Corrigan, "Late Marx: Continuity, Contradiction and Learning," in Teodor Shanin (ed.), *Late Marx and the Russian Road: Marx and the "Peripheries of Capitalism"* (New York: Monthly Review Press, 1983), 77-94; see also, in the same volume, Shanin's "Late Marx: Gods and Craftsmen," 3-39. These two articles argue, with interesting differences of opinion, for a reevaluation of the late Marx in the light of his own consideration of the Paris Commune and Russian revolutionary populism. I am indebted to these articles for the version of Marx that follows, and to Terry Cochran for making me aware of this book.

39. See Jacques Rougerie, *Procès des Communards*, 125-34, for a systematic breakdown of the backgrounds of the Communards. See also Manuel Castells, "Cities and Revolution: The Commune of Paris, 1871," in *City and the Grassroots* (Berkeley: University of California, 1983), 15-26.

40. Prosper-Oliver Lissagaray, *Histoire de la commune de 1871* (1876; reprint, Paris: Maspero, 1967), 110.

41. See Lucio Colletti's discussion of Marx's critique of Hegel in his introduction to Karl Marx, *Early Writings*, trans. Rodney Livingstone and Gregor Benton (New York: Vintage, 1975), 7-56, esp. 41-45.

42. Karl Marx, *Critique of Hegel's Doctrine of the State* in *Early Writings*, 189-90.

43. Ibid., 190.

44. Marx, preface to the 1872 German edition of *The Communist Manifesto*, ed. D. Ryazanoff (New York: Russell & Russell, 1963), 260.

45. Marx, ibid., 153. See also Sayer and Corrigan, "Late Marx," 88.

46. Shanin, "Late Marx," 20-29.

47. Stewart Edwards (ed.), *The Communards of Paris, 1871* (Ithaca, N.Y.: Cornell University Press, 1973), 9.

48. Karl Marx, *Capital* (Harmondsworth: Penguin, 1979), I, 91.

49. Aimé Césaire, *Discours sur le colonialisme* (Paris: Présence Africaine, 1955), 45.

50. I borrow the use of this term from Teodor Shanin, "Marxism and the Vernacular Revolutionary Traditions," in *Late Marx and the Russian Road*, 243-79.

51. Ibid., 249.

Chapter 1
The Transformation of Social Space

I

Attempts to discuss Rimbaud in terms of the events of 1871 have for the most part been limited to frenzied interrogations by literary historians and biographers anxious to ascertain his precise physical whereabouts during the months of March to May 1871.[1] Was Rimbaud an active participant in the insurrection? Which informants are to be believed? Even to pose the question in this form reveals the anxiety of the empiricist working in the service of reductivism—a reductivism that most likely has political (recuperative) motivations. Would Rimbaud's absence, definitively proved, from the scene of the crime, in turn definitively silence the social and political repercussions of his work? Would an eyewitness account of his presence on the barricades give a political interpretation of his poetry more validity?

The actual, complex links binding Rimbaud to the events in Paris are not to be established by measuring geographic distance. Or, if they are, it is perhaps by considering Rimbaud's poetry, produced at least in part within the rarefied situation of his isolation in Charleville, as one creative response to the same objective situation to which the insurrection in Paris was another. In what way does Rimbaud figure or prefigure a social space adjacent—side by side rather than analogous—to the one activated by the insurgents in the heart of Paris?

To begin to answer this question I propose postponing for now a discussion of Rimbaud's most explicitly and thematically "political" poems—poems like "Les Mains de Jeanne-Marie," which praises the revolutionary actions of women during the Commune, or "Chant de guerre parisien," announced by Rimbaud under the rubric of a "contemporary psalm" and featuring verbal caricatures of Favre and Thiers lifted straight from the stockpile of revolutionary imagery used in political cartoons and gravures produced during the early months of 1871. Such overtly political verse is important for an ideological reading of Rimbaud, but no more so, I hope to show, than the early Charleville erotic verse (or, for that matter, than the late "hermetic" prose poems)—in Rimbaud there is little distance between political economy and libidinal economy. And the significance of the Commune is most evident in what Marx called its "working existence": in its *displacement* of the political onto seemingly peripheral areas of everyday life—the organization of space and time, changes in lived rhythms and social ambiences. The insurgents' brief mastery of their own history is perceptible, in other words, not so much on the level of governmental politics as on the level of their daily life: in concrete problems of work, leisure, housing, sexuality, and family and neighborhood relations. Revolutionary struggle is diffuse as well as specifically directed, expressed throughout the various cultural spheres and institutional contexts, in specific conflicts and in the manifold transformations of individuals rather than in some rigid and polar opposition of capital and labor. Taking seriously such a "displacement of the political" can point us in the direction of certain of Rimbaud's poems thematically at a distance from the turbulence in Paris: the early ironic and erotic everyday Rimbaud of kisses, beer, and country walks.

Like much of Rimbaud's early lyric poetry, "Rêvé pour l'hiver" (1870) puts forth a particular imagination of the nineteenth-century commonplace of "the voyage." The poem opens with the dream of an enclosed, infantile universe:

> L'hiver, nous irons dans un petit wagon rose
> Avec des coussins bleus.
> Nous serons bien. Un nid de baisers fous repose
> Dans chaque coin moelleux.

> [In winter we shall travel in a little pink railway carriage
> With blue cushions.
> We'll be comfortable. A nest of mad kisses lies in wait
> In each soft corner.]

The interior of the carriage is created oppositionally to the winter outside; inside is warmth, well-being and comfort (the simplicity of "Nous serons bien"), repose and restfulness. The muted pastel colors suggest a nursery; the carriage is a nest where the violence and jolts of the voyage are cushioned and where all sensation or sound of moving through space is dulled. The passage will not be noticed.

But if the carriage is a nest, it is also the container of nests—a potential disturbance in the nursery is suggested by the adjective "mad," whose threat is for the moment attenuated by the verb *repose*. Madness is there, a violence oddly separated and detached from the actors and seemingly part of the environment, but it is, at least at present, a sleeping *folie*.

> Tu fermeras l'oeil, pour ne point voir, par la glace,
>> Grimacer les ombres des soirs,
> Ces monstruosités hargneuses, populace
>> De démons noirs et de loups noirs.

> [You will close your eyes, so as not to see through the window
>> The evening shadows grimacing,
> Those snarling monsters, a swarm
>> Of black devils and black wolves.]

The second stanza opens out onto the landscape, continuing the childlike tone whereby shadows are frozen into grimaces not unlike the anthropomorphized nature illustrations in the popular children's books (*petits livres d'enfance*) Rimbaud mentions in "Alchimie du verbe." Still, it is the gesture of cushioning, or refusing the experience of voyaging, that appears to hold sway. You will close your eyes to the outside, shutting off vision—that which continually makes and undoes relations between the voyager and the outer world. You will believe yourself intact because surrounded by the walls of the carriage. But the refusal of vision is double-edged: it is also a relinquishing of the mastery involved in any viewer/viewed relation, the domination of the look. To stop seeing the horrifying exterior through the window is, by the same token, to shut off the possibility of defining the interior by its contrary. Gone then is the protection of being distanced from the outside world that would remain there, detached, frozen into an illustration. The closing of the eyes makes the illustration come alive and awakens the sleeping madness:

> Puis tu te sentiras la joue égratignée . . .
> Un petit baiser, comme une folle araignée,
>> Te courra par le cou . . .

> Et tu me diras: "Cherche!" en inclinant la tête,
> —Et nous prendrons du temps à trouver cette bête
>> —Qui voyage beaucoup . . .

> [Then you will feel your cheek scratched . . .
> A little kiss, like a mad spider,
>> Will run about your neck . . .

> And you'll say to me "Find it!" bending your head,

—And we'll take a long time to find that creature
—Who travels far . . .]

A kiss begins its journey; as a spider, it shares with the outer world the quality of darkness; its threatening aspect is underlined by the repetition of the adjective "mad." The outside invades the inside, the nursery is threatened by erotic madness. Closing the eyes awakens the possibility of haptic perception—touch rather than an abstracted and distanced mastery of the scenery. The word *égratignée* signals the movement from *voir* to *faire*; the violence of contact is reminiscent of key moments in many of the poems of *opening*, moments when seams are exposed, the instant of scratching the surface: the fingernails on the child's scalp in "Les Chercheuses de poux," the *picotement* of "Sensation," the holes in the pockets and trousers in "Ma Bohème"; "A blast of air pierces gaps in the partitions, . . . blows away the limits of homes" ("Nocturne vulgaire"). Rimbaud's poetry as a poetry of transformation is crystallized in this moment: the phenomenon of an absolutely commanding perception of the transformation brought on in us by the event of "contact," "opening," "rupture." Thus the importance of the reflexive form in many of these moments: "Puis tu *te* sentiras . . ."

The adjective *petit* used to describe the carriage in the first verse is repeated apropos of the kiss; the kiss shares with the carriage the properties of motion and time as well. The movement of the poem follows the invisible silent machine, the carriage, tracing its passage through space, and the spider/kiss, tracing its passage along the microgeography of the woman's body. These two transgressive movements become one, and what has initially functioned as a mode of separation, an enclosed module transporting its passengers through space, becomes in the intruding spider/kiss what articulates or breaks down the division between interior and exterior. Roland Barthes, speaking of the more extensive and dramatic play with the boundary between inner and outer space that occurs in Rimbaud's "Bateau ivre," calls this the move beyond a psychoanalysis of the cavern to a true poetics of exploration.[2] And indeed, the lover's exclamation, "Cherche!" the only sound in the poem, becomes a true *invitation au voyage*—the invitation to conceive of space *not* as a static reality but as active, generative, to experience space as created by an interaction, as something that our bodies reactivate, and that through this reactivation, in turn modifies and transforms us. The space of the voyage, whose unmapped itinerary lies in the dashes and ellipses that crowd the end of the poem, merges with a temporal passage ("And we'll take a long time . . .") that guarantees that the voyagers will not be the same individuals at the end of the trip that they were at the beginning.

The poem, as such, constitutes a movement and not a tableau, a *récit* rather than a map. Instead of the abstract visual constructions proper to the stasis of a geographic notion of space, the poem creates a "nonpassive" spatiality—space as a specific form of operations and interactions. In the late 1860s the expression "chercher la petite bête" was prevalent slang for wanting to know the inner workings of a thing, the hidden reasons of an affair—like a child wanting to know what lies beneath a watch face. But it was also a slang expression popular among literati, who used it to signify amusing oneself on the level of stylistics instead of bearing down on serious matters of content.[3] The turns and detours of the spider—ruse, madness, desire, passage—are at once the turns and detours of figures of style, an erotics, and a manner of moving through the world. It is this prefiguration of a reactivated space that in turn becomes transformative that we will take as our point of access to the event or "working existence" of the Commune.

II

In his *Mémoires*, Gustave-Paul Cluseret, the Commune's first Delegate of War, reflects on the lessons to be learned from the street fighting at the end of the Commune, and, in the process, details the philosophy and strategic use of that topographically persistent insurgent construction, the barricade. The building of barricades was, first of all, to be carried out as quickly as possible; in contrast to the unique, well-situated, and centralized civic monument, whose aura derives from its isolation and stability, barricades were not designed around the notion of a unique "proper place": street platoons were to set up as many barricades as they could as quickly as possible. Their construction was, consequently, haphazard and makeshift:

> It is therefore not necessary for these barricades to be perfectly
> constructed; they can very well be made of overturned carriages, doors
> torn off their hinges, furniture thrown out of windows, cobblestones
> where these are available, beams, barrels, etc.[4]

Monumental ideals of formal perfection, duration or immortality, quality of material and integrity of design are replaced by a special kind of *bricolage*—the wrenching of everyday objects from their habitual context to be used in a radically different way. A similar awareness of the tactical mission of the commonplace can be found in Rimbaud's parodic "Ce qu'on dit au poète à propos de fleurs" where standard Parnassian "tools" are rendered *truly* utilitarian: "Trouve, ô Chasseur, nous le voulons, / Quelques garances parfumées / Que la Nature en pantalons / Fasse éclore!—pour nos Armées! . . . Trouve des Fleurs qui soient des chaises!!" ("Find, O Hunter, we desire it, / One or two scented madder plants / Which Nature may cause to bloom into trousers—For our Armies! . . . Find Flowers which are chairs!") In this poem and elsewhere Rimbaud's paradoxical solution to the sterility of Parnassian imagery is, on the one hand, an unqualified return to the full range of ordinary experience—everyday life—at its most banal and, on the other hand, a breakthrough to a distinctly utopian space. Similarly, anything, writes Cluseret, can serve as building material, anything can be a weapon—"explosives, furniture, and in general, anything that can be used as a projectile"—and any person can be a soldier:

Passersby were stopped to help construct the barricades. A battalion of National Guards occupied the area, and the sentries called on everyone passing to contribute their cobblestone willy-nilly to the defense effort.[5]

But perhaps the most crucial point to emphasize concerning the barricades was their strategic use: they were *not*, as Auguste Blanqui also makes clear in his *Instructions pour une prise d'armes*, to be used as shelter. Barricades, writes Cluseret, "are not intended to shelter their defenders, since these people will be inside the houses, but to prevent enemy forces from circulating, to bring them to a halt and to enable the insurrectionists to pelt them with . . . anything that can be used as a projectile." Cluseret's remarks are reflections that took place after the event on how the defense should have been carried out; in fact, much of the actual fighting, particularly during the final massacres of the *semaine sanglante*, took the form of traditional hand-to-hand combat. Nevertheless, some of the urban guerilla strategies outlined or prescribed by Cluseret and Blanqui seem to have been followed. In the memoirs he dashed off immediately after the demise of the Commune, Catulle Mendès describes the difficulties experienced by the disciplined Versaillais soldiers in gaining access to certain Parisian *quartiers*:

But at other points in Paris, military operations were less successful. In the Faubourg Saint-Germain, the army advances very slowly, if it advances at all. The federalists fight with a heroic brutality; from street corners, from windows, from atop balconies ring gunshots, rarely ineffective. This sort of war tires the soldiers, whose discipline does not allow them to respond with similar maneuvers. In Saint-Ouen as well, the forward march of the troops has been halted; the barricade on the rue de Clichy holds strong and will hold for a long time.[6]

The immediate function of the barricades, then, was to prevent the free circulation of the enemy through the city—to "halt" them or immobilize them so that they, the enemy, could become targets. The insurgents, meanwhile, who have mobility on their side, offer no targets: "offering them no targets. . . . No one is in sight. This is the crucial point." To this end Blanqui advocated the strategy known as "piercing the houses":

When, on the line of defense, a house is particularly threatened, we demolish the staircase from the ground floor, and open up holes in the floorboards of the next floor, in order to be able to fire on the soldiers invading the ground floor.[7]

Cluseret writes of a "lateral piercing" of the houses: "Troops guard the ground floor while others climb quickly to the next floor and immediately break through the wall to the adjoining house and so on and so forth as far as possible.'' Houses are gutted in such a way that the insurgents can move freely in all directions through passageways and networks of communication joining houses together; the enemy on the street is rendered frozen and stationary. ''Street fighting does not take place in the streets but in the houses, not in the open but undercover.'' Street fighting depends on mobility or permanent displacement. It depends on changing houses into passageways—reversing or suspending the division between public and private space. ''A blast of air pierces gaps in the partitions . . . blows away the limits of homes'' (''Nocturne vulgaire''). Walter Benjamin writes that for the *flaneur* at the end of the Second Empire, the city is metamorphosed into an interior; for the Communards the reverse is true: the interior becomes a street.

III

Commentators on the Commune from Marx and Engels on have singled out the Communards' failure to attack that most obvious of monumental targets, the Bank of France:

> The hardest thing to understand is certainly the holy awe with which they remained outside the gates of the Bank of France. This was also a serious political mistake. The Bank in the hands of the Commune—this would have been worth more than 10,000 hostages.[8]

Engels evaluates the ''serious political mistake'' by calculating a rate of exchange between bank and hostages. Not surprisingly, his analysis is situated soundly in the realm of political economy. In the early 1960s the Situationists— a group whose project lay at the intersection of the revolutionary workers' movement and the artistic ''avant-garde''—proposed another sort of analysis, one that altered the sphere of political economy by bringing transformations on the level of everyday life from the peripheries of its analysis to the center. To the extent that the Situationist critique of everyday life was inseparable from the project of intervening into, transforming lived experience, the activities of the group can be seen to fall under the dual banner of Engels's ''making conscious the unconscious tendencies of the Commune'' and Rimbaud's ''Changer la Vie.'' In the failure of the Commune—its failure, that is, in the classical terms of the workers' movement, to produce what later, more ''successful'' revolutions produced, namely, a state bureaucracy—in that failure the Situationists saw its success. To view the Commune from the perspective of the transformation of everyday life would demand, then, that we juxtapose the Communards' political failure or mistake—leaving intact the Bank of France—with one of their more ''monumental'' achievements: the demolition of the Vendôme Column, built by Napoléon to glorify the victories of the Grand Army. On the one hand, a reticence, a refusal to act; on the other, violence and destruction as complete reappropriation: the creation, through destruction, of a positive social void, the refusal of the dominant organization of social space and the supposed neutrality of monuments. The failure of the Communards in the "mature" realm of military and politico-economic efficacy is balanced by their accomplishments in the Imaginary or preconscious space that lies outside specific and directly representable class functions—the space that could be said to constitute the realm of political desire rather than need.

What monuments are to the Communards—petrified signs of the dominant social order—the canon is to Rimbaud:

> Les blancs débarquent. Le canon! Il faut se
> soummettre au baptème, s'habiller, travailler.
> J'ai reçu au coeur le coup de grâce. Ah! je ne
> l'avais pas prévu!
>
> [The whites are landing. The cannon! We will
> have to submit to baptism, get dressed, and work.
> I have received in my heart the stroke of
> mercy. Ah! I had not foreseen it!]

This imaginary historical reconstruction, which occurs near the middle of the "Mauvais Sang" section of *Une Saison en enfer*, depicts a scene in the colonization of everyday life. In his attempt to rewrite his genealogy, to find another history, another language, the narrator has adopted the persona of an African. Precisely at that moment, the colonists arrive. The "coup de grâce" is also the shot of the cannon: in this context, the word *canon* should be taken, as Rimbaud said elsewhere, *littéralement et dans tous les sens*—not only as a piece of artillery or as a law of the church, but as the group of books admitted as being divinely inspired. The cannon is also an arm that implies an economic investment that only a state apparatus can make.

(The issue of canonization should play an important role in any discussion of Rimbaud *today*, given the ideologically significant modification of the "place" of Rimbaud in the literary canon that has occurred over the last twenty years. Dominant methodological or theoretical concerns have always generated a list of chosen texts that best suit their mode of analysis. Literary theory of the last twenty years—from structuralism to deconstruction—is no exception. It has, to a certain extent, brought about a rewriting of the canon that has elevated Mallarmé while visibly neglecting Rimbaud; this rewriting in and of itself attests to Rimbaud's resistance to a purely linguistic or "textual" reading.)

It is, however, the most extended sense of the word *canon*—the set of rules or norms used to determine an ideal of beauty in the Beaux Arts—that dominates

Une Saison en enfer. Beauty appears in the opening lines of the poem, capitalized and personified, seated on the knees of the narrator and cursed by him: "Un soir, j'ai assis la Beauté sur mes genoux. Et je l'ai trouvée amère. Et je l'ai injuriée." ("One evening I sat Beauty on my knees. And I found her bitter. And I cursed her.") It is the transformation of this idealized beauty into a "decanonized," lowercase form by the end of the narrative—"Je sais aujourd'hui saluer la *beauté*"—that constitutes, along with the gradual construction of a plural subject, the primary direction and movement of the poem. But the decanonization of beauty is not just a change in the object; it is a transformation in the relation of the narrator to the object—a transformation signaled by the verb *saluer* (a greeting that is both a hello and a farewell): thus, a relation to beauty that is no longer timeless or immortal, but transitory, acknowledging change and death.

The verb *saluer* appears again near the conclusion in one of the poem's most celebrated passages:

> Quand irons-nous, par delà les grèves et les monts, saluer la naissance du travail nouveau, la sagesse nouvelle, la fuite des tyrans et des démons, la fin de la superstition, adorer—les premiers!—Noël sur la terre!

> [When will we journey beyond the beaches and the mountains, to hail the birth of new work, new wisdom, the flight of tyrants and demons, the end of superstition; to adore—the first!—Christmas on earth!]

Here *saluer* is unambiguous and the poem concludes with the anticipation of, the unmitigated yearning for, the birth of new social relations figured in properly spatial terms: the as yet to emerge revolutionary space of "Noël sur la terre." The various geographic synonyms for "Noël sur la terre" that spring up at the end of the poem, the "splendid cities," the "beaches without end," are all situated in a future time, which suggests that "Noël sur la terre" is to be construed not as the founding of a new "proper place" but rather as that which, in its instability, in its displacement or deferment, exists as the breakdown of the notion of proper place: be it heaven or hell, Orient or Occident, winter or summer. The dizzying religious or vertical topography of the poem, with its meteoric descents and ascensions ("I believe myself to be in hell, so I am"; "hell is certainly *below*—and heaven above"; "Ah! to climb back up into life"; "It's the flames which rise up with their damned one"), is resolved in the narrative's final sections by a horizontal and social topography ("I, who called myself magus or angel, exempt from all morality, I am given back to the earth, with a task to pursue"), a kind of lateral vision that is not so much a vision as a movement ("The song of the heavens, the march of peoples!"), and not so much a movement as a future movement: "Let us receive all the influx of vigor and real tenderness. And, at dawn, armed with an ardent patience, we will enter into splendid cities.''

To the extent that the particular revolutionary realization of the Commune can be seen in its political understanding of social space, we can speak here of an analogous breakdown of the notion of "proper place." Class division is also the division of the city into active and passive zones, into privileged places where decisions are made in secret, and places where these decisions are executed afterward. The rise of the bourgeoisie throughout the nineteenth century was inscribed on the city of Paris in the form of Baron Haussmann's architectural and social reorganization, which gradually removed workers from the center of the city to its northeastern peripheries, Belleville and Menilmontant. An examination of the voting records in the municipal elections organized by the Commune shows this social division clearly: less than 25 percent of the inhabitants of the bourgeois *quartiers*, the 7th and 8th, voted in the election; only the 10th, 11th, 12th, and 18th, workers' *quartiers*, and the 5th, the university district, voted at more than half.[9] The workers' redescent into the center of Paris followed in part from the political significance of the city center within a tradition of popular insurgency, and in part from their desire to reclaim the public space from which they had been expelled, to reoccupy streets that once were theirs.

If workers are those who are not allowed to transform the space/time allotted them, then the lesson of the Commune can be found in its recognition that revolution consists not in changing the juridical form that allots space/time (for example, allowing a party to appropriate bureaucratic organization) but rather in completely transforming the nature of space/time. It is here that Marx's "Transform the World" and Rimbaud's "Changer la Vie" become, as the Surrealists proclaimed, the same slogan. The working existence of the Commune constituted a critique pronounced against geographic zoning whereby diverse forms of socioeconomic power are installed: a breakdown of a privileged place or places in favor of a permanent exchange between distinct places–thus, the importance of the *quartier*. Lefebvre's work is especially important in emphasizing the disintegration of the practical, material foundations and habits that organized daily life during the hardships of the siege of Paris in the fall and winter of 1870.[10] In the midst of this disintegration sprang up new networks and systems of communication solidifying small groups: local neighborhood associations, women's clubs, legions of the National Guard, and, above all, the social life of the *quartier*—groups whose often avowedly revolutionary aspirations were allowed to develop freely in part because the government lacked both the means and the authority to police the city. The local *arrondissement* gained a considerable degree of autonomy, and the heavily populated popular districts had come close to being self-governing. The siege allowed new ambiences, new manners of encountering or of meeting with one another to develop that are both the product and the instrument of transformed behavior.

The breakdown of spatial hierarchy in the Commune, one aspect of which was the establishment of places of political deliberation and decision making that were no longer secret but open and accessible, brought about a breakdown in temporal division as well. The publicity of political life, the immediate publication of all the Commune's decisions, and proclamations, largely in the form of *affiches*, resulted in a "spontaneous" temporality whereby citizens were no longer informed of their history after the fact but were actually occupying the moment of its realization. If the city and its streets were in fact reappropriated by the Communards, this undoubtedly entailed a Communard reinvention of urban rhythms: white nights and "revolutionary days" that are not simply certain days marked off on a calendar, but are rather the introduction to and immersion in a new temporal movement. Journals and accounts of everyday life during the Commune written by people active in the insurrection suggest a particular and contradictory movement of time, a duration experienced as being at once more rapid and more slow than usual.[11] We will return to this peculiar temporality at some length in the next chapter; for now, we can describe the sensation as being a simultaneous perception of events passing by quickly, too quickly, and of each hour and minute being entirely lived or made use of: saturated time.

The workers who occupied the Hôtel de Ville or who tore down the Vendôme Column were not "at home" in the center of Paris; they were occupying enemy territory, the circumscribed proper place of the dominant social order. Such an occupation, however brief, provides an example of what the Situationists have called a *détournement* — using the elements or terrain of the dominant social order to one's own ends, for a transformed purpose; integrating actual or past productions into a superior construction of milieu.[12] *Détournement* has no other place but the place of the other; it plays on imposed terrain and its tactics are determined by the absence of a "proper place." Thus, the *détournement* of churches: using them to hold the meetings of women's clubs or other worker organizations. *Détournement* is no mere Surrealist or arbitrary juxtaposition of conflicting codes; its aim, at once serious and ludic, is to strip false meaning or value from the original:

> When the Club Communal of the Salle Molière took over the church of Saint-Nicolas-des-Champs, "a public monument that until then had served only a caste, born enemy of all progress," this was announced as a "great revolutionary act" by the population of the district.[13]

A similar aim is apparent in Rimbaud's "Ce qu'on dit au poète à propos de fleurs," where the literary code of Parnassian aestheticism is "deturned" by a jarring influx of social, utilitarian vocabulary:

> Ainsi, toujours vers l'azur noir
> Où tremble la mer des topazes,

Fonctionneront dans ton soir
Les Lys, ces clystères d'extases!

[Thus, continually toward the dark azure
Where the sea of topazes shimmers,
Will function in your evening
Lilies, those enemas of ecstasy!]

Here the echo to Lamartine at his most elegiac ("Ainsi toujours poussés vers de nouveaux rivages . . .") coexists with the most mechanistic and technical of jargons: *fonctionneront* and *clystères*. What is the effect of the audacious realism of a word like *fonctionneront*? Rimbaud's insertion of technical vocabulary is purely strategic, and the word takes on significance only in the context of its Parnassian surroundings—of its relations with it and in dynamic criticism of it. Rimbaud's lexical anomalies, in other words, should not be considered as the mutation of isolated elements. We should always bear in mind that change lies in the *relation* of elements to each other: the particular dynamic created by what we might call lexical shock, incest, bastardism, or other such arrangements. Nor should the oppositional dynamic at work in "Ce qu'on dit . . ." be understood as accidental or haphazard—an arbitrary, extrinsically conceived assemblage of juxtaposed disparate parts or discourses. Rather, the poem produces its own parts by active differentiation that in turn reform themselves into a new unity.

Certainly, the introduction of a jarringly "nonpoetic" word like *fonctionneront*, placed in such close proximity to "shimmering topazes," serves to assault the elite enclosure of Parnassian aesthetic isolationism, marooned and cut adrift as it was from the world of working relations and wider social institutions. It lays bare the Parnassian high bourgeois flight from the realm of utility—a flight governed, it would seem, by fear of the very contagion the poem enacts: fear of contact with the popular, fear of industrial "progress" conceived of as social equality. But Rimbaud's gesture is double-, perhaps triple-edged. For although his use of technical vocabulary allies him with a class culture whose concerns—science, politics, social organization—are distinct from the aesthetic and metaphysical interests of orthodox Parnassian culture, it does not, on the other hand, imply his entrenchment in some distinct, preconceived, countercultural identity. By the same token, the abrupt shock of lexical juxtaposition manages on a formal level to keep at bay the smooth ideological agenda—the whole reasoned march of progress regulated by instruction, by scientific principles and by the general interest, progress as the dominant explication of the social order, and of a society that thinks itself under the aegis of perfectibility—associated with the vocabulary of utility.

Elsewhere in Rimbaud's poetry, a similar subversion is carried out by the trivial, commonplace nature of the represented object, the introduction of the detail that is neither distinguished nor abject, the detail that has no higher significance than itself: the clove of garlic in "Au Cabaret-Vert."

IV

Accounts of the Commune and accounts of the "phenomenon" of Rimbaud rely on a shared vocabulary:

> Rimbaud erupts into literature, throws a few lightning bolts and disappears, abandoning us from then on to what looks like twilight. We had hardly time to see him. . . . This is enough for the legend to be born and develop.[14]

> The seventy-two days from 18 March to 28 May 1871, the length of time Paris was able to hold out against the National Government at Versailles and its army, though too short to carry out any permanent measures of social reform, were long enough to create the myth, the legend of the Commune as the first great workers' revolt.[15]

Brevity, eruption, lightning flash, myth, legend—these are the words that recur. Mallarmé, for example, uses the metaphor of a meteor when speaking of Rimbaud; René Char writes of his "sudden evaporation." Qualities of speed, brevity, and brilliance are transferred from the biographical phenomena to the production and reception of the work: anarchist art and literary critic Félix Fénéon, one of the first serious readers of the *Illuminations*, describes these poems in 1887 as having "suddenly appeared, scattered by shocks into radiant repercussions";[16] Leo Bersani writes of Rimbaud's work as that of someone who wants to " 'stay' in language as briefly as possible."[17] Neither Rimbaud, "the first poet of a civilization that has not yet appeared" (Char), nor the Commune, that "unplanned, unguided, formless revolution,"[18] reached maturity. Perhaps it is this joint lingering in the liminal zone of adolescence—what Mallarmé, referring to Rimbaud, called "a perverse and superb puberty"—that tends to create anxiety. For it is striking to see the way in which narratives of both subjects, for the most part, adhere to a traditional developmental model, concluding almost invariably with a consideration of the reasons for the failure of the Commune to become stabilized, of Rimbaud to remain loyal to literature, and ensuing motifs: the silence of Rimbaud, the demise of the Commune. Speculations abound as to what "fulfillment" or "adulthood" *might have* looked like: the poems Rimbaud would have written in Africa, the social reforms the Commune would have put through had it been given the time to stabilize.

But such an omniscient theoretical viewpoint gives way to easy proofs that the Commune was objectively doomed to failure and could not have been fulfilled. This viewpoint, as the Situationists point out, forgets that for those who really lived it, the fulfillment was *already there*. And as Mallarmé said of Rimbaud, "I think that prolonging the hope for a work of maturity would harm, in this case, the exact interpretation of a unique adventure in the history of art."[19] It is in this sense that Marx should be understood when he says that the most important social measure of the Commune was its own *working existence*.

The Commune, wrote Marx, was to be a working, not a parliamentary, body. Its destruction of hierarchic investiture involved the displacement (revocability) of authority along a chain or series of "places" without any sovereign term. Each representative, subject to immediate recall, becomes interchangeable with, and thus equal to, its represented.

The direct result of this kind of distributional and revocable authority is the withering away of the political function as a specialized function. Rimbaud's move beyond the idea of a specialized domain of poetic language or even of poetry — the fetishization of writing as a privileged practice — begins not in 1875 with his "silence" but rather as early as 1871 with the "Lettres du voyant." In these letters, writing poetry is acknowledged as one means of expression, action, and above all of *work* among others:

> I will be a worker: that is the idea that holds me back when mad rage
> drives me toward the battle of Paris — where so many workers are dying
> as I write to you!

The *voyant*, as has been frequently pointed out, "*se fait* voyant": "I *work* at making myself a *voyant*." The emphasis here is on the work of self-transformation as opposed to the Romantic commonplace of poetic predestination. The *voyant* project emerges in the letters as the will to combat not merely specific past or contemporary poetic practices, but the will eventually to overcome and supersede "poetry" altogether. Like the "abolition of the state," the process outlined by Rimbaud is a long and arduous revolutionary process that unfolds through diverse phases. The work is not solitary but social and collective: "other horrible workers will come: they will begin at the horizons where the first one has fallen!" In fact, the *voyant* project can be taken, in its totality, as a figure for nonalienated production in general. Its progress is to be measured, Rimbaud implies, by the degree to which "the infinite servitude of women" is broken: "When the unending servitude of woman is broken, when she lives by and for herself, when man — until now abominable — has given her her freedom, she too will be a poet!" An exclamation from the letters like "Ces poètes seront!" must be placed in the context of the emergence, particularly in Rimbaud's later work, of a collective subject: the *nous* of the concluding moments of *Une Saison* ("Quand irons-nous . . ."), of "A une Raison," of "Après le Déluge." Masses in movement — the human geography of uprisings, migrations, and massive displacements — dominate the later prose works: "the song of the heavens, the march of peoples" ("*Une Saison*"); "migrations more enormous than the ancient invasions" ("Génie"); "the uprising of new men and their march forward" ("A une Raison"); "companies have sung out the joy of new work" ("Villes"). The utopian resonance of *travail nouveau*—"to greet the advent of new work"—can be found even in the project of *voyance*: an enterprise of self- and social transformation which implies that poets themselves accept their own uninterrupted transformation—even when this means ceasing to be a poet.

Notes

1. The one notable exception is Steve Murphy, in his "Rimbaud et la Commune?" In Alain Borer (ed.), *Rimbaud Multiple. Colloque de Cérisy* (Gourdon: Bedou & Touzot, 1985), 50-65. I came across Murphy's very valuable and erudite research as I was completing this book; although our arguments and findings frequently overlap, Murphy's goal, as I take it, to enhance explications of particular poems by Rimbaud, is more circumscribed than mine.

2. Roland Barthes, "Nautilus et Bateau ivre," *Mythologies* (Paris: Seuil, 1957), 91.

3. Alfred Delvau, *Dictionnaire de la langue verte* (Paris: Marpon & Flammarion, 1883), 87.

4. Gustave-Paul Cluseret, *Mémoires du général Cluseret*, vol. II (Paris: Jules Levy, 1887); citations taken from 274-87.

5. Louis Rossel, *Mémoires, procès et correspondance* (Paris: J. J. Pauvert, 1960), 276.

6. Catulle Mendès, *Les 73 journées de la Commune* (Paris: E. Lachaud, 1871), 311.

7. Auguste Blanqui, *Instructions pour une prise d'armes* (Paris: Editions de la tête de feuilles, 1972), 61.

8. Friedrich Engels, introduction to Karl Marx and V. I. Lenin, *The Civil War in France: The Paris Commune* (New York: International Publishers, 1940), 18.

9. Pierre Gascar, *Rimbaud et la Commune* (Paris: Gallimard, 1971), 66.

10. See Henri Lefebvre, *La Proclamation de la Commune* (Paris: Gallimard, 1965).

11. See, especially, Louis Barron, *Sous le drapeau rouge* (Paris: Albert Savine), 83-87, for one of the best descriptions by an active Communard of the sense of daily life under the Commune.

12. For a description of *détournement*, see especially Guy-Ernest Debord and Gil J. Wolman, "Mode d'emploi du détournement," *Les lèvres nues*, no. 8 (May 1956); reprinted in Gil Wolman, *Résumé des chapitre précédents* (Paris: Editions Spiess, 1981), 46-53; English version in Ken Knabb (ed. and trans.), *Situationist International Anthology* (Berkeley, Calif.: Bureau of Public Secrets, 1981), 8-14.

13. *Bulletin Communal*, May 6, 1871, cited in Stewart Edwards, *The Paris Commune 1871* (Devon: Newton Abbot, 1972), 284.

14. Gascar, *Rimbaud et la Commune*, 9.

15. Stewart Edwards (ed.), *The Communards of Paris, 1871*, (Ithaca, N.Y.: Cornell University Press, 1973), 9-10.

16. Félix Fénéon, "Arthur Rimbaud: *Les Illuminations*," in Joan Halperin (ed.), *Oeuvres plus que complètes*, vol. II (Geneva: Massot, 1970), 572.

17. Leo Bersani, "Rimbaud's Simplicity," in *A Future for Astyanax: Character and Desire in Literature* (Boston: Little, Brown, 1976), 247.

18. Edwards (ed.), *The Communards of Paris, 1871*, 10.

19. Stephane Mallarmé, *Oeurves complètes*, ed. Henri Mondor and G. Jean-Aubry (Paris: Gallimard, 1945), 518.

Chapter 2
The Right to Laziness

The origin of the Commune dates back in effect to the time of Genesis, to the day when Cain killed his brother. It is envy that lies behind all those demands stuttered by the indolent [des paresseux] whose tools make them ashamed, and who in hatred of work prefer the chances of combat to the security of daily work.

Maxime du Camp

"Ideology" is perhaps the fact that each person does what he or she is "supposed to do." . . . *Ideology is just the other name for work.*

Jacques Rancière

I

In his essay "Le Chant des sirènes," Maurice Blanchot places Rimbaud's *Une Saison en enfer* within a curious constellation of texts, in the community of narratives he calls *récits*: the tale of Ulysses and the Sirens, for example, *Moby-Dick*, Nerval's *Aurélia*, *Nadja*. The constituent elements of the genre, or rather antigenre, *récits* are, at least initially, relatively straightforward; the *récit* is the narrative of a single episode: "something has happened, something which someone has experienced who tells about it afterwards."[1] I say antigenre because Blanchot defines the *récit* in opposition to the novel; the distinction he proposes

47

between the two kinds of narrative is primarily a temporal one: the *récit* recounts the exceptional event, while the propelling force of the novel is everyday, mundane time. The novel's space is "the world of the usual sort of truth," and its concerns are those of verisimilitude. The *récit*, on the other hand, takes off where verisimilitude stops.

The *récit* for Blanchot functions as a kind of transhistorical antigenre that flowers in opposition to the dominant generic compromise formation of any given historical moment. By designating *Une Saison* a *récit* Blanchot invites an examination of its oppositional stance to the dominant generic project of its historical moment: the novelistic one, what in English is variously called the novel of education or acculturation, in French the *roman de formation*, and the more vast bourgeois cultural project of which the novel of apprenticeship forms perhaps something of a subset—that of biography or autobiography. The novel of formation shares with autobiography a very general project: the recounting of the formation of a personality.

The novel of acculturation, which interests me here not as a collection of specifically designated texts but rather as the exemplary bourgeois cultural project whose outlines we can begin to determine, leads a character through a variety of encounters and experiences and brings him or her out the other end a changed and generally morally [re]formed figure. Georg Lukács, in his chapter on *Wilhelm Meister* in *The Theory of the Novel*, describes the goal or telos of the genre as "the reconciliation of the problematic individual, guided by his lived experience of the ideal, with concrete social reality."[2] The alienated youth is reintegrated and accommodated to a generally conservative moral and social order through a process involving trial and error, exposure to the wisdom and experience of others, the acquiring of independent judgment, and the ensuing recognition of the individual's role in the objective social world.

In their writings on the bourgeois novel, Lukács and Jean-Paul Sartre join together in underlining two elements essential to the genre of the novel of acculturation. The first of these is an almost atmospheric emanation of *calm*, which Lukács locates in the social optimism of the beginnings of the genre and in the relativization of the central character into a universal and ideal bourgeois subjectivity (bourgeois *as* universal). Sartre, writing about the late nineteenth century—his exemplary author is Maupassant—locates the same calm in the novel's retrospective narration, in the great distance from which the narrator looks back on the turbulent events of his youth. The novel of youth, in other words, is ventriloquized out of the mouths of the aged, narrators freed from the exigencies of desire who consider the escapades of their youth both lucidly and indulgently:

> His heart is calm like the night. He tells his story with detachment. If it has caused him suffering, he has made honey from this suffering. He looks back upon it and considers it as it really was, that is, *sub specie*

aeternitatis. There was difficulty to be sure, but this difficulty ended long ago. . . . Thus the adventure was a brief disturbance which is over with. It is told from the viewpoint of experience and wisdom; it is listened to from the viewpoint of order.[3]

Neither the author nor the reader of these novels, says Sartre, is running any risks: the event, the turbulence, is past, catalogued, understood, and recounted by a stabilized bourgeoisie at the end of the century who have lived through 1848 and the Commune and who are confident that "nothing else will happen."

We can now begin to gauge the chasm dividing Rimbaud from this project of bougeois acculturation, of constructing the bourgeois subject, of even recounting a life. To do so we must return to Blanchot's category of the *récit*. The event, in the late nineteenth-century novel, is, for Sartre, passed, catalogued, and understood. The event for Blanchot, however, is essentially to come:

Yet if we regard the *récit* as the true telling of an exceptional event that has taken place and that someone is trying to report, then we have not even come close to sensing the true nature of the *récit*. The *récit* is not the narration of an event, but that event itself, the approach to that event, the place where that event is made to happen—an event that is yet to come and through whose power of attraction the *récit* can hope to come into being too. (109)

If we agree, at least for the moment, with Blanchot's designation of *Une Saison* as *récit*, we can say that it bears a distinctly different relation to the event than one of cataloguing or understanding; it materializes as a thought taken up with, vitally engaged with exterior forces, a problem-thought rather than a narrated, completed thought. "My fate," Rimbaud writes, "depends on this book." The genre of the "novel of youth" is formed out of the interplay between the transformational energies it derives from the energy of youth, and the formal limitations imposed by the necessity that youth must come to an end.[4] Rimbaud, on the other hand, proposes the impossible: a narrative that consists of pure transformational energy, pure transition or *suradolescence*; a voice that speaks from the place of youth rather than ventriloquizes it; the movement of a thought conjugated *with and in view of* (not after) the event; and the impossible notion that youth might not have to come to an end. Rimbaud's narrative, formally marked by the upheaval of its multifaceted transformations, is not calm.

The second and, for our purposes, more important element that both Lukács and Sartre deem essential to the novel of acculturation is the centrality of the role of métier in the narrative construction of the bourgeois subject:

It follows . . . given by the theme itself, of effective action in social reality, that the organization of the outside world into professions, classes, ranks, etc., is of decisive importance for this particular type of personality as the substratum of its social activity. (Lukács, 133)

The reconciliation of the aspirations of the subject to the objective limitations imposed on him or her by an alienated world is charted through the subject's gradual accession into the world of work. The individual learns to internalize the jarring shocks of encountering the objective limitations set by the social world (''I learned from my mistakes''): this process of internalization is called apprenticeship.[5] Along the way the individual makes errors; learning to internalize these errors leads not only to a comprehension of and reconciliation with the world — it provides the very motor energy of the plot. The gentleman who has arrived at the moment of his life when the mistakes of his life can be imparted as moral lessons is, according to Sartre, ''always a professional by experience, a doctor, soldier, artist . . . neither the general nor the doctor impart their memories in a raw state: they are experiences that have been distilled, and we are warned as soon as they begin to speak that their story has a moral'' (134). That moral is both the result and the proscription of the choice and acquisition of a *métier*.

The regime of work, then, is inseparable from the development of form, to which corresponds the formation of the subject.[6] Rimbaud's narrator, in the ''Mauvais Sang'' section of *Une Saison en enfer*, categorically refuses the choice of *métier*:

J'ai horreur de tous les métiers. Maîtres et ouvriers, tous paysans, ignobles. La main à plume vaut la main à charrue. — Quel siècle à mains! — Je n'aurai jamais ma main. Après, la domesticité mène trop loin. L'honnêteté de la mendicité me navre. Les criminels dégoûtent comme les châtrés: moi, je suis intact, et ça m'est égal.

[I have a horror of all trades. Bosses and workers, all of them peasants, and common. The hand that holds the pen is as good as the one that holds the plow. (What a century for hands!) I'll never learn to use my hands. Then, domesticity leads too far. The propriety of beggary shames me. Criminals are as disgusting as castrates; I'm intact, and I don't care.]

Lest we take *métiers* in the opening sentence of this passage to mean ''trades'' as opposed to the more bourgeois ''professions,'' the rest of the paragraph makes clear that the narrator refuses the very structure of work, the social division of labor itself that in the nineteenth century is beginning to be pushed to the limits of overspecialization. He is refusing the narrow horizon resulting from being imprisoned in one's trade — the *idiotisme*, both in the sense of the idiocy and the idiom, of the *métier*: seeing only the problems and preoccupations of one's specialty, whether one's role be that of boss or worker: "Bosses and workers, all of them peasants, and common."

"Quel siècle à mains!" *Manus*, in Latin, indicates the fist, power, that which wields the weapon or the tool, strength, authority, the "authorial" authority of the writer, even the conjugal authority of the man over the woman who gives him hers. "I'll never learn to use my hands. Then, domesticity leads too far." The narrator places himself outside a set of power relations that includes conjugal domesticity as much as it does the division of labor, even that most primitive of hierarchies that privileges intellectual over manual work, professions of initiative, intelligence, and command—those "proper" to the bourgeoisie—over those requiring physical effort, obedience, and the execution of orders. In Rimbaud the other of the proletariat is not so much the capitalist, the person of property, as the intellectual or artist, the man of words: "The hand that holds the pen is as good as the one that holds the plow."

Writing is an activity of the hand as much as is plowing: the importance lies in the relation of the hand to a tool, even if the tool is as light as a pen. "Je n'aurai jamais ma main," which Paul Schmidt translates convincingly as "I'll never learn to use my hands," announces the will to resist participation in a society where workers' activities—those of artists or farmers—are projected outside of and against them, in a work process in which the previous social labor, which has produced the tools, the pens, the plows, the language with which work is done, appears as a dead structure automatizing labor and worker at once. It is not work that forms the worker but only his or her expropriation—apprenticeship is "realized" only when work has become a power completely alien to the worker. "Je n'aurai jamais ma main": Rimbaud here indicates the will to resist that compromise solution of finding the contradictions of the objective structure to be complex and alienated but nonetheless *manipulable*. The poet, in fact, is identified with the instrumentally manipulated and dominated; if we understand *ma main* as in the French expression *de la main de quelqu'un*, then "I will never have my signature," my oeuvre: a body of artistic work that exists as an alienated or detached object. To have a *métier*, a trade, a specialty—even an antisocial *métier* like beggar or criminal (both professionals who "live by their hands"; in French, *tendre la main* means "to beg")—is to lose one's hand as an integral part of one's body: to experience it as extraneous, detachable, in service to the rest of the body as synecdoche for the social body, executing the wishes of another. To give birth to myself, to become my own work: by placing myself outside the regime of work I can remain intact. "Criminals are as disgusting as castrates; I'm intact, and I don't care." Intact, which is to say, not castrated.[7]

The native infirmity of the worker is castration, the expropriation of the body by the institution of wage labor: the economic obligation of people who cannot otherwise survive to sell the only commodity they possess, their labor power, their "hand," on the labor market. Mutilation is a *consequence* of war (as in "Le

Dormeur du Val''); it is, however, as Rimbaud makes clear, a *condition*, a presupposition of the state apparatus and the organization of work. In the ''Nuit de l'enfer'' section of *Une Saison*, the space of hell—which is at one and the same time the Christian concept of eternal damnation (''hell; the old one, the one whose doors the son of man opened'') and the increasing standardization of everyday life under late nineteenth-century capitalism—is characterized by mutilation: ''But I am still alive! Suppose damnation is eternal! A man who wants to mutilate himself is certainly damned, isn't he?'' ''Ah! To return to life! To stare at our deformities.''

The ''Mauvais Sang'' section of the poem, which, it seems clear from the letters, provided the genesis for the entire narrative, opens with the construction of an ''oppositional'' ancestry:

> J'ai de mes ancêtres gaulois l'oeil bleu blanc, la cervelle étroite, et la maladresse dans la lutte. Je trouve mon habillement aussi barbare que le leur. Mais je ne beurre pas ma chevelure.
>
> Les Gaulois étaient les écorcheurs de bêtes, les brûleurs d'herbes les plus ineptes de leur temps.
>
> D'eux, j'ai: l'idolatrie et l'amour du sacrilège; — oh! tous les vices, colère, luxure, — magnifique, la luxure; — surtout mensonge et paresse.
>
> [From my ancestors the Gauls I have white-blue eyes, a narrow brain, and awkwardness in competition. I think my clothes are as barbaric as theirs. But I don't butter my hair.
>
> The Gauls were the most inept hide-flayers and hay-burners of their time.
>
> From them I inherit: idolatry and love of sacrilege–oh, all sorts of vice: anger, lust–terrific, lust–above all, lying and laziness.]

We must look closely here at the first of what will be a lengthy series of identifications or *devenir-autres* on the part of the narrator. A lineage or racial ancestry is established, at least initially, through the legacy of specifically antibourgeois moral qualities bequeathed by the barbarian ancestors: clumsiness, inattention to dress, ineptitude or incompetence, idolatry, anger, lust, and, above all, dishonesty and laziness. Later we will see more clearly how this racial identification, among others, functions strategically in the narrative as a rewriting of autobiography: an apparently subjective and individual narrative is little by little generalized to the point of forming a collective, world-historical subject. It has never been sufficiently emphasized that the narrator's ''identifications'' throughout the poem are always *group* identifications and not individual, psychological, or sentimental ones. In Rimbaud the minimal real unity is not the word or the individual subject or the concept, but rather the *arrangement*, the process of arranging or configurating elements. *Une Saison en enfer* is about the production of collective utterances that are the products of such arrangements: the voices and experiences of populations—here barbarian hordes—multiplicities, territories, migrations. Thus the acquisition in this passage of what appear initially to be psychological or rather moral characterological traits by the narrator-heir is of importance only within the larger social framework, which places those qualities in dynamic opposition to bourgeois values. Hence, for example, the embrace of lying, which undercuts, of course, the confessional or autobiographical validity of the narrative. (A similar purpose is served in the opening dedication of the whole work to the figure of Satan, "you who value in a writer all lack of descriptive or didactic flair." This opening should be relieved once and for all of any cheap "Satanic" or demonic interpretation. For if it is, what emerges is a formal refusal analogous to the narrator's refusal of work in "Mauvais Sang": Rimbaud's prose work will contain none of the didactic or moralizing posture of the nineteenth-century prose described by Sartre.)

"Above all, lying and laziness." How are we to understand this *éloge* to laziness, which amounts to a placing of the entire poem under its aegis? Certainly it is the antibourgeois value par excellence, the contrary to the justifying myth (industry and utility) of that unproductive and laborious class. But Rimbaud's relationship to laziness is a long and complex one that we can only begin to examine here. Laziness is frequently thematized, in more or less overt ways, throughout the poetry, beginning perhaps with the figure of the *bohème* in "Ma Bohème" and "Sensation" ("Et j'irai loin, bien loin comme un bohémien") and the conscious opposition of sexual and archaic drives to the reality and performance principles of Nina's work world in "Les Réparties de Nina." "Nina" is perhaps the first of the poems where the sharp division between spaces of lived time and the possibility of desire are placed over against the compartmentalized clock time of the adult, work world. In later works like "Vagabonds," this opposition is highlighted by pairing *oisif* and *luxe*, as in the preceding description of the Gauls. The intact body, the body unmarked by work, is the body that experiences intense sensation; *paresse* is linked throughout Rimbaud's work to intensity of physical sensation and, at the same time, to a kind of weightlessness affiliated with pure speed. By a striking paradox, laziness, remaining outside the work order, is not standing still but moving fast, too fast.

Fredric Jameson has written about Rimbaud's unparalleled production of the "adolescent body"; he reads this production in the poetry in terms of a lived experience of "fermentation": the perseverance of identity through metamorphosis.[8] The choice of fermentation is governed in Jameson's argument by the need to construct a physiological, individual, or subjective homology to the objective historical change in mode of production—the transition from the market stage of capitalism to the monopoly stage—marked by Rimbaud's work. Jameson's underlining of the specificity of the adolescent body in Rimbaud is a powerful perception; however, grounding it in the phenomenological experience of fermentation, with all its connotations of ripeness and maturity, is incongruous and textually unconvincing. Is not a full, sensory approximation of the *male* adolescent body more readily apparent in the almost reptilian combination of absolute torpor and absolute speed with which that body emerges in Rimbaud's text? Thus, on the one hand, the famous *sommeil* of Rimbaud, the languorous "wine of indolence" of "Les Chercheuses de poux," of "Délire II": "I lay about idle, consumed by an oppressive fever: I envied the bliss of animals—caterpillars, who portray the innocence of Limbo; moles, the slumber of virginity!" "He'll never work; he wants to live like a sleepwalker" ("Délire I"); "The best thing is a drunken sleep, stretched out on some strip of shore" ("Mauvais Sang"). And, on the other, a gesture that is most like a darting, sudden reptilian precipitation; a brusque, usually oral aggression or rapid discharge of emotion—emotion, not sentiment but affect that takes a projectile form. This gesture is most prevalent in Rimbaud's early, erotic thematics—look, for instance, at the early prose work "Les Déserts de l'amour" or the poem "Tête de Faune," or recall the ending to "A la Musique" in which the leisurely contemplation of the girls' bodies is suddenly disrupted: "Et mes désirs brutaux s'accrochent à leurs lèvres"—but it is apparent in other contexts as well, in the violent way, for instance, in which Rimbaud allows the category of the social to disrupt the sleepy genre of pastoral in "Le Dormeur du Val" by suddenly blasting two bullet holes into the middle of the tableau.

What distinguishes the adolescent body, then, as it is figured in Rimbaud's work, is a particular corporeal relation to speed: the body is both too slow and too fast. Periods of apparent lulls are broken by violent, spasmodically unbridled explosions, but even this is something of an optical illusion: the heavy torpor or seeming somnambulance of the body qualified by *paresse* hides a body that is in fact moving too fast. In his memoirs of the Commune, poet and songwriter Louis Barron detects a similar atmosphere prevailing in mid-May in the streets of Paris: "There is in Paris that excess of torpor and excess of exuberance that precedes catastrophe."[9] Laziness for Rimbaud is a kind of absolute motion, absolute speed that escapes from the pull of gravity. (One thinks, in the context of Rimbaud's relation to speed, of the almost unbelievable rapidity of diction, the semantic *acceleration* of the *Illuminations*; and, in a related context, of Delahaye's description of Rimbaud reading his poetry aloud: "that convulsive haste he had when he recited verse.")[10] Laziness hides an activity not subordinated to certain necessities, an activity that is not the everyday action of subsistence or industry ("Action isn't life; it's merely a way of ruining a kind of strength, a means of destroying nerves. Morality is water on the brain"; "Délire II"). Immobility in Rimbaud can in some cases be composed of pure speed: the sudden darting of desert reptiles on whom lies the fatigue of centuries. The adolescent body is both too slow and too fast to submit to the regime of work: "Work makes life blossom," writes Rimbaud later in "Mauvais Sang," "an old idea, not mine; my life doesn't weigh enough, it drifts off and floats far beyond action, that third pole of the world [*ce cher point du monde*]." In later sections of *Une Saison en enfer* we will hear diatribes against the sluggishness of work and against the engulfing of the understanding of the civil world by the canons of knowledge used in the physical sciences: "Careful, mind. Don't rush madly after salvation. Train yourself! Ah, science never goes fast enough for us!" ("L'Impossible"). Or:

> —Qu'y puis-je? Je connais le travail; et la science est trop lente. Que la prière galope et que la lumière gronde . . . je le vois bien. C'est trop simple, et il fait trop chaud; on se passera de moi. J'ai mon devoir; j'en serai fier à la façon de plusieurs, en le mettant de côté.

> [What more can I do? Labor I know, and science is too slow. That praying gallops and that light roars; I'm well aware of it. It's too simple, and the weather's too hot; you can all do without me. I have my duty; but I will be proud, as others have been, to set it aside.]

> Non! non! à présent je me révolte contre la mort! Le travail parait trop léger à mon orgeuil: ma trahison au monde serait un supplice trop court. Au dernier moment, j'attaquerais à droite, à gauche.

> [No! No! Now I rise up against death! Labor seems too easy for pride like mine: to betray me to the world would be too slight a punishment. At the last moment I would attack, to the right, to the left.]

The adolescent body, at once too slow and too fast, acts out the forces that perturb bourgeois society's reasoned march of progress. For that progress is disrupted by two phenomena: it can be slowed down by the superstitious and the lazy, and it can be thrown offtrack by the impatient, violent rush of insurrection.

II

Rimbaud's own lived experience of resistance to work is well known to any who have read his letters. A few days after returning from his first flight to Paris he writes to Izambard: "I am out of place [*dépaysé*], sick, furious, dull, upset; I hoped to lie in the sun, I hoped for infinite walks, rests, trips, adventures, wanderings [*des bohémienneries*]" (August 25, 1870). To Izambard again three months later: "I returned to Charleville the day after leaving you. My mother received me, and I'm here . . . completely lazy [*oisif*]." And the following year, after the three famous instances of "vagabondage"—twice to Paris and once to Belgium—he is back in Charleville, under the strict and watchful eye of his mother:

> More than a year ago I left ordinary life behind for the one you know about. Locked up forever in that indescribable Ardennes country, seeing

nobody, burdened with wretched work, incompetent, mysterious, obstinate, answering questions or crude, mean addresses with silence. . . . She [his mother] wanted to force me to work—forever, in Charleville (Ardennes!). Find a job by such and such a day, she said, or get out.—I refused that life without giving any reasons: it would have been pathetic. (August 28, 1871)

Poetic work, as well, is problematic. To Verlaine he writes in 1872, "Work is as far away from me as my fingernail from my eye." And two years later in London, when Rimbaud appears to be engaged in a frantic search for a position as an instructor of languages, his mother and sister come to London and wait for him to find a position: "There *are* positions," his sister complains. "If he had wanted one, he would have had one and we would have already left. If he had wanted, we could have already been gone today."[11]

Psychobiographical data like Rimbaud's flights from Charleville, his "vagabondage," have been used most frequently to support any of the various mythic constructions of Rimbaud as *poète maudit*. Designed largely to promote a vulgarized notion of the experience of exile and expatriation, such interpretations rely on the simple and traditional model of the poet as "outsider" and "genius"—outsider even within his own community. The banal imagery invoked by such models is all too familiar: the fixed gap between isolated and misunderstood, but clairvoyant, prodigy and the inauthentic society. Rimbaud's running away from home at sixteen becomes the proof of the irrepressible and singular nature of his genius, his uniquely "poet's" need to distance himself from the petty tyrannies of the provinces and his mother. Nothing, in fact, shows Rimbaud's uniqueness or originality less.[12] Between the years 1830 and 1896, convictions for vagrancy (vagabondage) increased sevenfold in France; in 1889, 600,000 children—one-eleventh of the educable population—had fled school.[13] In most cases vagabondage corresponded to the ritualization of the entry into the work force at the end of school—that abrupt passage into a new age, itinerary, group of friends: with the onset of work came the moment of rupture. Particularly widespread was the phenomenon of youthful vagabondage: youths "of a bohemian and lazy character, vicious or incorrigible, unable or unwilling to stay and work for bosses in the countryside,"[14] who fled rural life to come to the cities. Charles Portales, author of a book on the phenomenon, wrote in 1854 that "soon laziness and debauchery will propel . . . into the cities thousands of corrupt young men who will threaten propriety."[15] By the middle of the century, vagabondage as a social problem was being analyzed and discussed in print by an assortment of educators, prison supervisors, and social reformers. While some of these writers showed at least an initial sensitivity, speaking, for example, of "the extreme difficulty presented by the question of vagabondage . . . since the problem touches on the primordial rights of human liberty,''[16] most resorted to a particularly lurid brand of rhetoric:

> Outside of the society that it frightens and repels, lives a class of individuals for whom there is no family, no regular work, no fixed domicile.
> That class is the class of vagabonds.[17]

The Belgian inspector general of prisons, Edouard Ducpetiaux, writing in a tone that typifies the pamphlets of the period, warns against vagabondage as the male equivalent to prostitution; what looks like aimless wandering, he alerts his readers, is in fact a greased path to the gallows:

> Ordinarily vagabondage means the first step taken in a career that leads to prison and sometimes to the gallows: vagabondage is for the apprentice what prostitution is for the young woman worker. A sort of proclamation of independence, it is the first act of defiance against the social order.[18]

Vagabondage is a pure creation of penal law, a word of repression; it has no existence apart from a legally constituted infraction. A vagabond is a vagabond because he or she is arrested. What is particularly disquieting about vagabondage is its ambiguous status: technically, vagabonds have not violated any laws (except the laws against vagabondage), they have not committed any crimes. But their "way of life" places them in a state that supposes the *eventual* violation of laws: vagabonds are always virtual, anticipatory. One writer describes the ambiguity in this way: you can't say to a vagabond, as you might to a criminal who has committed a crime, "Don't do it again"; instead, you would have to say, "Change your way of life, take up the habits of work, etc."[19] Their existence in "virtuality" or "potentiality" of misdeed makes them more threatening, as Maupassant's 1887 story "Le Vagabond" makes clear, than the more predictable criminal. Vagabonds are victims of dangerous heredity and carriers of the fatal germ of *dégénérescence*; "contagious," in both the medical and social sense of the term, they are the incarnation of a social illness that strikes not so much an individual as a family, a generation, a lineage.[20] Their problem, like Rimbaud's, is "bad blood." The vagueness of the vagabond's "potential" for evil is, after the Commune, given a precise identity, a face. Vagabonds are now potential political insurgents:

> It is easy to understand what the support of such people [vagabonds] must be for the enemies of the established order, those who are pushed by various motives of ambition, desire, anger, and who want to rise up against the established order. These will always find in vagabonds men of action, always ready to do anything, those who, for a cigar or a glass of eau-de-vie, would set fire to all of Paris.

Vagabonds are the most dangerous enemies of society . . . they live among us as savage animals would . . . deplorable from the point of view of society; for the vagabond, having nothing to lose in moments of social upheaval, desires such moments and helps out in the hopes of gaining something . . . vagabondage being not only a fact, but a state, a sort of moral infirmity.[21]

Methods of treating the problem ranged from the preacherly ("Men must be taught, not only by laws and by speeches, but also by example, that nothing is more beautiful than work")[22] to the severely repressive. Concerning Rimbaud's being sent back to Charleville after his arrest in Paris, the official police document reads: "Came from Charleroi to Paris with a ticket for Saint-Quentin and without a domicile or means of supporting himself."[23] In fact, the French penal code of 1810 (article 270) defines the vagabond not only as someone without a home but specifically as someone without a *métier*: "Vagabonds or people without a place [*gens sans aveu*—the expression in the Middle Ages referred to people who were not tied to a lord, and who thus had no protection under the law] are those who have neither an assured domicile nor means of existence, and who generally have no trade [*métier*] or profession." Rimbaud profited from an 1832 revision of the penal code that established a legal distinction between adults and adolescents; while adults were liable to six months in prison, youths sixteen or younger were, depending on the circumstances, sent back to their parents or placed under police surveillance until the age of twenty-one, if they had not, by that age, obtained a place in the armed services.

Later in the century the French government would learn to apply to vagabondage—"that nervous mania of locomotion and laziness that appears to be one of the ways in which the free life of the savage is preserved"[24]—a more effective, if homeopathic, treatment. From vagabondage would come organized wandering in the form of geographic exploration and colonial expedition, a solution that had been advocated for some time by writers on the topic:

One day when I was sitting in the correctional chamber of the Court of Appeals in Rouen, we had to judge a young man who had been found guilty of vagabondage, and who already had been convicted four times for the same crime.

"Why are you appealing?" the President asked him. "In the first place you were only condemned to six months in prison, which is the penalty you just saw being given men for their first offense."

"Why am I appealing?" responded the guilty man. "I am appealing so that you will send me to the colonies. There perhaps I could do something better than what I am doing in France."[25]

As for transportation, if the state would only grant the transport and establishment of vagabonds on Algerian soil . . .[26]

Let another asylum be opened for them, and, in the same way that
Rome had a law decreeing that rebel beggars be sent to the colonies, let
a new law open up those magnificent domains that France possesses
beyond the seas for her vagabonds.[27]

III

In the *Voyant* letters written at the time of the Commune, it is clear that the *élan*
propelling Rimbaud toward a structural identification with the workers in Paris
arises at the precise moment when "work," as such, has definitively stopped:

> Je serai un travailleur: c'est l'idée qui me retient quand les colères folles
> me poussent vers la bataille de Paris, — où tant de travailleurs meurent
> pourtant encore tandis que je vous écris! Travailler maintenant, jamais,
> jamais; je suis en grève.

> [I will be a worker: that's what holds me back when a wild fury drives
> me toward the battle in Paris, where so many workers are still dying
> while I am writing to you! Work, now? Never, never. I'm on strike. (To
> Izambard, May 13, 1871)]

"Workers" in this identificatory structure are not those whose time/space is rig-
idly defined and allotted by a dominant class; they are people who have become
aware of their position in a structure of oppression. Rimbaud's identification is
with a group-subject whose joint activity is not work but in this case combat. "I
will be a worker": it is only at some future moment when the project of new
social relations, a radical transformation in the structure of work, has been
achieved that Rimbaud will be a worker; now, however, he refuses work. But the
refusal of work is not an absence of activity, nor, obviously, is it leisure since
leisure reinforces the work model by existing only with reference to work; it is a
qualitatively different activity, often very frenetic, and above all combative. The
strategic refusal of work presupposes a collective subject as well — the *nous* of the
final sections of *Une Saison*, the *horribles travailleurs* whose future existence is
affirmed in the letter to Demeny (May 15, 1871): "Other horrible workers will
come; they will begin at the horizons where the other has fallen!"

"Mauvais Sang" develops the strategy of nonwork:

> Mais! qui a fait ma langue perfide tellement, qu'elle ait guidé et
> sauvegardé jusqu'ici ma paresse? Sans me servir pour vivre même de
> mon corps, et plus oisif que le crapaud, j'ai vécu partout.

> [But who has made my tongue so treacherous, that until now it has
> counseled and kept me in idleness? I have not used even my body to get
> along. More idle than a toad, I have lived everywhere.]

The intact body is the body "safeguarded" from work and from the hierarchy of its organs inflicted by the work model: the mind that commands, the hand that executes. Laziness, the refusal to make use of the body or turn it into a tool, is here linked to a kind of radical mobility. I have lived everywhere. I have lived many lives. (Later, "J'ai connu tous les fils de famille" — the sexual sense of the verb is clear.) This is not the proverbial mobility of the industrial worker under capitalism, who migrates to the urban capitals from the countryside, "free" to move about because "free" to sell his or her labor. This is the impossible liberty of having exempted oneself from the organization of work in a society that expropriates the very body of the worker.

A pamphlet written about five years after *Une Saison en enfer*, a text that is in many ways its double in the field of political theory, sheds light on Rimbaud's celebration of laziness as ideological refusal: Paul Lafargue's *Le Droit à la paresse* (1880). Born in Cuba of mixed ancestry (Jewish, Cuban mulatto, French, Caribbean Indian), Lafargue came to France to study medicine but became involved in left-wing politics. At first a follower of Proudhon, he became friends with Marx and his family in London and later married Marx's daughter Laura. He participated actively in the Commune and took exile in London at the same time as Rimbaud, Verlaine, Vermersch, Pottier, Clément, and many other ex-Communards.[28] He resettled in Paris in 1880 and became a leading propagandist for the Parti ouvrier français. Militantly anticlerical, he was a strong supporter of women's rights. His colonial background helped him become a leading critic and uncannily prescient analyst of imperialism; he was, as well, one of the pioneering figures in the new fields of anthropology and ethnology.

Le Droit à la paresse was written as a parodic refutation of the document that elevated the "right to work" to the status of a revolutionary principle, the 1848 *Droit au travail*. It was to have an enormous effect in France and elsewhere; of all nineteenth-century political pamphlets it was second only to *The Communist Manifesto* in the number of languages into which it was translated. The pamphlet sets out to prove, at a time when labor was being virtually deified, that all individual and social miseries in capitalist society are born of the working classes' conditioned passion and demand for work. Like Rimbaud, Lafargue stages highly dramatic imaginary dialogues and tableaux; his hyperbolic, parodic, and colorful prose in and of itself shows a proto-Brechtian suspension of the opposition between entertainment and instruction. His subtitles ("A nouvel air, chanson nouvelle") recall the *nouvelle harmonie*, the veritable crescendo of "the new" that we find in Rimbaud's "Départ," "Génie," and the conclusion to *Une Saison*. Much time is spent detailing the grotesque physicality and degradation of both worker and bourgeois resulting from the inscription on their bodies of the division of labor — that great sale of human labor that makes merchandise of people and an immense boutique of society. ("For sale," writes Rimbaud in "Solde," "bodies without price, outside any race, any world, any sex, any lineage!") The bourgeoisie, for example, obliged to devote themselves to overconsumption as their definitive activity or *métier*, strikingly resemble the Charleville music listeners in "A la Musique"; traces of Lafargue's medical training can be seen in the precise anatomical vocabulary he uses to depict the bourgeoisie "squatting" (*accroupie*, that favorite word of Rimbaud's) in their *absolute* laziness:

> With this occupation [*à ce métier*], the organism decays rapidly, hair
> falls out, teeth loosen, the abdomen loses its shape, the stomach is
> ruined, respiration is hampered, all movement grows heavy, the joints
> stiffen, the phalanxes become twisted.[29]

By proclaiming the right to laziness Lafargue is not turning his back on the tradition of utopian socialism—even if his pamphlet was greeted more favorably in anarchist than in socialist circles.[30] He is, however, "deconstructing" the most definitive and time-honored semantic opposition of that tradition—the opposition, dating back to the 1789 Revolution and at first a solely economic one, between "one who works and produces" (*travailleur*) and "one who produces nothing and is a social parasite" (*oisif*).[31] By the 1830s, the term *travailleurs*, in the collective plural, had taken on strong moral as well as economic value within revolutionary vocabulary, defined antonymically to the pejorative connotations of *oisif* (and its synonyms, *capitaliste*, *exploiteur*, *bourgeois*). With the problem of the "right to work" dominating the June insurrection, the revolution of 1848 definitively consecrates the opposition; the revolutionary content of the term *travailleur* develops throughout the Second Empire, and what had once expressed a solely economic relationship by the time of the Commune takes on its full social and political resonance. By depicting the *absolute* laziness of the bourgeoisie, Lafargue operates within the traditional socialist opposition. His emphasis, however, on workers claiming what the bourgeoisie reserved for itself (leisure, pleasure, intellectual life), on workers *abandoning* the world of work, gives the pamphlet its shock value. Lafargue suggests a revolutionary praxis whereby the true threat to existing order comes not from some untainted working class but from a challenge to the boundaries *between* labor and leisure, producer and consumer, worker and bourgeois, worker and intellectual.

My concern in articulating Rimbaud's and Lafargue's "attack" on labor is to document a moment or strategy in an oppositional culture that itself cannot be detected as long as one approaches cultural production uniquely from the perspective of the relentless "it couldn't have been otherwise" logic of the commodity. Studies of the nineteenth-century commodification of leisure, of the rise of the department store or the opulent life of the demimonde under the Second Empire, have little to say about such specific oppositional strategies that were operative at the same time. It is crucial in this context, therefore, not to mistake laziness for leisure. Laziness, for Rimbaud and Lafargue, constitutes a kind of third term outside the programmed dyad of labor and leisure.

The interest of Lafargue lies particularly in his refusal to participate in the construction of the "good worker," that image type central to pre-Commune moralizing discourse directed at workers by right-wing philanthropists, moralists, and factory managers. In the decade following the Commune, it is the left that takes over the task of constructing the "good worker"—largely in reaction to inflammatory right-wing diatribes against the prostitutes, *pétroleuses*, drunkards, and vagabonds who set Paris aflame. Many left-wing histories of the Commune written in the 1870s are immediately concerned with depicting the Communard as model worker: a good family man who never touched eau-de-vie and who wanted nothing more than to devote himself fifteen hours a day to his *métier*.

Lafargue begins his pamphlet by quoting Thiers as the representative mouthpiece of bourgeois utility. He allows Thiers to establish the basic opposition between work and pleasure that will structure his own text:

I want to make the clergy's influence all powerful, because I am
counting on it to propagate that good philosophy that teaches man that
he is here below to suffer, and not that other philosophy that tells man
the opposite: take pleasure [*jouis*]. (119)

Rimbaud sums up the alliance between bourgeois rationalization and Christian asceticism even more succinctly in *Une Saison*: "Monsieur Prudhomme was born with Christ" ("L'Impossible"). The value judgments that found the distinction between classes, which privilege intellectual over manual work, have their roots in the primacy of mind over matter, intellectual and moral life over the life of the body, that is the founding premise of the Christian tradition. The new and dominant bourgeois ideology of scientific knowledge as a nonbelief is nothing more than the last refuge of belief, of religiosity. " 'Nothing is vanity; on toward knowledge!' cries the modern Ecclesiastes, which is *Everyone*" ("L'Eclair"). "Science doesn't deny God, it does better, it makes Him unnecessary."[32] In Lafargue and Rimbaud, capitalist morality and Christian morality unite in making anathema the body of the worker.

Lafargue's strategy, like Rimbaud's in "Mauvais Sang," is to begin his historical narrative by establishing an "alternative" history; like Rimbaud he will call his alternative narrative a "barbarian" or "pagan" history. (The original title for *Une Saison en enfer* was *Livre païen* or *Livre nègre*.) He begins his narrative with the historical moment when the bourgeoisie, locked in struggle against the nobility, "had happily taken up the pagan tradition once more and glorified the flesh and the passions" (119). Now, of course, gorged with pleasures and with goods, the bourgeoisie preaches abstinence; formerly, its inferior, combative posture allowed for an "adoption" of the pagan tradition.

Like Rimbaud in "Mauvais Sang" ("Pagan blood returns!" and, "Since I cannot express myself except in pagan terms, I would rather keep quiet"), Lafargue uses the notion of a pagan tradition as a hinge between the celebration of the body (*jouissance, paresse*) in the past—the European antecedents—and "New World" alternatives to Western bourgeois ideology: the indifference or outright hostility of peasants and tribespeople to participation in the market economy as wage laborers. Complaining that work in capitalist society is the cause of all intellectual degeneration and all organic deformation, Lafargue conjures up a "precolonial" tableau picturing the native that "the missionaries of trade and the traders of religion have not yet corrupted with Christianity, syphilis, and the dogma of work" (121). Rimbaud's trio of oppression in "Mauvais Sang" is, if we recall, almost identical: "The white men are landing! The cannon! Now we must be baptized, get dressed, and go to work." Just as older civilizations and the beginnings of Christianity "corrupt the barbarians of the old world," so aging Christianity and modern capitalist society corrupt the inhabitants of the New World, manipulating the same rhetoric used to justify class warfare in Europe to condemn the seemingly irrational resistance of tribespeople new to the modern wage-labor situation to be drawn into a marketing mentality in which people are seen as commodities. Lafargue then undertakes a vaguely ethnographic survey, quoting in passing F. LePlay's *Les Ouvriers Européens* (1864); he admires Le Play's talent for observation while rejecting all of his sociological conclusions. The passage he selects praises the seminomadic *paresse* of the *bachkirs* (shepherds from the Asian side of the Urals):

> The propensity of the *bachkirs* for laziness, the leisures of nomadic life,
> the habits of meditation these give rise to even in the least gifted
> individuals often lend these people a distinction of manners, a fineness
> of intelligence and of judgment rarely seen at the same social level of a
> more developed civilization. (122)

Lafargue forms his "pagan" constellation out of the European bourgeoisie at the moment of its struggle against the nobility, the precolonial native, aborigines from Oceania, the Goths and other barbarian tribes, the Eskimo, Indian tribes in Brazil, and the *bachkirs*. On the other side of the spectrum he provides examples of races who "love to work, races for whom work is an organic necessity": Auvergnats, Scots, and Chinese. Within capitalist society he specifies the classes that love work for work's sake: "landowning peasants and the petite bourgeoisie, the former stooped over their lands, the latter entombed in their shops, moving around like moles in their underground world" (213). (It is striking to note that Rimbaud's class background unites exactly these two: his mother was a landowning peasant, his father, petit bourgeois.)

If Rimbaud's and Lafargue's alternative or oppositional constellations are roughly the same, so are the forces each chooses to castigate within the filiation of the oppressive bourgeois order. In fact, the opposition between what I am calling a "constellation" on the one hand, which might be defined as an oppositional rapport based on a kind of acentered, nonhierarchical mobility and alliance, and the familial relation of "filiation" on the other plays a crucial role in both texts. A familial or filial rhetoric dominates those passages in both texts that deal with the oppressive, official history: "I recall the history of France, the oldest daughter of the Church" ("Mauvais Sang"); "Bourgeois men of letters . . . have sung loathsome songs in honor of the god Progress, the oldest son of Work" (Lafargue, 126). The thematics of the orphan, which are prevalent throughout Rimbaud's early poetry (for example, "Les Etrennes des Orphelins," "Ma Bohème," "Rêvé pour l'hiver," "Les Effarés," or the opening of the early prose work, "Les Déserts de l'amour": "These writings are of a young, a very young man, whose life evolved in no particular place; without a mother, without a country") and, if we are to believe Delahaye, in his conversation ("What work, everything to be demolished, to be erased in my head! Oh! how happy the abandoned child, brought up any which way, reaching adulthood without any idea inculcated by teachers or by a family: new, clear-headed, without principles, without ideas, — since everything they teach us is false — and free, free from everything"),[33] reach their high point in the figure of the poet-speaker of "Mauvais Sang" — dispossessed, without a family, without even a proper language or material form. "If only I had a link to some point in the history of France! But instead, nothing"; "I don't remember much beyond this land, and Christianity. I will see myself forever in its past. But always alone, without a family; what language, in fact, did I used to speak?" And:

"Weakness or strength: you exist, that is strength. . . . You don't know where you are going or why you are going; go in everywhere, answer everyone. No one will kill you, any more than if you were a corpse."
In the morning my eyes were so vacant and my face so dead that the people I met *may not even have seen me.*

Is it surprising, then, to find Rimbaud, an adolescent, and Lafargue, a Creole, both of whose political imaginations were irrevocably marked by participating in the event of the Commune, joined together at the precise historical moment of the acceleration of capital into what would become its imperialist heyday, both articulating the refusal — the very same as that of "primitive" societies — to allow work and production to engulf them?

But are we really seeing anything here distinct from the standard oppositional discourse adopted en masse by nineteenth-century bourgeois intellectuals and writers — Mallarmé and Flaubert being the best examples — to the hegemonic discourse and workings of their own class? In the face of the creeping domination of the world, including the world of art, by a market economy, the midcentury artistic avant-garde institutes a radical disjunction between the world of poetry and the perceived vulgarity of socioeconomic existence: the realm of utility. Flaubert's dialectical negation takes the form of an enshrined, privatized notion of the

Beautiful: an aesthetic realm freed from the contamination of mediocre, "common," extraliterary considerations. Mallarmé, as is well known, is preoccupied with asserting language's autonomy and self-sufficiency. A poetic language of "evocation" must be rescued from drowning in the base and dominant language of "precision": the rationalist, analytic discourse of science, technology, and material production. Mallarmé's fetishization of the poetic text—the thing which appears without a producer, which appears, according to Mallarmé's famous dictum, with "the elocutory disappearance of the poet"—in fact ends up promoting the reification it sought to resist. Thus the canonical avant-garde stance—what was then called art for art's sake and what has evolved via the formalists into the aestheticism and empty formalism of many strains in our own contemporary criticism—can be seen as a transformation of the old aristocratic doctrine that manual work, work related to concerns of practicality or utility, is the attribute of inferiority.[34]

How different, then, the embrace of inferiority by Rimbaud: "I am well aware that I have always been of an inferior race"; and, "Priests, professors, and doctors, you are mistaken in delivering me into the hands of the law. I have never been one of you; I have never been a Christian; I belong to the race that sang on the scaffold" ("Mauvais Sang"). The narrator's desires or investments are, quite simply, those of the "inferior race." That "race" shows up in the margins of official French history in the form of the undifferentiated horde of serfs "who owe their existence to the Declaration of the Rights of Man," recruited to fight in the Crusades:

> Je me rappelle l'histoire de la France, fille aînée de l'Eglise. J'aurais fait, manant, le voyage de terre sainte; j'ai dans la tête des routes dans les plaines souabes, des vues de Byzance, des remparts de Solyme; le culte de Marie, l'attendrissement sur le crucifié s'éveillent en moi parmi mille féeries profanes. —Je suis assis, lépreux, sur les pots cassés et les orties, au pied d'un mur rongé par le soleil. —Plus tard, reître, j'aurais bivaqué sous les nuits d'Allemagne.
>
> Ah! encore: je danse le sabbat dans une rouge clairière, avec des vieilles et des enfants.
>
> [I remember the history of France, the Eldest Daughter of the Church. I would have gone, a village serf, crusading to the Holy Land; my head is full of roads in the Swabian plains, of the sight of Byzantium, of the ramparts of Jerusalem; the cult of Mary, the pitiful thought of Christ crucified, turns in my head with a thousand profane enchantments—I sit, a leper among broken pots and nettles, at the foot of a wall eaten away by the sun. —And later, a wandering mercenary, I would have bivouacked under German nights.
>
> Ah! one more thing: I dance the Sabbath in a scarlet clearing, with old women and children.]

This passage is striking for several reasons, not the least of which is the spatial, geographic presentation of world history we begin to find here—a kind of slide-show projection of side-by-side world-historical scenes with no apparent transition or continuity—that will become so overwhelmingly prevalent in the *Illuminations*. That Rimbaud should produce a historical narrative of discrete, disjointed tableaux at the point in the poem when he is seeking to disassociate himself from the history of official France and of the Church is not surprising; as Gramsci points out, the history of subaltern social groups is necessarily fragmented and episodic. And Rimbaud's history is resolutely subaltern: "I never see myself in the councils of Christ, nor in the councils of the Lords [*Seigneurs*], Christ's representatives."

The subaltern figures of the village serf, the leper, the reiter, the witch are implicitly opposed to the canonical ghost trio of "priests, professors, doctors" who appeared earlier in the poem. A *manant*, in the Middle Ages, was the inhabitant of a village subjugated to seigneurial justice, a rude, uneducated man, the opposite of a gentleman: a *paysan* (a word that has the same etymology as *pagan*, from the Latin *paganus*, villager). A reiter in the Middle Ages was a German warrior; in the nineteenth century the term came to mean "mercenary." The marginality of the leper and the witch needs no comment; it is, however, striking that it should be at this moment that the verb tense underlines a particular relation: "I *would have gone* , a village serf," and "a wandering mercenary, I *would have bivouacked*," but "I *sit*, a leper," and "I *dance* the Sabbath." Hugo Friedrich, in *The Structure of Modern Poetry*, speaks of Rimbaud's use of what he calls "absolute metaphor," one that is no longer a mere figure of comparison but instead creates an identity.[35] (Théodore de Banville was perhaps the first to notice this propensity in Rimbaud when he complained about the opening of "Le Bateau ivre." The poem would be clearer, more successful, he advised, if Rimbaud were to replace the audacious "I" of the first line with a more digestible formula like "I am *like* a boat that . . ." The true program of such language is, like that of Artaud's Theater of Cruelty, to verge *beyond* representation, to function as a machine to produce, not reproduce, the real. Thus Rimbaud's affinity with the slogan, with invective, with any language that, like the peculiar status of the vagabond, is latent or "virtual"—on the verge of passing over into action—and his affinity as well with the performative, libidinal politics of the Situationists, Deleuze, Guattari, and others of the post-May 1968 generation.) Here the present tense of the "I" as leper is given the weight of one of Friedrich's "absolute metaphors"; it is important first as an underlining of the theme of mutilation, the body in Rimbaud being at all times at issue. But it also serves to clarify the peculiar dimensions of Rimbaldian subjectivity. There is no I-Rimbaud who suddenly hallucinates an identity with various marginal characters; instead there is something like a Rimbaud-subject who passes through a series of affective states and who identifies the proper names of history—and later geography—to these states. *Une Saison en enfer* lasts for much longer than a season, and its expanse is not limited to hell: a whole parade of universal history, races, cultures, populations will be played out on the body of the speaker. This kind of relation is certainly not the static, familial one of identification, based on relations of resemblance or generation, the "I take myself for . . ." or the "I take after Uncle Todd," the composite, metaphorical figures of Freudian condensation; it is instead the essentially nonrepresentative "crowd" process—"I dance the Sabbath . . . *with* old women and children"—the becoming-other of "Je est un autre."

Thus the transition from the ending of the fourth section of "Mauvais Sang," "De profundus, Dominé, suis-je bête!" to the middle of the next section: "*Je suis* une bête, un nègre" (my emphasis): the rhetorical exclamation "materializes" into a *devenir-bête*, a *devenir-nègre*. This is the longest and most celebrated metamorphosis in "Mauvais Sang": the poet's becoming African at the precise moment of the arrival of Christianity and the colonialists ("The white men are landing! The cannon! Now we must be baptized, get dressed, and go to work"). The last term in this trio alerts us to the fact that it is in terms of *métier* or the work order that Rimbaud establishes the opposition between the bad faith of the Western, European bourgeois—the *faux nègres* who are singled out and identified by their professional titles—and the "true kingdom of the children of Ham":

> Oui, j'ai les yeux fermés à votre lumière. Je suis une bête, un nègre.
> Mais je puis être sauvé. Vous êtes de faux nègres, vous, maniaques,
> féroces, avares. Marchand, tu es nègre; magistrat, tu es nègre; général,
> tu es nègre; empereur, vieille démangeaison, tu es nègre. . . . Le plus
> malin est de quitter ce continent, où la folie rôde pour pourvoir d'otages
> ces misérables. J'entre au vrai royaume des enfants de Cham.

> [Yes, my eyes are closed to your light. I am a fool, a nigger. But I can
> be saved. You are fake niggers; maniacs, savages, misers, all of you.
> Businessman, you're a nigger; judge, you're a nigger; general, you're a
> nigger; emperor, old scratch-head, you're a nigger. . . . The best thing
> is to quit this continent where madness prowls, out to supply hostages
> for these wretches. I enter the true kingdom of the children of Ham.]

Gilles Deleuze and Félix Guattari in *Mille Plateaux* have provided a useful distinction between the "work regime" and another model of motor activity they call *action libre*.[36] Work, in their account, is a motor cause that must overcome resistances, operate on the exterior, be consumed or spent in its effect, and which must be renewed from one instant to another. *Action libre*, on the other hand, has no resistance to overcome; just as much a motor cause, it operates only on the mobile body itself, is not consumed in its effect, and is continuous between two instances. The work model is characterized by relative speed and the importance of gravity—the force exerted by the weight of a unified body. "Absolute" speed and the way in which parts of the body escape from gravitational pull in order to occupy a nonstratified, nonpunctual space characterize "free action." "Work makes life blossom," writes Rimbaud. "An old idea, not mine; my life doesn't weigh enough, it drifts off and floats far beyond action." And in an earlier Commune poem, "Qu'est-ce que pour nous, mon coeur," the spectacular physics of the whirlwind—a word that both literally and figuratively means agitation: the group in rapid movement or that which propels a rapid, irresistible movement—is opposed to that of work:

> Qui remuerait les tourbillons de feu furieux,
> Que nous et ceux que nous nous imaginons frères?
> A nous! Romanesques amis: ça va vous plaire.
> Jamais nous ne travaillerons, ô flots de feu!

> [Who will stir up whirlwinds of furious fire
> If we do not, and those whom we call brothers?
> Join us, Romantic friends! Forget all others!
> And never will we work, O waves of fire!]

"Free action," a kind of whirlwind, free expenditure, holds sway in the brief moment before the arrival of the whites:

Connais-je encore la nature? me connais-je? — *Plus de mots*. J'ensevelis les morts dans mon ventre. Cris, tambour, danse, danse, danse, danse! Je ne vois même pas l'heure où, les blancs débarquant, je tomberai au néant.
Faim, soif, cris, danse, danse, danse, danse!

[Do I understand nature? Do I understand myself? *No more words*. I shroud dead men in my stomach. Shouts, drums, dance, dance, dance, dance! I can't even imagine the hour when the white men land, and I will fall into nothingness.
Thirst and hunger, shouts, dance, dance, dance, dance!]

The articulated language of the dance, in a kind of fast forward of the process of colonial domination, will be replaced in the next scene by the parodic, staccato recitation of catechism lessons ("I am reborn in reason. The world is good. I will bless life. I will love my brothers . . . God is my strength and I praise God"), and finally, in the concluding moments of "Mauvais Sang," by the slow, torturous movement of a slave caravan:

Assez! voici la punition. — *En marche!*
Ah! les poumons brûlent, les tempes grondent! La nuit roule dans mes yeux, par ce soleil! Le coeur . . . les membres . . .

Où va-t-on? au combat? Je suis faible! les autres avancent. Les
outils, les armes . . . le temps! . . .
Feu! feu sur moi! Là, où je me rends. —Lâches! —je me tue! Je me
jette aux pieds des chevaux!
Ah! . . .
—Je m'y habituerai.
Ce serait la vie française, le sentier de l'honneur!

[Stop it! This is your punishment . . . ! *Forward march*!
Ah! my lungs burn, my temples roar! Night rolls in my eyes, beneath
the sun! My heart . . . my arms and legs . . .
Where are we going? To battle? I am weak! the others go on ahead
. . . tools, weapons . . . give me time!
Fire! Fire at me! Here! or I'll give myself up! —Cowards! —I'll kill
myself! I'll throw myself beneath the horses' hooves!
Ah! . . .
—I'll get used to it.
That would be the French way, the path of honor.]

Once again, power relations are inscribed on the body as the regulated movement
of the march overcomes the whirlwind, nomadic language of the dance. Space is
stratified in a single direction: ''the French way, the path of honor.'' Tactile and
auditory sensations, speed and movement succumb to the natural gravity of the
state apparatus, one of whose principal affairs is to fix, to make sedentary, to
regulate work, and create a work force.

The dance of the blacks before the arrival of the colonialists, like the *paresse*
and inactivity of the Gauls, consists of movements whose material and variations
have not been controlled by or submitted to the spatiotemporal framework of the
state. Lafargue, outlining the results of overproduction in ''advanced'' countries—the necessity of capital to find new markets in undeveloped, unterritoria-
lized lands—uses the verb *lézarder*, recalling the reptilian, adolescent body in
Rimbaud, to describe the free action of noncolonized space:

Capital abounds like merchandise. The financiers no longer know where
to put it; and so they go into happy nations where people lounge
[*lézardent*] in the sun smoking cigarettes, to build their railroads, set up
factories, and bring in the malediction of work. (132)

Political anthropologists like Pierre Clastres in *Society against the State* (1977)
have argued that primitive societies do not, in our sense, work, even if their activities are extremely constrained and regulated. An earlier, more powerful version
of Clastres's argument can be found in the striking first pages of what many
maintain is the first African novel, René Maran's *Batouala* (1921). The novel

opens with the main character, a tribal leader in a colony within French Equatorial Africa, struggling to get out of bed in the morning:

> And didn't it take an immense effort for him just to stand up? He was the first to admit that making that decision could appear to be of the utmost simplicity to white men. As for him, he found it infinitely more difficult than one might believe. Ordinarily, waking up and work go hand in hand. Certainly work didn't frighten him excessively. Robust, stout-limbed, of excellent stride, he knew no rival when it came to throwing a spear or an assagai, hunting or fighting.
>
> So work couldn't frighten him. Only, in the language of the white men, this word took on a surprising sense, signifying fatigue without immediate tangible result, worries, grief, pain, bad health, the pursuit of chimerical designs.
>
> Aha! white men. So what did they come looking for, so far from their home, in black lands. How much better for them, all of them, to go back to their lands and to never leave them again.
>
> Life is short. Work is only pleasing to those who never understand life. Idleness [la fainéantise] cannot degrade anyone. In this it differs profoundly from sloth [paresse].
>
> In any case, whether you agreed with him or not, he firmly believed, and would not have given in until proved wrong, that to do nothing was, in all good nature and simplicity, to avail oneself of everything that surrounded you.[37]

For Clastres, work is the imperative of a state apparatus, and primitive societies are societies without a state: "Two axioms seem to have guided the advance of Western civilization from the outset: the first maintains that true societies unfold in the protective shadow of the state; the second states a categorical imperative: man must work."[38] The work model is the invention of the state in that people will only work or produce more than their needs require them when forced to. What are disparagingly called "subsistence economies," societies where one works to satisfy one's needs and not to produce a surplus, are to be seen, according to Clastres, as operating according to a refusal of a useless excess of *activity* ("There were days when all men of action seemed to him like the toys of some grotesque raving. He would laugh, horribly, on and on"; "Délire I"). Work, then, appears only with the constitution of a surplus; work begins, properly speaking, *as* overwork, it originates as alienated labor. Where there is no state apparatus or overproduction, there is no work model.

After the Commune—the moment in the history of Western society that comes closest to a dismantling of the state apparatus—the late nineteenth century is figured in Rimbaud's poetry as the epoch of the triumph of the work model, the moment when all activities are translated into possible or virtual work. "It's the vision of numbers," writes Rimbaud in "Mauvais Sang" in a succinct encapsulation of all of Weberian rationalization: the organization of people's productive capacities and nature's resources into markets, their rationalization according to cost accounting, their unity broken into smaller and smaller quantifiable subcomponents—the gearing of a society to accumulation for its own sake. The vision of numbers: the stage reached when everything, as Henri Lefebvre has put it, is calculated because everything is numbered—money, miles, degrees, minutes, calories.[39] It is also the moment, as Rimbaud makes clear in poems like "Le Bateau ivre" and "Démocratie," when even the most distant and exotic lands are beginning to be opened up to European commercial interests.

Rimbaud's peculiar achievement in *Une Saison en enfer* is to have articulated the strategic position and pathos of the adolescent body approaching and entering what "the vision of numbers" designates as adulthood. "Quick! Are there any other lives?" "It seemed to me that everyone should have had several *other* lives as well" ("Délire II"). "Je veux travailler libre," writes Rimbaud to Demeny in 1871, three months after the Commune: his strategy of resistance, even flight— from *métier*, from "formation," but no less from morals, values, nations, religions, and private certitudes—should in no way be confused with a quasi-Mallarmean denegation of the social, that canonical avant-garde doctrine according to which self-realization can only be attained outside the functioning of the social. Rimbaud's flight is at all times a profoundly social investment; it opens at every step onto a sociohistorical field. The gradual disassembling of the vertical, religious scaffolding of *Une Saison en enfer* in its final sections is both the event and the possibility of the event—the utopian possibility, that is, of transformed work relations, the resolutely social and nonnostalgic vision of "Noël sur la terre." In this sense we could say that the *récit* in its entirety ends on the note of "Je serai un travailleur": I *will be* a worker—but only at the moment when work, as we know it, has come to an end.

Notes

1. Maurice Blanchot, "The Song of the Sirens," in *The Gaze of Orpheus*, trans. Lydia Davis (Barrytown, N.Y.: Station Hill Press, 1981), 109.

2. Georg Lukács, *The Theory of the Novel*, trans. Anya Bostock (Cambridge, Mass.: MIT Press, 1971), 132.

3. Jean-Paul Sartre, *What Is Literature?* trans. Bernard Frechtman (New York: Braziller, 1965), 134.

4. Franco Moretti, "The Novel of Youth" (lecture delivered at the University of California at Santa Cruz, May 1985). See also his study of the *bildungsroman*, *The Way of the World* (London: Verso, 1987).

5. See Max Weber for the role of apprenticeship, or "the calling," in the rationalization of economic life: "Labor must . . . be performed as if it were an absolute end in itself, a calling. But such an attitude is by no means a product of nature. It cannot be evoked by low wages or high ones alone, but can only be the product of a long and arduous process of education." *The Protestant Ethic and the Spirit of Capitalism*, trans. Talcott Parsons (New York: Scribners, 1958), 62.

6. "Formation," a term assuring the link between the psychological and the professional, takes precedence over "Instruction" as a goal in mid-nineteenth-century French schooling; the adolescent's purely technical education is downplayed in favor of "apprenticeship": preparation in view of social position as well as technique. See Jean-Claude Monier, "L'Apprentissage de sa condition," in Jean Borail (ed.), *Les Sauvages dans la cité* (Paris, 1985), 161-69.

7. It is here, in this urgent need to reassume the body, to eradicate or prevent its expropriation, to take back one's words—"Burn them, *I insist*, and I think you will respect my wish like that of a dead man, burn *all the poems I was stupid enough* to give you" (Rimbaud to Demeny, June 1871)—to recompose oneself, that Rimbaud's connection to Artaud can most convincingly be determined. Compare, for example, Rimbaud's "I became a fabulous opera"—opera, from the Italian meaning *oeuvre*—"I became a fabulous work," with Artaud's "Moi, Antonin Artaud, je suis mon père, ma mère," etc. See my "Artaud and Van Gogh: Reading in the Imaginary," *Enclitic* 7 (Fall 1984): 116-25.

8. Fredric Jameson, "Rimbaud and the Spatial Text," in Tak-Wai Wong and M. A. Abbas (eds.), *Re-writing Literary History* (Hong Kong: Hong Kong University Press, 1984), 66-93. This is an extremely suggestive essay with which I am mostly in agreement; my quarrel lies with the importance Jameson grants the motif of "fermentation."

9. Louis Barron, *Sous le drapeau rouge* (Paris: Albert Savine, 1889), 165.

10. Ernest Delahaye, cited in Henri Matarasso and Pierre Petitfils, *Vie d'Arthur Rimbaud* (Paris: Hachette, 1962), 86.

11. Vitalie Rimbaud, *Journal*, in Arthur Rimbaud, *Oeuvres complètes*, ed. Rolland de Renéville and Jules Mouquet (Paris: Gallimard, 1967), 582.

12. In the discussion of vagabondage that follows, I am less concerned with allegorizing the social position of the vagabond and the aesthetic position of Rimbaud than with calling attention to the material conditions of Rimbaud's gesture. I want to show how the mythification of the artist works: on the one hand (in traditional accounts), Rimbaud runs away *because he is a poet*, but the fact that this gesture marks his participation in a social collectivity is ignored and deemed irrelevant to his development *as a poet*.

13. Phillipe Meyer, "Le Territoire de l'aveu," in Jacques Berque (ed.), *Nomades et vagabonds* (Paris: 10/18, 1975), 72, 76.

14. C. Rollet, *Enfance abandonnée, vicieux, insoumis, vagabond* (Clermont-Ferrand: Mont-Louis, 1899), 8.

15. Charles Portales, *Des Mendiants et des vagabonds* (Nimes: Baldy & Roger, 1854), 5.

16. Louis Rivière, *Un Siècle de lutte contre le vagabondage* (Paris: Bureaux de la revue politique et parlémentaire, 1899), 5.

17. Théodore Homberg, *Etudes sur le vagabondage* (Paris: Forestier, 1880), ix.

18. Cited in Meyer, "Le Territoire de l'aveu," 69.

19. Homberg, *Etudes sur le vagabondage*, 9.

20. See Jean-Claude Beaune, "Images du mauvais pauvre. Anti-travail et anti-éducation: la figure du vagabond au XIX siècle," in Jean Borail (ed.), *Les Sauvages dans la cité*, 184-201.

21. Homberg, *Etudes sur le vagabondage*, 24-25, 243-48.

22. Portales, *Des Mendiants*, 8.

23. Cited in Pierre Petitfils, *Rimbaud* (Paris: Juillard, 1982), 70.

24. Published in the newspaper, "La Providence," in Meyer, "Le Territoire de l'aveu," in Berque (ed.), 74.

25. Homberg, *Etudes sur le vagabondage*, vii-viii.

26. Homberg, *Etudes sur le vagabondage*, 250.

27. Portales, *Des Mendiants*, 10-11.

28. It was in London, in the intimate circle of Communard exiles, that the paths of Lafargue and Rimbaud intersected. Vermersch, Vallès, Lissagaray, and others formed a "Cercle d'études sociales"

dedicated to counteracting Versaillais anti-Commune propaganda with its own publications about the Commune. Rimbaud and Verlaine were part of this group, which Lafargue frequented as well. Although there is no documented evidence of Rimbaud and Lafargue actually meeting, they traveled in the same small circle. In November 1872, for instance, Paul and Laura Lafargue attended a lecture by Vermersch on Gautier; Rimbaud and Verlaine were also present. See Steve Murphy, "Rimbaud et la Commune?" In Alain Borer (ed.), *Rimbaud Multiple. Colloque de Cérisy* (Gourdon: Bedou & Touzot, 1985), 53-55, and Olga Meier (ed.), *The Daughters of Karl Marx: Family Correspondence 1866-1898*, trans. Faith Evans, intro. Sheila Rowbotham (New York: Harcourt Brace Jovanovitch, 1982), 113.

29. Paul Lafargue, *Le Droit à la paresse*, (Paris: Maspero, 1965), 136.

30. Lafargue was apparently engaged in translating Engels's *Socialism Utopian and Scientific* at the same time (early 1880) that he was writing the pamphlet. While proclaiming himself a "scientific socialist," he maintained that socialist convictions were awakened not only by "the entrails of reality" but by a "far off memory" of a communist epoch preceding the era of private property, by "a memory of that golden age, of that earthly paradise which religions speak to us about." See his *Idéalisme et matérialisme dans la conception de l'histoire* (Paris: de Lille, 1901), 43. Compare Rimbaud's utopian opening to *Une Saison*: "Long ago, if I remember well, my life was a feast where all hearts opened, where all wines flowed."

31. For a diachronic study of the term *travailleur*, see Jean Dubois, *Le Vocabulaire politique et social en France de 1869 à 1872* (Paris: Larousse, 1962), 37-40. While the term had a thickness of revolutionary connotation during the Commune this was not always to be the case. The diffusion of a specifically Marxist vocabulary in the next few decades made prevalent the term *classe ouvrière*; writers whose political activities and memories linked them to the Commune and who continued to use the term *travailleur* were frequently criticized in the late nineteenth century for "sloppy thinking." In fact such a usage proved their link–like that of Rimbaud–to a precise historical period.

32. Paul Lafargue, cited in J. Tchernoff, *Le Parti républicain au coup d'état et sous le Second Empire* (Paris: Pedone, 1901), 354.

33. Cited in Petitfils, *Rimbaud*, 57.

34. For a study of the modes of opposition or "counterdiscourses" of bourgeois writers and intellectuals to the increasing standardization of culture in a rapidly industrializing France, see Richard Terdiman, *Discourse/Counter Discourse: The Theory and Practice of Symbolic Resistance in Nineteenth-Century France* (Ithaca, N.Y.: Cornell University Press, 1984). Rimbaud, symptomatically, is relegated to a footnote in this book; he is, as Terdiman rightly puts it, "beyond the limits of counter-discursive protocol."

35. Hugo Friedrich, *The Structure of Modern Poetry*, trans. Joachim Neugroschel (Evanston, Ill.: Northwestern University Press, 1974), 51.

36. See Gilles Deleuze and Félix Guattari, *Mille Plateaux* (Paris: Minuit, 1980), 494-96, for a discussion of the work model vs. *action libre*.

37. René Maran, *Batouala* (Paris: Albin Michel, 1965), 20-21.

38. Pierre Clastres, *Society against the State*, trans. Robert Hurley (New York: Urizen Press, 1977), 163. It is crucial to point out that Clastres is forced to admit, almost inadvertently, that his basic argument—"Primitive societies are societies without a state; a state is necessary to impose work: there is no 'work' in primitive societies"—pertains to only one half of the population of primitive societies: the men. Consider this description of the Tupi-Guarani tribe in South America: "The economic life of those Indians was primarily based on agriculture, secondarily on hunting, fishing, and gathering. The same garden plot was used from four to six consecutive years, after which it was abandoned, owing either to the depletion of the soil, or, more likely, to an invasion of the cultivated space by a parasitic vegetation that was difficult to eliminate. The biggest part of the work, performed by the men, consisted of clearing the necessary area by the slash and burn technique, using stone axes. This job, accomplished at the end of the rainy season, would keep the men busy for a month or

two. Nearly all the rest of the agricultural process—planting, weeding, harvesting—was the responsibility of the women, in keeping with the sexual division of labor. This happy conclusion follows: the men (i.e., one-half of the population) worked about two months every four years!'' (164-65). Happy for some. The sexual division of labor creates an underclass, women, whose activity, according to Clastres's own definition, would have to constitute ''work,'' alienated labor.

For other valuable analyses of precapitalist or ''primitive'' relations to work, see Michael T. Taussig, *The Devil and Commodity Fetishism in South America* (Chapel Hill: University of North Carolina Press, 1980); John M. Coetzee, ''Anthropology and the Hottentots,'' in *Semiotica* 54 (1985): 87-95; and Marshall Sahlins, *Stone Age Economics* (Chicago: Aldine Atherton, 1972).

39. Henri Lefebvre, *La Vie quotidienne dans le monde moderne* (Paris: Gallimard, 1968), 44.

Chapter 3
Spatial History

Rimbaud, it appears, was a topic of discussion between Bertolt Brecht and Walter Benjamin. In his journals Benjamin relates some of his friend's musings about Rimbaud, the poet with whom Brecht felt the closest connection:

> He thinks that Marx and Engels, had they read "Le Bateau ivre,"
> would have sensed in it the great historical movement of which it is the
> expression. They would have clearly recognized that what it describes is
> not an eccentric poet going for a walk, but the flight, the escape of a
> man who cannot live any longer inside the barriers of a class which—
> with the Crimean War, with the Mexican adventure—was then beginning
> to open up even the most exotic lands to mercantile interests.[1]

Brecht's phrase "an eccentric poet going for a walk" is an efficient way of summing up and dismissing the various mythic interpretations of Rimbaud as *poète maudit* or *enfant terrible*. The audacity of his praise of "Le Bateau ivre" as a *historical* narrative, and specifically as a lyric poem that encompasses or expresses the moment of the passage from market capitalism into a far-flung and geographic world system—the imperialist heyday of the late nineteenth century—bears examination. Does not its audacity lie in its strong linking of two pairs of elements that are not frequently brought together in either literary criticism or political thought, namely, lyric poetry and politics, and, second, history and space? At the same time that Brecht affirms the narrative, diachronic power of Rimbaud's verse, he is concerned with portraying historical development in terms of a massive, synchronic expansion or spatial movement: the late nineteenth-century European construction of space *as* colonial space. In Brecht's statement, time and space are not where they should be: history has gone spatial, and the lyric—that unique, evanescent, exceptional moment—tells a story.

Rimbaud's later poetry is marked by a distinct proliferation of geographic terms and proper names: poles and climates, countries, continents and cities—a kind of charting of social movement in geographic terms. A fairly neat division can in fact be established, as Fredric Jameson has suggested, between the erotic microgeography and more or less individual thematics of Rimbaud's early work—the kiss that wanders over the woman's body in "Rêvé pour l'hiver"—and the move to a global, planetary space in the later works.[2] A vast geography of mass displacements, movements of populations and human emigrations dominates not only *Une Saison en enfer*, but a large number of the *Illuminations* as well: "Parade," "Barbare," "Promontoire," "Soir Historique," "Mouvement," the "Villes" poems, "Démocratie," and others. In fact, given the flood of geographic terms in the *Illuminations* and *Une Saison* I was at first tempted to correlate the opening up of geographic space in Rimbaud's work to his transition from verse to prose. But such a correlation corresponds too neatly with traditional assumptions regarding prose as privileged vehicle for objective or political themes and verse for subjective, personal, or individual ones. More important, it reinforces the widespread notion that there exists a social production of reality on the one hand, and a desiring production that is mere fantasy on the other. Rimbaud's poetry—and Commune culture in general—seemed to me to collapse or render artificial such a division between the psychoanalytic and the social.

The geopolitical perception I will examine in this chapter can in fact be already detected in verse Rimbaud writes in 1870 and 1871—not only, as Brecht points out, in "Le Bateau ivre," or in the long verse poem "Ce qu'on dit au poète à propos de fleurs," which we will consider later, but in such passages as the conclusion to "Qu'est-ce pour nous, mon coeur":

> Europe, Asie, Amérique, disparaissez.
> Notre marche vengeresse a tout occupé,
> Cités et campagnes!—Nous serons écrasés!
> Les volcans sauteront! et l'océan frappé . . .
>
> Oh! mes amis!—mon coeur, c'est sûr, ils sont des frères:
> Noirs inconnus, si nous allions! allons! allons!
> O malheur! je me sens frémir, la vieille terre,
> Sur moi de plus en plus à vous! la terre fond . . .
>
> [Europe, Asia, America, vanish!
> Our avenging advance has ravished and sacked
> Towns and countryside! We will be punished!
> Volcanoes will explode! And Ocean attacked . . .

Oh, friends! Be calm, these are brothers, my heart:
Dark strangers, suppose we begin! Let's go, let's go!
Disaster! I tremble, the old earth,
On me, and yours, ah, more and more! The earth dissolves. . . .]

A spatial or geopolitical preoccupation does not appear linked to prose rather than verse. Consider, in more detail, the spatial agenda already apparent in one of Rimbaud's earliest poems, "A la Musique," a poem that documents, in an almost Balzacian grotesque realism, the paltry vanities and habits surrounding the Thursday afternoon summer concert in the town square at Charleville. In this poem, placement is everything; the proper name "Place de la Gare, Charleville" below the title, far from evoking an exotic geography, serves instead to *ground* the poem in the triviality and specificity of its petit bourgeois portraiture. Indeed, the poem opens with a description of the square; the small provincial town as nature that has been worked over and subdivided, rendered sordid and mediocre, as lacking in generosity or air as its wheezing inhabitants:

> Sur la place taillée en mesquines pelouses,
> Square où tout est correct, les arbres et les fleurs,
> Tous les bourgeois poussifs qu'étranglent les chaleurs
> Portent, les jeudis soirs, leurs bêtises jalouses.

> [On Railroad Square, laid out in little spots of lawn,
> Where all is always order, the flowers and the trees,
> All the puffing bourgeois, strangling in the heat,
> Parade their envious nonsense on Thursday afternoon.]

Here, the stuffiness and claustrophobia evoked by words like *poussifs* and *étranglent*, reduplicate the carefully segmented metric space—the grid—of the town center. Although lacking in air or inspiration, the bourgeois are nevertheless *jalouses*: envious, rapacious, acquisitive. The enjambment of the last line places the verb *porter* in relief and establishes it as the bourgeois verb or posture par excellence: both in the sense of "to bear the weight of" (with all its foreshadowing of "the white man's burden") and "to display," to parade. The class of possessors, weighed down by and displaying their possessions—here, their envy.

The military band, the source of the music in the title, is situated in the spatial center of the square:

> —L'orchestre militaire, au milieu du jardin,
> Balance ses schakos dans la *Valse des fifres*:
> —Autour, aux premiers rangs, parade le gandin;
> Le notaire pend à ses breloques à chiffres:

> [In the middle of the garden a military band is
> Playing, helmets jiggling to "Lady of Spain";

By the benches in front dawdle the dandies;
The notary dangles from his own watch chain.]

An earlier version of the poem shows a different last line: "les notaires mon-trent leurs breloques à chiffres" ("The notaries display their watch chains"). Obvious differences accompany the verb change; by altering the notary's relation to his watch chain from one of "displaying" to one of "hanging from," the "display" meaning of *porter* gives way to that of weight or burden. (The "display" side of the tension is maintained in the stanza through a subdivision of "types": if the notary "hangs," the dandy, on the other hand, displays or pa-rades himself as aesthetic object. *Gandin*, a midcentury slang word, had come to signify very specifically in Rimbaud's time a wealthy do-nothing who ruined himself for women; the word derived most likely, Delvau speculates, from the luxurious gloves [*gants*] these men gave their lovers.) Hanging, which develops the strangling or choking theme from the first stanza, shows the bourgeois func-tionary as someone who has lost control of his possessions; his possessions deter-mine, control, even strangle him. The notary is specifically controlled by his watch, by his schedule, his *horaire*: the numerical emblem and reflection of his own *métier* (time is money) lurks in "breloques à *chiffres*." Time, then, is reg-ulated, divided, calculated to the same extent that space is "managed" in the small town.

A word is in order here on the notary as nineteenth-century type. The arbiter in most small-town business deals, and often, in the late 1800s, the mayor of his own village, the notary is the necessary intermediary in small-town movement of property and capital. Notaries, viewed as usurers, were persecuted during the Revolution more than any other profession, some say more than the aristocracy. When Baudelaire hurls invective against the school of *bon sens*, he attacks the "honest bourgeoise" and above all, the notary, the person such women hold in respect. In Balzac, and, as we will see, in "A la Musique," the notary as type functions in binary opposition to the artist or lover:

When a notary has not got the immobile and gently rounded face you
can recognize, if he does not offer to society the unlimited guarantee of
his mediocrity, if he is not the polished steel cog that he ought to be, if
there is left in him any suggestion that he is in the least bit an artist,
capricious, passionate, or a lover, he is lost.

The next stanzas of the poem are cluttered with an enumeration of fetishized possessions:

Des rentiers à lorgnons soulignent tous les couacs:
Les gros bureaux bouffis traînent leurs grosses dames
Auprès desquelles vont, officieux cornacs,
Celles dont les volants ont des airs de réclames;

Sur les bancs verts, des clubs d'épiciers retraités
Qui tisonnent le sable avec leur canne à pomme,
Fort sérieusement discutent les traités,
Puis prisent en argent, et reprennent: "En somme!"

Epatant sur son banc les rondeurs de ses reins,
Un bourgeois à boutons clairs, bedaine flamande,
Savoure son onnaing d'où le tabac par brins
Déborde—vous savez, c'est de la contrebande;—

[Private incomes in pince-nez point out all the false notes
Great counting-house desks, bloated, drag their fat wives—
Close by whom, like bustling elephant keepers
Walk women whose flounces remind you of sales.

On the green benches, clumps of retired grocers
Poke at the sand with their knob-top canes,
Gravely talk of trade agreements, move closer,
Take snuff from silver boxes, then resume: "To sum it up . . ."

Spreading his global bottom on a bench,
A pale-buttoned bourgeois—a Flemish gut—
Sucks his smelly pipe, whose flaky tobacco
Overflows—"You realize, it's smuggled, of course . . ."]

The pince-nez of the *rentiers* are granted the same function as the fat wives dragged along by the clerks (or *bureaux*: in an audacious metonymy the place of work, the container, is used to name the person). Rimbaud's use of the word *réclame* shows his characteristic move of cannibalizing contemporary specialized vocabulary: *réclame* takes on the meaning of advertisement, announcement, or poster in commercial vocabulary only in 1869. The language of numbers dominates the next stanza where retired grocers earnestly discuss trade agreements; their quoted remarks ("To sum it up . . .") "economically" and playfully reduce their conversation to an exchange of numbers, a reductive discourse used to master material, to control its variations and movements. In the next stanza the "b" sound that began with "les gros bureaux bouffis" becomes more aggressively oppressive: "un *b*ourgeois à *b*outons clairs, *b*edaine flamande"; the bourgeois is designated by the synecdoche *bedaine*—stomach—a variation on the popular working-class shorthand for the propertied class, *ventres* (another working-class slang expression for the bourgeoisie, *épiciers* [grocers], was used earlier in the poem).

The first five stanzas state and restate in the form of static description a dialectic between, on the one hand, a portrait of limitation and stagnation, of a controlled (*taillée*) reductive discourse where everything, nature as well as sexual and social relations, evaporates into numerical relations, and, on the other, a posture of voracious acquisition. The tobacco, a guilty, contreband pleasure, overflows its container, and the enjambment gives full weight to the verb "overflow" (*déborder*: literally, to go beyond one's borders, and, in the popular slang of the period, to vomit because of overeating). Squared-off angles versus overflowing, greedy bodies that are somehow too big for the picture, exceeding their own boundaries.

These relations are established in the poem largely by way of spatial prepositions; the first five stanzas are dominated by the preposition *sur* ("sur la place taillée," "sur les bancs verts," "épatant sur son banc les rondeurs de ses reins")—a preposition that emphasizes not only the static, stationary quality of the population but also a relationship of power or domination, of possession. The etymology of the word "possession" (from the Latin *possidere*: *s'asseoir sur*, to sit upon) is worth recalling here in the light of this poem, as well as in the light of Rimbaud's more extended diatribes against "Les Assis"—the seated ones—or against "Accroupissements"—the squattings—in those poems and elsewhere. In the Commune poem "Chant de guerre parisien," for instance, the rural monarchist landowners (*Ruraux*) who joined forces with the Versaillais to wipe out the Commune, are shown in their emblematic posture of squatting: "Et les Ruraux qui se prélassent / Dans de longs accroupissements" ("And the Rustics who loll about / In long squattings"). The only thing worse than the sedentary provincial population, is that population "on the move":

> . . . cette benoîte population gesticule, prud'hommesquement spadassine. . . . C'est effrayant, les épiciers retraités qui revêtent l'uniforme! C'est épatant comme ça a du chien, les notaires, les vitriers, les percepteurs, les menuisiers et tous les ventres, qui, chassepot au coeur, font du patrouillotisme aux portes de Mézières; ma patrie se lève! . . . Moi, j'aime mieux la voir assise: ne remuez pas les bottes! c'est mon principe.

> [. . . this sanctimonious population gesticulates like so many swashbuckling M. Prudhommes. Retired grocers dressed up in their uniforms are a terrifying spectacle! It's astonishing to see how smart they look, notaries, glaziers, tax-collectors, carpenters and all the fat-bellied dignitaries with rifles over their hearts, patriotically patrolling shit-scared at the gates of Mézières: my country rises up! I like it better sitting down. Don't stir an inch, that's my motto. (August 25, 1870)]

Thus a new spatial preposition, *Le long des* (along side of), opening the sixth stanza of "A la Musique" can be immediately taken as announcing a moment of rupture, of opening in the poem:

Le long des gazons verts ricanent les voyous;
Et, rendus amoureux par le chant des trombones,
Très naïfs, et fumant des roses, les pioupious
Caressent les bébés pour enjôler les bonnes . . .

[Along the grass borders, slum kids laugh in derision
Chewing on roses, fresh-faced young soldiers
Melt to love at the sound of trombones,
And fondle the babies to get round their nurses . . .]

We have moved to a marginal situation vis-à-vis the town square and to a marginal group of inhabitants; both age and class separate the maids, the *voyous*, and the soldiers from the "seated ones." The very same music heard from this distance is no longer military music or "false notes" but music that awakens desire, a *chant* and not a *couac*. Distance from the town center *allows* the possibility of laughter, desire, melody—all of which appear for the first time.

—Moi, je suis, débraillé comme un étudiant
Sous les marronniers verts les alertes fillettes:
Elles le savent bien, et tournent en riant,
Vers moi, leurs yeux tout pleins de choses indiscrètes.

Je ne dis pas un mot: je regarde toujours
La chair de leurs cous blancs brodés de mèches folles:
Je suis, sous le corsage et les frêles atours,
Le dos divin après la courbe des épaules.

J'ai bientôt déniché la bottine, le bas . . .
—Je reconstruis les corps, brûlé de belles fièvres.
Elles me trouvent drôle et se parlent tout bas . . .
—Et mes désirs brutaux s'accrochent à leurs lèvres.

[Me, I follow, disarrayed like a student
Under the green chestnuts, the lively young girls
—Which they know very well, and they turn to me, laughing,
Their eyes full of indiscreet things.

I don't say a word: I just keep looking
At the skin of their white necks embroidered with stray locks:
I go hunting, beneath bodices and thin attire
The divine back below the curve of the shoulders.

Soon I've discovered the boot and the stocking . . .
I re-create the bodies, burning with fine fevers.
They find me absurd, talk together in low voices . . .
And my savage desires fasten onto their lips . . .]

The poet-speaker makes his appearance immediately following the move toward spatial and social marginalization; the "I" is unsituated in terms of a *métier*—not even a student, but *like* a student (recalling a similarly vague "I" in "Sensation" who is not a bohemian but "*like* a bohemian"—in a posture of flight from the very organization of *métier*). In poems like "La Maline," "Les Douaniers," *Une Saison en enfer*, and "Les Réparties de Nina," Rimbaud reveals an almost Proustian tendency to construct the world as what Benjamin called a "physiology of chatter"—to mimic voices, accents, speech patterns, slang, specialized vocabularies as a means of "situating" a person—establishing that person's class, *métier*, region. In so doing he underlines the social contingency of semiotic behavior. Here the "I" says not a word, and thus definitively absents himself from or defers participation in this system of identification; the use of this strategy by the poet/speaker of "Mauvais Sang" is, as we saw in the preceding chapter, all the more exaggerated.

The word *débraillé* suggests open clothing and disarray as opposed to the encumberment of bibelots dragging down the bourgeois; the girls are similarly unencumbered ("thin attire")—in fact, the ambiguity of "Je suis" ("I follow . . . the lively young girls" and "I am . . . the lively young girls") even suggests an almost narcissistic identification with the girls and their position. *Débraillé* also has the sense of an indiscreet conversation, an exchange lacking in reserve (versus the grocers' characteristic move to "sum it up")—echoed elsewhere in the poem by the derision of the *voyou*'s laughter, and the indiscretion of the girls' glances, their laughter, their alertness. The speaker's relation is given as *under* the chestnuts rather than *upon*, and *following* the young girls, rather than *dragging* the fat wives. His activities in the final stanza are those of the artist-/lover; his work, unlike that of the notary, takes place in the imaginary: while the notary hangs from his schedule, the poet is riveted to the lips of the girls (with as much desire to know what they are saying about him as desire *for them*).

The poem establishes two distinct spaces: the first governed by dimensional, metric division where material (people and things) is organized according to ready-made forms, and space is governed by optical perception and by gravity. The final stanzas establish an alternative space of flight as the space of affect and of possible (latent) event: the exchanged glance between the girls and the poet, a space of intensities, noises, laughter, music, and connivance—tactile and sonorous qualities. It is true that the bodies of the girls, like that of the bourgeois, are fragmented, part-objects ("the curve of the shoulders")—but there is a crucial difference between designating a man as a "Flemish stomach" and evoking a group of girls as "the curve of the shoulders." The first amounts to a synecdochic designation of an entire class while the second blurs the outlines of a person, or rather of a group, into a vague essence, a material quality—roundness. The curve: what changes directions without forming angles, what is not straight, what is distinct from the fixed, metric, and sedentary essences of the town square grid.

All this is apparent in the two possible meanings of the title. "To the Music": a dedication rife with all of Rimbaud's early spatial optimism to a fleeting lyrical moment of desire and escape—the song rather than the squawk; or "At the Concert": Rimbaud's effort to record and expose, in specific utterances and bodily attitudes, the language and situation of a class, in order to strip that class of its ideological guarantee and its seamless self-confidence. The small-town slice of life, the accurately documented portrait of a class, a discourse (quantitative), and a bodily posture (parading, carrying) *overflowing*—a class on the edge of spreading out over the whole world. ("Contreband" and "trade agreements" already suggest the burgeoning realm of international commerce.)

"A la Musique" resembles nothing so much as one of the rural physiologies, with their descriptions and caricatures of "types" and *métiers*, or other such subgenres prevalent in the midcentury that provided a kind of ethnography of rural France. Such genres tended to manipulate direct, and above all *thematic* contestation. With a post-Commune work like "Ce qu'on dit au poète à propos de fleurs," we move to a more subtly formal and functional subversive strategy. And its scope, like the scope of the class it satirizes, has widened beyond small-town provincialism to encompass the international, exoticist penetration and expropriation enacted by bourgeois culture.

"Ce qu'on dit au poète à propos de fleurs" has been read as a parody of and manifesto against a certain dominant brand of aestheticism and rhetorical trickery practiced by the Parnassian poets. It was these poets—among them Banville (to whom the poem is dedicated or sent), Mallarmé, Mendès, and Leconte de Lisle—whom Rimbaud, recently arrived in Paris, was attempting to both impress and repudiate. The problem with Parnassian poets, Rimbaud makes clear early in the poem, is their excessive concern with mimesis—their dependence on the eye:

> De vos forêts et de vos prés,
> O très paisibles photographes!
> La Flore est diverse à peu près
> Comme des bouchons de carafes!
>
> Toujours les végétaux Français,
> Hargneux, phtisiques, ridicules,
> Où le ventre des chiens bassets
> Navigue en paix, aux crépuscules . . .
>
> [In the fields and forests of your verse
> —Oh, you peaceful photographers!—
> The flora is about as diverse
> As bottle corks and stoppers.

> Always this French vegetation abounds,
> Grouchy, coughing, silly and sick,
> Where the bellies of basset hounds
> Wallow through the growing dark . . .]

Whether confined to describing the flora of the immediate suburbs of Paris, or "free" like Leconte de Lisle, satirized in the next section of the poem as a kind of Great White Hunter—

> O blanc Chasseur, qui cours sans bas
> A travers le Pâtis panique,
> Ne peux-tu pas, ne dois-tu pas
> Connaître un peu ta botanique?

> [O White Hunter, bootless in a
> Panicky Pasture, it
> Might really help to recall
> Your botany a bit.]

. . . free to travel to exotic lands to conduct a panicky search, like Chateaubriand and a whole lineage of Western writers before and after him, for fresh raw materials with which to revitalize his writing, these poets are guilty of a kind of "landscapism": they describe what they see. Rimbaud is not alone in making this kind of accusation. Future Communard Eugène Vermersch, in whose London apartment Rimbaud and Verlaine would take refuge in 1872, was also quick to link Parnassian exoticism to an elitist artistic posture and its attendant racism. In his *Les Hommes du jour*, a satiric series of brief portraits of the more visible men and women in Parisian society written some time in the early 1870s, Vermersch adopts a tone similar to Rimbaud's when he addresses Catulle Mendès:

> Too many, far too many asokas, Monsieur Mendès. What could all this
> mean to us, the Bhandiras, the Gangas, the Vacu, the devas, the
> Mangou, the Tchandra Star, the Maharchis, the Cudras, the Malicas?
> Could it be that you are only writing for the dozen or so of your little
> friends who lean back in their chairs at your gatherings and swoon at
> the readings of your verse, and for the young Chinese who follows six
> steps behind you when you deign to show yourself to the people?[3]

The asoka, apparently an Indian tree, figures in the title of Parnassian Louis Menard's 1855 poem; for Vermersch and Rimbaud that obscure plant became a synecdoche for the work produced by what Rimbaud would playfully accuse Verlaine of aspiring to be—a "bon Parnassian." The asoka surfaces in later stanzas of "Ce qu'on dit":

L'Ode Açoka cadre avec la
Strophe en fenêtre de lorette;
Et de lourds papillons d'éclat
Fientent sur la Pâquerette . . .

Oui, vos bavures de pipeaux
Font de précieuses glucoses!
—Tas d'oeufs frits dans de vieux chapeaux,
Lys, Açokas, Lilas et Roses.

[The Ode on Asokas is as bad as
The Stained-Glass-Window stanza;
And heavy, vivid butterflies
Are dunging on the Daisy . . .

Yes, the droolings from your flutes
Make some priceless glucoses!
—A pile of fried eggs in old hats,
Those Lilies, Lilacs, Lotuses and Roses!]

Neither Mendès nor Leconte de Lisle would have denied the accusation of "land-scapism." Giving voice to what was to become the dominant avant-garde stance in the nineteenth century, Leconte de Lisle situates the "poetic" definitively on the side of the socially irrelevant: "The first concern of anyone who writes in verse, or in prose for that matter, must be to emphasize the picturesque side of things."[4] For de Lisle and the Parnassians, the archaic, the suburban, or the exotic picturesque would automatically procure what was needed to compensate for a world become prosaic to the extent of its scientific and technological progress.

Landscapism was not to be confined to a purely aesthetic debate; a veritable *science* of landscapism, the science of objective space par excellence, university geography, took form during the era of the Parnassians. University geography *began* in the 1870s: it was then that the subject was first institutionalized as an academic discipline in France. During this decade the enormously influential French school of geography began to take shape around the figures of Emile Levasseur, the great initiator who showed the necessity of the instruction of geography as a discipline, Ludovic Drapeyron, founder of the *Revue de géographie*, and, most important, Vidal de la Blache, later to be canonized, significantly enough, by Lucien Febvre and other leading thinkers associated with the Annales School of Historiography, as the "Father of French Geography."[5] The Vidalian model would exert a hegemonic control over geographic studies until the 1950s.

Febvre's embrace of the work of Vidal de la Blache is not surprising. Annales historians in the 1920s and 1930s established a historiography that brought to the forefront elements most often considered geographic or spatial: climate, demography, the immutable rural life associated with time conceptualized as *longue durée*.[6] History tells us that French geography was born in the 1870s, the bastard offspring of history. Levasseur, Drapeyron, and Vidal were all trained initially as historians, and each turned to more geographic pursuits after the French defeat of 1870: spatial history. Vidal, writing later about his own metamorphosis, attributes the change to an itinerary well traveled by and memorialized by the Parnassian poets of the day: he was seduced into geography, he writes, by his frequent voyages in Egypt, Greece, and Asia Minor, where he would travel as a young man to explore ancient ruins.

Vidal was to supply classical French geography with both a definition and a method. The definition was concise and enduring: "Geography is the science of landscape." Vidalian geography takes its model from the taxonomic dream of the natural sciences and is resolutely turned toward description; the geographer finds himself facing a landscape: the perceptible, visible aspect of space. When Vidal wrote what was to become the master text of French geography, he called it *Tableau de la géographie de la France*, a title that revealed not only the contents of the book—an inventory of the typical landscapes of France—but the situation of its author as well: the geographer as landscape painter.

The method Vidal provided and which was to spread the renown of the French school can be summed up as follows: the geographic description of any country consists of presenting and describing the regions that make it up. Space is divided into regions that exist as distinct "individualities," "personalities"; the role of the geographer is to detail a region's physiognomy and show how its traits result from a harmonious and permanent interaction between natural conditions and old historical heritages. It would be many generations before people noticed that Vidal's regions were not natural "givens": that Brittany, for example, was not a God-given designation.

What are the implications of Vidal's definition and methodology? First, the definition of the object of study as "landscape" imposes solely visual criteria and makes of the geographer an interpreter of natural conditions. Vidal defines landscape as "what the eye embraces with a look," or, in another formulation, "the part of the country that nature offers up to the eye that looks at it." One could speak at some length about the sexual metaphors operative in these definitions, about "space become feminine" and "offering itself up" to the viewer—all this as preparatory to the more blatant "penetration" metaphors favored by later geographer/explorers; here, I want rather to point out an ironic undercutting of Vidal's own fetishization of visual criteria. Radical geographers like Béatrice Giblin have convincingly shown that Vidal's landscapes cannot, in fact, *be seen* ; his masterful, almost Parnassian literary style masks the fact that he is concerned *not* with precise, localized landscapes—the observed landscape—but rather with the *typical* landscape that he constructs from abstract and derivative cliché formulations.[7] It is precisely this kind of synthetic and derivative mobilization of cliché that Rimbaud ridicules in Parnassian poetry:

> Tu ferais succéder, je crains,
> Aux Grillons roux les Cantharides,
> L'or des Rios au bleu des Rhins, —
> Bref, aux Norwèges les Florides:

> [I'm afraid you'd follow up
> Russet crickets with Cantharides,
> Blues of Rhine with Rio golds
> — in short, Norways with Floridas.]

Here the geographic proper name is in the plural — Floridas and Norways — and trivializes Parnassian practice as a relation to a series of detached, reified elements: Florida is not a place in all of its particularity, but a hodgepodge of exoticist clichés, textual citations, and trumped-up botanical references; by simply changing the bird, the insect, the color, PRESTO! We're in Norway.

Both Parnassian landscape and Vidalian landscape pose space as a natural referent. Vidalian geography, composed as it is in the late nineteenth century, is striking in its almost total evasion of ongoing historical developments like the industrial revolution or colonialism, famines or the rise of urbanism. Cities figure very little in Vidalian geography. The methodology of regionalism implies instead a geography of permanences: what in the countryside has been in place for a long time. To conceive of space in this way is to occult the social and economic contradictions of which space is the material terrain; the very concept of "the region" as it is developed by Vidal implies a homogeneous, unitary society at one with its natural milieu and united in its collective will to exist. In fact, "humanized landscapes" are quite rare in nineteenth-century academic geography; if humans appear at all they must do so in such a way as to reinforce the natural harmony of the region: the native, the peasant is *part of* the landscape, in a synecdochic relationship of décor.

Only when the evolution of capitalist society had created a greatly increased demand for scientific geography were specialist geographers sought. Vidalian geography was to play a large role in physically naturalizing the foundations of national ideology. That the privileged and exclusive status of space as a natural referent corresponds to the needs of Western colonialism would become more evident in the decades to follow. Western, Christian colonialism demands a certain construction of space that Vidalian, academic geography was to help provide: natural, which is to say, nonhistorical — and one where all alterity is absent. Another contribution to the construction of space as colonial space was to come from a surprising source: Saussurian linguistics. Saussure, interestingly enough, wrote his first major work in the 1870s. In order to understand how the Saussurian sign refers back to a doubly determined spatial referent—extralinguistic and above all *natural*—it would perhaps be enough to recall the canonical example by which each of us learned the explanation of the Saussurian sign. I say the word "tree" (the acoustical image, the signifier); the concept "tree" comes to your mind (at this point a tree is drawn on the blackboard), but this is not the *real* tree, which is *out there* (extralinguistic, spatial, and natural).[8]

Saussure insisted on the marginal role that denotation—the relation of the sign to the referent—played in his definition of the sign. Consequently denotation played a small and very vague role in his linguistics. The dominance of a Saussurian informed linguistics over French literary studies during the past thirty years has been the dominance of a linguistics preoccupied with the problem of signification, the relation of signifier to signified, and not that of reference. Saussure and his followers have given us a "spatiality" of language—but it is a particular kind of spatiality: one that results from rigorously distinguishing signifier from signified and from giving the former the leading role in what is called the "play" of language. This is then defined as a purely differential system of relations where each element is qualified by the place it occupies in an ensemble, and by the horizontal and vertical relations it entertains with neighboring elements. We are familiar with this Saussurian spatiality of language, as well as with its inaccessibility to either geometric space or, more important, the space of lived experience, everyday life. If we turn back to Rimbaud's poem, I think we will see another kind of spatiality at work. Rimbaud's linguistics is more concerned with the problem of reference ("the silk of seas and arctic flowers; [they do not exist]"; "Barbare"), of denotation, than with signification. Into the midst of Parnassian stage props, Rimbaud suddenly inserts the problem of the referent:

> La . . . Comme si les Acajous
> Ne servaient, même en nos Guyanes,
> Qu'aux cascades des sapajous,
> Au lourd délire des lianes!
>
> [Really, as if mahoganies
> Were only, even in our Guianas,
> Swings for swarms of monkeys
> In dizzy tangles of lianas . . .]

Rimbaud's later poetry is, as I have mentioned, characterized by a proliferation of geographic names, but his *use* of geography is, for the most part, distinct from and critical of the Orientalist or exoticist appropriation of place-names prevalent in nineteenth-century French literature. In this passage, for instance, instead of Floridas, Norways, we have not just "Guianas" but *our* Guianas. The possessive plus the proper name indicates an instance of what language philosophers following Russell call "definite description"—an instance, that is, of denotation, not connotation. This use of definite description is a referential function, a formulation capable of shifting its referent according to time, speaker, use context—in other words, according to history. The possessive here functions as a shifter, indicating the particular sociopolitical reality of its enunciation—thus, a use of geographic place-names in a historical, nontimeless way.

Two things draw our attention in this stanza. First, Rimbaud's explicit thematic argument against the strict Parnassian limits of what constitutes a proper subject for poetry. By arguing and enacting a definition of the poetic that embraces sociopolitical themes and practical, utilitarian concerns, Rimbaud sets himself against not only the Parnassians but against what would become the dominant nineteenth- and twentieth-century avant-garde stance, the one best exemplified by Mallarmé's lifelong concern with hygienically rescuing a truly "poetic" language of evocation from the hegemonic vulgarity of bourgeois utilitarianism and precision. More important, though, "our Guianas" and the many other examples from Rimbaud's poetry of demonstratives, shifters, proper names, and "definite descriptions," indicate a repeated insertion of the problem of the referent at a time when poetry was single-mindedly announcing its immunity to changes in denotation. Instead of the Mallarméan problematic of signifier and signified—consider, for example, such spatial experiments as Mallarmé's typographical arrangement of words on a page in "Un Coup de dés"—Rimbaud's concern is with the referent. Thus, as I will discuss in Chapter 5, his affinity with invective and with the slogan, with performative language that, in the case of Rimbaud, can be "frozen" and transported across generations, to be revived at certain moments of our own century, most notably during May 1968 in Paris. Contemporary theory's canonization of Mallarmé and Saussure at the expense of Rimbaud goes hand in hand with the priority given epistemology and aesthetics over social thought and the celebration of a romantic "politics" of textuality, that ludic counterlogic of semantic instability that characterizes much of French theory, and especially French theory readily imported in America, today.

Perhaps the best way to crystallize Rimbaud's opposition to the canonical avant-garde, and to the prevalent nineteenth-century class privilege of aestheticism, is to recall here, in the context of Rimbaud's poem about flowers, Mallarmé's famous remark about the missing flower: "Je dis: une fleur! et . . . musicalement se lève, idée même et suave, l'absente de tous bouquets" ("I say: a flower! and . . . musically there arises, precise and suave idea, the flower absent from all bouquets").[9] Poetic discourse "replaces" the referent; the word "flower" eliminates the flower. Poetic language speaks of things in their absence rather than in their presence. How different, then, Rimbaud, in this poem—a poem that poses the question, How does one write about flowers in 1870 without writing about the *fleur-de-lis*, with all of its connotations of French state power and hierarchy? Rimbaud's response is succinct: "Find flowers which are chairs." How different, too, the next stanza:

> Dis, front blanc que Phébus tanna,
> De combien de dollars se rente
> Pedro Velasquez, Habana . . .

> [Tell, pale-faced one tanned by Phoebus
> How many dollars are made a year
> By Pedro Velasquez, Havana . . .]

Rimbaud's use of a somewhat combative imperative is characteristic: not "I say" (as in "I say: a flower!"), but "say it." The imperative is a shifter; it indicates the historical moment and situation of the enunciation, the speaker and the spoken to. "Pedro Velasquez of Havana" may or may not exist; what counts is the denotative function of the proper names that allows a set of economic, socio-political relations to be constructed—denoted, not represented. In Rimbaud the minimal real unity is not the word, the individual concept, but rather the arrangement, the process of arranging or configurating elements. And the arrangement, as in this passage, is never a neutral exchange; here, it is not only the economic differential that is established but the racial one as well, and this by the use of another proper name, the timeless, mythological "Phoebus": the Parnassian poet, in contrast to "Pedro Velasquez" is figured synecdochically by his pale skin, tanned by mythology, by the whole stock of Western tradition: a textual tan.

Rimbaud's referent is thus neither the purely natural, ahistorical one of Saussure, nor the poststructuralist "textual," purely constructed referent of our own critical atmosphere. It is a constructed referent, certainly—but one that allows for historical change. Rimbaud peoples his landscapes, but peoples them in such a way that "Pedro Velasquez" functions neither as accessory nor as decor. Rimbaud's comprehension of space allows social relations to prevail: space as social space, not landscape.

At this point we must return to our tale of academic geography in order to point out that the institutionalization of "landscape geography" and the preeminence of Vidal de la Blache took place by way of a significant repression of the work of an anarchist geographer writing at the time: Elisée Reclus. Like Rimbaud, Reclus's political imagination, as well as his personal geography, was marked by his active participation in the Paris Commune; because of that participation he was exiled to Switzerland (his fame as a geographer prevented his deportation to New Caledonia), where he produced most of his major works. He participated in the quarrel that led to the scission between Marx and Bakunin in 1872, and defended anarcho-communism in numerous articles that appeared in journals like *Le Révolté* and *La Liberté*. His geographic informants included fellow anarcho-communists like Malatesta and Kropotkin, who supplied him with information on the terrains of Italy and Russia. In his political writings he advocated a Commune-inspired society organized from the base to the top, and addressed the problems of bureaucracy, *autogestion*, and the liberty of workers' organizations in relation to the party. His constant preoccupation was the problem of the state and its relation to the individual.[10] In 1879, when the French government granted official amnesty to Reclus, he refused to return to France until *all* Communards were granted amnesty as well.

Unlike his contemporaries Vidal, Drapeyron, and Levasseur, Reclus's earliest intellectual formation was not in history but rather theology. Whereas Vidal's decision to become a geographer was fueled by tours of the ancient ruins of Egypt and Greece, for Reclus it was his voyages in America and to Ireland, where he was moved by the devastations caused by the great famine, that solidified both his socialist convictions and his decision to write geography.

The first to have employed the term ''social geography,'' Reclus opposed the Vidalian definition of geography as the science of landscape with a different one: ''geography is nothing but history in space.'' As such, his analyses take space into account as a differentiated, nonstatic, changing ensemble: ''Geography is not an immutable thing. It is made, it is remade every day; at each instant, it is modified by men's actions.''[11] For the most part Reclus avoids the empiricist reification of space that occurs whenever one postulates in any way an autonomous existence of spatial facts, processes, or structures that would constitute the object of a spatial analysis. Space in Reclus's work is considered a social product—or rather, as both producer and produced, both determinative and determined— something that cannot be explained without recourse to the study of the functioning of society. Reclus refutes Vidal's definition of geography as ''the science of places and not of people'' by his constant preoccupation with analyzing relations of power between empires, states, and peoples. His analyses show, for example, with amazing intricacy, the changes provoked by colonization on indigenous populations and the organization of their space, thus anticipating many of the more modern theories of unequal development.

Much of Reclus's opposition to the geography of his time and to the ''geography movement'' took the form of a critique of specialization:

> It seems to me that Drapeyron's point of departure for the teaching of geography is very badly chosen. The study of geography according to him should no longer begin with cosmography as it did in the past, but with topography: that is understanding science in the most narrow of ways. Life cannot be accommodated to these arbitrary modes of instruction. Science should be a living thing or else it is nothing but a scholastic misery. Like a plant that draws its nourishment from afar through all its roots as well as through the pores of its leaves, geography should begin by everything at once: cosmography, natural history, history, topography.[12]

Reclus produced, in short, a kind of analysis that would be repressed and entirely disappear in the ensuing reduction of geography to a narrow and specialized pursuit.

"Ce qu'on dit au poète à propos de fleurs" concludes with a striking metaphor and a piece of advice:

> Voilà! c'est le Siècle d'enfer!
> Et les poteaux télégraphiques
> Vont orner,—lyre aux chants de fer,
> Tes omoplates magnifiques!
>
> Surtout, rime une version
> Sur le mal des pommes de terre!
> —Et, pour la composition
> De Poèmes pleins de mystère
>
> Qu'on doive lire de Tréguier
> A Paramaribo, rachète
> Des Tomes de Monsieur Figuier,
> —Illustrés!—chez Monsieur Hachette!
>
> [Look! This is the Infernal Age!
> And telegraph poles
> Will adorn—a lyre that sings a song of steel
> The splendor of your shoulder blades.
>
> Above all, give us a rhymed
> Account of the potato blight!
> —And, to compose Poems
> Full of mystery
>
> —Intended to be read from Tréguier
> To Paramaribo, buy
> A few volumes by Monsieur Figuier
> —Illustrated!—at Hachette's!]

In the first of these stanzas the poet's body has undergone an amazing transformation: no longer the detached observer, the "peaceful photographer" of the opening of the poem, the poet's body is directly implicated in the change in production and reproduction. His body has changed. At stake, here, in other words, is not a mere "thematic" change—the substituting of economic questions for aesthetic or picturesque ones. Instead, in this complex corporeal allegory of technology, the natural and the technological adhere as tightly to one another as they do in neologisms contemporary to Rimbaud like "steamhorse" or "horsepower": developed technology is fused with the natural, living creature and from that site will emanate another hybrid vaguely Whitmanian formation: a song of steel. The human body is permeated with apparatus-like elements not unlike the way, for example, the language of telegraphy is used in popular nineteenth-century scientific texts whenever the nervous system is described.

These popular science texts are advertised in the final stanza—"buy / A few volumes by Monsieur Figuier /—Illustrated!—at Hachette's." Louis Figuier, author of, among other things, *The Marvels of Science*, was the leading scientific vulgarizer of Rimbaud's time.[13] His *La Terre et les mers*, constantly reedited between 1864 and 1884, was perhaps the most popularly read "vulgar" geography in France. Figuier was not the only major figure to publish with Hachette; Hachette produced the, at that time, very popular atlases and geographic treatises of Elisée Reclus, works that Jules Verne, who also published with Hachette, consulted when he wrote his novels. Rimbaud was to follow his own advice a month later and borrow heavily, not only from Figuier, but also from the most libertarian of Verne's novels, *20,000 Leagues under the Sea*, from Poe's *Arthur Gordon Pym*, and from Parnassian Léon Dierx's "Le Vieux solitaire" (1871), when he composed "Le Bateau ivre."[14]

Historians of French colonial policy generally portray the rise of French interest in colonial expansion as a rather sudden development of the 1880s. But if we cannot speak of a full-fledged colonial movement during the 1870s, we can certainly recognize the existence of a genuine geographic one.[15] Geography, as the anticolonialist geographer Jean Dresch puts it, is not born *during* the triumph of the bourgeoisie; its development is *part and parcel of* that triumph.[16] In the decade following the Prussian victory and the suppression of the Commune, "geography fever" swept France. Signs of the new ardor for geography were everywhere: not only in the founding of academic geography by turncoat historians Levasseur, Vidal de la Blache, and others, but also in the improvement in the teaching of geography at every level of the school system, and in the number of national and international congresses held in France during that decade. Immediately after the war, pressure groups launched a national campaign to demand the opening of an Ecole supérieure de géographie in Paris. The mid-seventies saw the appearance of the first French journals—*L'Explorateur* and the *Revue de géographie*—devoted entirely to geography; the French geographic societies, which in 1881 were unanimously to applaud the conquest of Tunisia, experienced what can only be described as a meteoric expansion. Before 1871 there was only one such society, based in Paris, with never more than three hundred members; ten years later there were twelve important new societies and many lesser ones with over ninety-five hundred members.[17]

A Belgian geographer writes in 1881: "No country did more for developing and popularizing an isolated science than France, ever since the war of 1870."[18] The date and the event, 1870, are crucial. For France's defeat at the hands of the Prussians was popularly thought to have been caused by the French troops' knowing geography well enough. In 1874 when the *Révue de géographie* begins to appear, the first issue justifies its existence with these opening remarks: "We all remember those flawed maps supplied to our officers in 1870, that hardly provided the descriptions of the regions which were to be the theater of such a fatal war."[19] Not surprisingly, perhaps, the remarks are made by Ernest Picard, Thiers's minister of the interior and leading Versaillais strategist. Elisée Reclus, in exile in Switzerland four years after the Commune and eagerly awaiting the arrival of the first issue of the *Révue de géographie*, in which he hopes to publish some of his work, is appalled to find Picard, the notorious anti-Communard, resurfacing and enshrined in a new form in the journal's preface:

> You must have received Drapeyron's *Révue de géographie*. I must admit I expected better. That letter of Picard's, who doesn't know a word of geography, placed at the head of the journal like a flag planted on the large mast of a ship; that pretension of wanting to make geography administer politics, a pretension that in the end could have no other motive than to make geography serve political ambitions.[20]

Despite Reclus's prescient metaphor of the geography journal as ship of state, nothing, at least initially, objectively links the geographical societies and their publications, with whom Rimbaud was to publish several articles not too many years later sent from Africa, to colonial expansion: their goals, explicitly stated in the bulletins and minutes of the meetings, are to propagate interest in the "scientific interests" of geography and to aid in the postwar rehabilitation of France. But as the decade advances, the societies function increasingly as propaganda agencies for voyages and explorations — licensed vagabondage; the first French Society for *Commercial* Geography is founded in 1874; Drapeyron, writing in 1875, proclaims that "the world will belong to the one who knows it best." Calling for public subscriptions to finance explorers, the rhetoric of the bulletins of the geographical societies begins to show a complete assimilation of the figure of the geographer with the figure of the explorer, and later, with that of the *commerçant*:

> The end which the Societies of Geography propose to themselves consists in favoring explorations of unknown and still infrequently visited countries in order to draw from them products of the soil and to take there the objects of our industry and at the same time to effect the penetration of moral ideas which will elevate the intellectual level of races relatively inferior up to our own day. But in order to attain that end, a youth must have a relish for voyages and explorations and an exact knowledge of the geographical sciences. This last point is indispensable.[21]

The explorer/geographer, reads another bulletin, is he who sacrifices his life to give "a world to science, a colony to his country." In 1881 the *Révue de géographie* expressed the proud belief that its work facilitated French intervention in Tunis.[22] Prizes were offered by the geographic societies for accomplishments of global phantasmagoria that, for the most part, revealed the same "fantasy of the straight line" that had marked Baron Haussmann's transformations of Paris a decade earlier: finance capital's new and open Paris, a city of flowing traffic, intraurban arteries, and bold thoroughfares. A special prize was to be given, for example, to any voyager who could go from Algeria to Senegal by way of Timbuktu. At stake was the persistent dream of a trans-Saharan railroad that would unite the two most important existing French colonies, Algeria and Senegal. One of the most extravagant projects discussed, debated, and planned throughout the 1870s was that of creating a sea in the middle of the Sahara.[23] Placed beside such public fantasies as these, images from Rimbaud's *Illuminations* lose much of the occult difficulty or privatistic surrealism almost automatically ascribed to them.

Another curious project was to found a practical school of higher geographic studies that would undertake an "around the world" campaign of scientific exploration. To carry out the scheme its promoters hoped to find fifty rich travelers who could each contribute 20,000 francs. Their hopes were based on the astronomical success of a play based on Jules Verne's *Around the World in Eighty Days*; a further bizarre note was added when Verne himself consented to head the organizing committee.

If we look closely at this particular project of the first collective voyage around the world, we see that something has changed. In it we can detect the whole complex dialectic of mass tourism: the vestiges of the romantic ideology of the solitary explorer, who, seeking virgin territory, uncharted worlds, suddenly notices he has brought his whole world along with him in a tour bus. Perhaps no one understood as well as Rimbaud the futility of the flight of the bourgeois tourist from what was his own creation, a futility so well evoked by the Weininger aphorism that "one can never depart for liberty from a train station."[24] This can be seen if we turn to one of Rimbaud's last poetic works, an *Illumination* entitled "Soir historique":

> En quelque soir, par exemple, que se trouve le touriste naïf, retiré de nos horreurs économiques, la main d'un maître anime le clavecin des prés; on joue aux cartes au fond de l'étang, miroir évocateur des reines et des mignonnes; on a les saintes, les voiles, et les fils d'harmonie, et les chromatismes légendaires, sur le couchant.
>
> Il frissonne au passage des chasses et des hordes. La comédie goutte sur les tréteaux de gazon. Et l'embarras des pauvres et des faibles sur ces plans stupides!
>
> A sa vision esclave, l'Allemagne s'échafaude vers des lunes; les déserts tartares s'éclairent; les révoltes anciennes grouillent dans le centre du Céleste Empire; par les escaliers et les fauteuils de rocs un

petit monde blême et plat, Afrique et Occidents, va s'édifier. Puis un ballet de mers et de nuits connues, une chimie sans valeur, et des mélodies impossibles.

La même magie bourgeoise à tous les points où la malle nous déposera! Le plus élémentaire physicien sent qu'il n'est plus possible de se soumettre à cette atmosphere personnelle, brume de remords physiques, dont la constatation est déjà une affliction.

Non! Le moment de l'étuve, des mers enlevées, des embrasements souterrains, de la planète emportée, et des exterminations conséquentes, certitudes si peu malignement indiquées dans la Bible et par les Nornes et qu'il sera donné à l'être sérieux de surveiller.—Cependant ce ne sera point un effet de légende!

[On whatever evening, for example, when the simple tourist stands withdrawn from our economic horrors, the master's hand awakens the pastoral harpsichord; they are playing cards at the bottom of the pond whose face, a mirror, conjures up favorites and queens; you have saints, veils, threads of harmony, and legendary chromatisms in the setting sun.

He trembles at the passing of hunts and hordes. Drama drips on the stages of turf. And the superfluity of poor people and weak people on those stupid levels!

Before his captive vision, Germany goes scaffolding toward the moons; the deserts of Tartary light up; ancient revolts ferment in the heart of the Celestial Empire; on stairways and armchairs of rock, a little world, pale and flat, Africa and Occident, will be erected. Then a ballet of familiar seas and nights, worthless chemistry and impossible melodies.

The same bourgeois magic wherever your baggage sets you down! Even the most elementary physicist knows that it is no longer possible to submit to this personal atmosphere, to this fog of physical remorse, whose very diagnosis is a sickness itself.

No! This is the moment of the seething cauldron, of oceans boiling over, of underground explosions, of the planet swept away, of exterminations sure to follow; certitudes indicated with so little malice by the Bible and by the Nornes, which the serious person will be asked to watch out for. Yet there will be nothing legendary about it!]

The shifter "our economic horrors" establishes the present historical moment of the poem; the simple tourist is indicated precisely and by the whole rhetoric of vision and theater—the spectacle—which dominates the poem up to, but not including, the final paragraph: mirror, chromatisms, drama, stages, "before his captive vision," and so forth. The spectator in the poem is "withdrawn from our economic horrors," as befits a tourist who has fled the workplace for leisure; but the rest of the poem will erode the possibility of such a withdrawal.

It soon becomes clear that it is a whole spectacular panorama of world history that is being displayed before the tourist's captive vision. The tour guide's weary formulas ring out in the opening paragraph's revival of a waning aristocratic or feudal stage set: favorites and queens, hunts and hordes, you have saints, veils, etc.

The flood of geographic names in the third paragraph announces the triumph of the bourgeoisie: we are once more back to the present historical moment of the poem. Rimbaud presents this triumph less as a movement of social homogenization than one of spatial homogenization, for while the *rise* of the bourgeoisie is indicated by a vertical, ascending topography (Germany goes scaffolding up, deserts light up, stairways, etc.), all this upward effort and energy results in a chilling spatial platitude: ''a little world, pale and flat,'' ''the same bourgeois magic wherever your baggage sets you down,'' ''a ballet of familiar seas and nights, worthless chemistry.''

The tension operating in the poem between the temporal homogeneity, the repetition and redundance of ''on whatever evening,'' and the historical singularity announced by the title; between the spatial homogeneity of ''the same bourgeois magic'' everywhere and the convulsive upheaval of the final paragraph; between the figure of the tourist, the detached and affectless observer of spectacular images (or landscapes), and the serious one who will undergo the event— all this becomes apparent with the apocalyptic ending of the poem.

It is as if in the face of the monolithic force of bourgeois spatial conquest, the social upheaval, the ''event'' announced by the title, could only be played out on a global scale. If administrative rationalization, if a total colonization of all social and cultural relations eliminates the possibility of exercising freedom, then nothing less than an apocalyptic reversal of this fate and a cataclysmic break in the continuum of history can set an emancipatory dynamic in motion. The exploded earth doubles a social antagonism that has already, in the preceding paragraph, become ''atmospheric,'' a ''fog''—that is, climatic or geographic.

The full effect of the geological cataclysm of the last lines can only be felt if we recall once again the dialectically opposed reaction provided by the example of Mallarmé. Faced with and experiencing the same perceived hegemony of bourgeois platitude, Mallarmé's reply takes the form of a poetics of allusion designed to exclude the real because it is vulgar, designed to disrupt any referentiality outward. Rimbaud's reply to Mallarmé's fetishization of the poetic text, best summed up by the latter's famous dictum ''Tout au monde existe pour aboutir à un Livre'' (the whole world is made to end up in a book), occurs in the last line of ''Soir historique'': ''There will be nothing legendary about it.''

Notes

1. Walter Benjamin, ''Conversations with Brecht,'' in Brecht, *Aesthetics and Politics*, trans. Stuart Hood (London: New Left Books, 1977), 87.

2. See Fredric Jameson, ''Rimbaud and the Spatial Text,'' in Tak-Wai Wong and M. A. Abbas (eds.), *Re-writing Literary History* (Hong Kong: Hong Kong University Press, 1984), 66-93.

3. Eugène Vermersch, *Les Hommes du jour* (Paris: Towne, 187? [n.d.]), 11.

4. Leconte de Lisle, *Oeuvres diverses*, vol. IV (Paris: Société d'edition, 1978), 477.

5. Several excellent introductions to and analyses of the history of French academic geography have appeared in recent years; my own summary owes much to these works, in particular, Rodolphe de Koninck, "La Géographie critique," in A. Bailly (ed.), *Les Concepts de la Géographie humaine* (Paris: Masson, 1984); Yves Lacoste, *La Géographie, ça sert d'abord à faire la guerre* (Paris: Maspero, 1982), 1982; articles by Béatrice Giblin published in the radical French geography journal *Hérodote* over the last ten years. See also the American equivalent or "sister journal" to *Hérodote*, *Antipode*; in particular, Brian Hudson, "The New Geography and the New Imperialism: 1870-1918," *Antipode* 9 (September 1977): 12-19.

6. In 1922 Febvre wrote *La Terre et l'évolution humaine*, the book that formulated the theoretical positions of Vidal, and subtitled it *Introduction géographique à l'histoire*; it was the first epistemological reflection on geography and the history of geography.

7. See Béatrice Giblin, "Le Paysage, le terrain et les géographes," *Hérodote* 9 (1978): 74-89. See also Yves Lacoste, "A bas Vidal . . . Viva Vidal!" in *Hérodote* 16 (1979): 68-81.

8. In the context of an analysis of Zionism, Uri Eisensweig has persuasively argued the relation between Saussurian linguistics and the Western construction of colonial space. See his *Territoires occupés de l'imaginaire juif* (Paris: Christian Bourgois, 1980). Eisensweig's argument is relevant beyond Zionism to the larger context of nineteenth-century imperialism.

9. Stephane Mallarmé, *Oeuvres complètes*, ed. Henri Mondar and G. Jean-Aubry (Paris: Gallimard, 1945), 368.

10. Thus Reclus's problematic relation with the "official" Marxism of his time. In his preface to F. Domela Nieuwenhuis's *Le Socialisme en danger* (Paris: Stock, 1897) he writes: "See how that powerful individual Marx is treated, in whose honor hundreds of thousands of fanatics raise their arms to the sky, promising to religiously observe his doctrine! Doesn't an entire party, a whole army with several dozens of deputies in the German Parliament, now interpret that Marxist doctrine in a precisely opposite sense to the thought of the master? He declared that economic power determines the political form of societies, and now his followers affirm that economic power will depend on a party majority in the Political Assemblies. He proclaimed that 'the State, to abolish pauperism, must abolish itself, for the essence of evil lies in the very existence of the State!' And in his shadow his followers devote themselves to conquering and directing the State! If the politics of Marx triumph, it will be, like the religion of Christ, only on the condition that the master, adored in appearance, be disowned in practice" (viii).

11. Elisée Reclus, *L'Homme et la terre*, vol. V (Paris, 1905-8), 335.

12. Reclus, *Correspondance*, vol. II (Paris: Schleicher, 1911), 182-83.

13. Vermersch provides us with a satirical portrait of Figuier's "collage" method of composition: "*La Cuisinière bourgeoise* says: 'To make a jugged hare, take a hare . . .' Monsieur Louis Figuier says, 'To make a book, take some other books.' He then arms himself with a pair of gigantic scissors and cuts to the right, to the left, in works that are scientific and in those that are not, in newspapers where he makes as much use of the *faits divers* as he does of the serials [*feuilletons*]; then when he has a sufficient weight of these fragments, he makes them into a book. All these bits and pieces, taken from three hundred authors, follow one another without order, without any agency, without connection, contradicting one another and forming an admirable harlequin's costume which parents buy for their children on New Year's, but which, fortunately, the children don't read" (*Les Hommes du jour*, 78).

14. Dierx's "Le Vieux solitaire," published in the second *Parnasse contemporain* a few months before the composition of "The Drunken Boat," reads like an early, primitive draft of Rimbaud:

> Je suis tel qu'un ponton sans vergues et sans mats,
> Aventureux débris des trombes tropicales

Et qui flotte, roulant des lingots dans ses cales,
Sur l'Océan sans borne et sous de froids climats.

Les vents sifflaient jadis dans ses mille poulies.
Vaisseau désemparé qui ne gouverne plus,
Il roule, vain jouet de flux et du reflux,
L'ancien explorateur de vertes Australies.

Il ne lui reste plus un seul des matelots
Qui chantaient sur la hune en dépliant sa toile.
Aucun phare n'allume au loin sa rouge étoile.
Il roule abandonné tout seul sur les grands flots.

Luc Decaunes (ed.), *La Poésie parnassienne de Gautier à Rimbaud* (Paris: Seghers, 1977), 138-39.

15. Excellent analyses and histories of the French geographic societies can be found in Agnes Murphy, *The Ideology of French Imperialism* (Washington, D.C.: Catholic University of America Press, 1948); and D. Vernon McKay, "Colonialism in the French Geographical Movement 1871-1881," *Geographical Review* 33 (April 1943): 214-32. My own description of the societies is indebted to these two works.

16. Jean Dresch, quoted in Milton Santos, *Pour une géographie nouvelle* (Paris: Publisud, 1984), 19.

17. Guillaume Depping, "Le Mouvement géographique," *Journal officiel de la République française*, October 23, 1881, 1.

18. H. Wagner, cited in Numa Broc, "L'Etablissement de la géographie en France: diffusion, institutions, projets (1870-1890)," *Annales de le géographie* 83 (September-October 1974): 564.

19. Ernest Picard, *Révue de géographie*, 1 (January-June 1877): 2. One of a flurry of articles like the following by Levasseur, entitled "On the Study and Teaching of Geography," suggests that the problem was not the maps: "We do not want our country to be the prey of foreigners. We have now understood all the advantages that the knowledge of geography gives. When the Prussians entered our territory, the public imagined that they possessed marvelous maps, because they are very painstaking about that kind of work, but these maps were only and could only have been the copy of our own maps, with some slight corrections. Their advantage consisted in having them in their baggage and in using them, because the habit of geography has for some time taught their officers of all ranks how important it is to know the terrain on which one is operating. Most of our officers, who neither in school nor in the world learned to appreciate that science, took off without maps and didn't even notice they were missing anything." Emile Levasseur, "L'Etude et l'enseignement de la géographie," *Séances et travaux de l'Académie des science morales et politiques* 46 (1871): 425.

20. Reclus, *Correspondance*, vol. II, 182.

21. "The Teaching of Geography Given by the Societies of Geography," *Bulletins de Bordeaux* 4 (1881): 213-14 (unsigned).

22. Ludovic Drapeyron, "Le But, la méthode et l'oeuvre de la *Révue de géographie*," *Révue de géographie* 9 (1881): 1-8.

23. See Murphy, *Ideology of French Imperialism*, pp. 70-93, for an entertaining description of this project. To follow the debate, read, for instance, Jules Gros, "La Mer Saharienne et le Capitaine Roudaire" in *L'Exploration: Journal des conquêtes de la civilisation sur tous les points du globe*, 1 (1876), 220-24.

24. Otto Weininger, quoted in Hans Enzensberger, "Une Théorie du tourisme," in *Culture ou mise en condition?* Trans. Bernard Lortholary (Paris: Juillard, 1965), 86.

Chapter 4
The Swarm

Writing in 1881 on a theme dear to Rimbaud and Lafargue, Friedrich Nietzsche concludes his own critique of the ideology of work by alluding to a peculiar dialectic of atomization and collectivity:

> *The eulogists of work.* Behind the glorification of "work" and the tireless talk of the "blessings of work" I find the same thought as behind the praise of impersonal activity for the public benefit: the fear of everything individual. At bottom, one now feels when confronted with work—and what is invariably meant is relentless industry from early till late—that such work is the best police, that it keeps everybody in harness and powerfully obstructs the development of reason, of covetousness, of the desire for independence. For it uses up a tremendous amount of nervous energy and takes it away from reflection, brooding, dreaming, worry, love, and hatred; it always sets a small goal before one's eyes and permits easy and regular satisfactions. In that way a society in which the members continually work hard will have more security: and security is now adored as the supreme goddess. And now—horrors!—it is precisely the "worker" who has become dangerous. Dangerous individuals are swarming all around. And behind them, the danger of dangers: the individual.[1]

Atomization and collectivity, or, in Nietzsche's terms, individuality and the swarm: the threat of the swarm and the threat of individual desire are the same threat; the swarm's collective desire masks the desire of the individual. In this instance Nietzsche's terms echo the principal tenet of the anarchist critique of capitalism, a critique that developed and emerged as a distinct movement during the nineteenth century alongside those of socialism and Marxism. According to this tenet, liberation on the mass social level—in other words, liberation of whole classes in economic and political terms—is inseparable from liberation on the level of the individual. Mankind, as Bakunin put it, is at once "the most individual and the most social of animals":

> All social life is simply this continued mutual dependence of individuals and the masses. Even the strongest and most intelligent of individuals . . . are at every moment of their lives both promoters and products of the desires and actions of the masses.[2]

Elisée Reclus, Bakunin's friend and an articulate defender of anarcho-communism, returned again and again in his writings to the themes that he and other libertarian anarchists debated in the early 1870s with the Marxists: problems of bureaucracy, of *autogestion* (self-management), of the liberty of workers' organizations in relation to the party.[3] Throughout his work Reclus reasoned in terms of class struggle while never omitting to consider the fundamental role of individual liberty. In what is perhaps his most concise formulation of the methodology and goal of social geography, these two factors—and a third, harmony or balance—are decisive:

> Class struggle, the quest for equilibrium, and the sovereign decision of the individual—these are the three orders of facts revealed to us by the study of social geography.[4]

Anarchist convictions and doctrines are based on a negative view of liberty: freedom is the freedom *from* some obstacle or impediment. Chief among these impediments, of course, is the state (thus the Commune, for Bakunin, as well as for Marx at his most "anarchist," was "a bold, clearly formulated negation of the State").[5] It is this view of freedom that Walter Benjamin affirms when he writes in his essay on surrealism that since Bakunin Europe has lacked a radical concept of freedom. Benjamin goes on in that essay to allude to something like a scattered, anarchist subculture of the 1870s: "Between 1865 and 1875 a number of great anarchists, without knowing of one another, worked on their infernal machines."[6] He is specifically referring to the trio of Dostoyevsky, Rimbaud, and Lautréamont—these last two, the two French adolescent writers working roughly at the same time, isolated and unaware of each other's existence, on their great prose poem antiautobiographical epics (this peculiar genre, the world-historical prose poem as antiautobiography, would be expanded a few years later to include another exemplum: Nietzsche's *Ecce Homo*).[7]

The anarchist notion of individual liberty, of individual*ity*, has always, then as much as now, run the risk of being mistaken for the individual*ism* that animates capitalist society.[8] An example from Rimbaud's moment provides a case in point.

Many recent cultural histories of the late nineteenth century have treated the subject of capitalism's "ordered disorganization" of urban space under the Second Empire and the decades that followed. The chief example brought to bear is the planned confusion of the department store, so well documented in Zola's novel *Au bonheur des dames*. The reader of this novel witnesses crowds of confused and muddled women shoppers led to consume more and more in a frenzy of greed and disorientation.[9] (The newspaper's fragmented layout is also cited as exemplary of capitalism's tendency to promote discontinuity; both the department store and the newspaper bear witness to a commodity structure wherein each article is conceived as autonomous and detachable.) How are we to distinguish between the "ordered disorganization" promoted by capitalist culture, and the "long, boundless, and reasoned disordering of all the senses" advocated by Rimbaud in a well-known slogan—between, that is, the anarchic chaos of Rimbaud and the anarchic chaos of high capitalism? Any reader of Zola can attest to the systematically disoriented sensorial experience of the women shoppers he represents.

In fact, Rimbaud's "reasoned disordering of all the senses" and capitalist "ordered disorganization" are dynamically opposed. They work at historical cross-purposes. Rimbaud's *target* is the closure of the fields of socially available perception—that closure that is precisely the *work* and *by-product* of capitalism's "ordered disorganization." In the department store, for instance, the unequal relation between seller and buyer acts to increase consumption without the buyer's awareness, thus doing violence to the buyer's individuality, and promoting the domination of the product, not only over its producer, but also over its consumer. Individualism animates capitalist society and *by the same token* does violence to individuality. Further, capitalist development, as the example of the department store makes clear, reduces not only the "free space" necessary for the existence of individuality but also the very desire for such "free space." Rimbaud's project, on the other hand, works against the grain—to forestall this erosion of individuality. Rimbaud calls for a hypersensorial, more-than-human perception. Grotesque, hyperbolic, extraordinary, superhuman perception is advocated in opposition to what capitalist development is at that moment defining (in the sense of setting the limits) *as* human, as *ordinary* perception.

Contemporary readers of Rimbaud can still be found promoting the confusion of individuality with individualism—often in veiled ways. Rimbaud's lexical anomalies, for example, his foraging in the dictionaries of specialized vocabularies, his predilection for peculiar slang and regional usages, his fondness for abrupt and unmotivated juxtaposition so prized by the Surrealists—these factors have contributed to his reputation for being a predominantly "lexical" poet, a poet of the individual Word. Tzvetan Todorov, for instance, writes that "as opposed to the 'syntactician' Mallarmé, Rimbaud is a lexical poet: he juxtaposes words which, innocent of any articulation, retain individually all of their urgency.''[10] But can Rimbaud's juxtapositions really be ''innocent of any artic-ulation''? For ''articulation'' read ''syntax,'' and for ''syntax'' read the struc-tural principle of a coherent social whole; Rimbaud, innocent of all articulation, is the Wild Child, unable to formulate his assertions within the bounds of socially instituted intelligibility. As such, his poetry can have no bearing on that intelli-gibility, it participates in no dialogue with the social, it is an atomized utterance.

But is not Rimbaud's atomism rather a mask for incipient dynamism? Rim-baud's lexical anomalies are not mere fragmentary gestures or morsels of spon-taneist thought; behind the individual word or lexical peculiarity in fact lies a swarm of relations; or rather the premonition of a change in the relations of ele-ments to each other, and not the random mutation of separate elements. If I begin, then, this analysis of Rimbaud and the swarm on the lexical level, I do so keeping in mind that Rimbaud's lexical anomalies are always, in some sense, propositions.

This lexical approach is made necessary by two factors. The first is the com-parative lack, on Rimbaud's part, of a thematizing of language, of tropology or rhetoric; unlike, for example, Mallarmé or Valéry, Rimbaud seems to possess a very sparse imaginary of language. There are no critical texts by Rimbaud to turn to—no metacritical reflection on linguistics. Rimbaud reflects on language little and theorizes it even less; only in the terse slogans of the Voyant letters, written during the Bloody Week of May 1871 (''Poetry will no longer give rhythm to action; it *will be in advance*''), can we detect something resembling a self-con-scious philosophy of language, and that ''philosophy'' suggests primarily a cri-tique of language's ''secondariness'' vis-à-vis action, and a confidence that lan-guage includes its own self-transcendence or verging *into* action. The second factor, which will mostly concern us in the next chapter, is the particular seman-tic instability of the highly compressed and contradictory period of Rimbaud's production—the Commune and the postrevolutionary years immediately follow-ing it. These two factors, Rimbaud's linguistic optimism and pragmatism, and the semantic destabilization of his historical moment, are of course not unrelated. Together they point to the usefulness of an approach by way of lexical fields or constellations—a field being not only semantic but also morphological, and having as its theoretical advantage the fact that it does not separate the use value (or content) of a given expression, and does not isolate signifier from signified.

One of the most striking features of Rimbaud's work is an absence: it does not possess the structures that allow for nostalgia. Put another way, it is rigorously forward-looking, and this fact alone dictates that one must always keep in mind the future(s) of Rimbaud's text. The future, in other words, is an indispensable dimension of Rimbaud's poetic dialogue with time and history. One of the most significant of these dialogues takes place between Rimbaud and the French-speaking contemporary poet most in his lineage, Aimé Césaire. (This, in fact, is the way that the tired topic of ''Rimbaud in Africa'' might be fruitfully addressed: by examining his dialogue with poets like Césaire and Edouard Glissant whose formations involved an early student identification with the posture and poetry of Rimbaud.) A lexical borrowing or *détournement* that Césaire performs on Rimbaud's text provides us with access to an important constellation. In "Cahiers d'un retour au pays natal," Césaire borrows or "evolves" a neologism Rimbaud invented and used twice in poems written in the summer and autumn of 1871. The verb, in the infinitive, is *bombiner*; in Rimbaud's "Les Mains de Jeanne-Marie," we find the lines "Mains chasseresses des diptères / Dont bombinent des bleuisons / Aurorales." The more celebrated use of the neologism occurs in his "Voyelles": "des mouches éclatantes / Qui bombinent autour des puanteurs cruelles." Early, faulty editions of "Voyelles" show the word as *bombillements* instead of *bombinements*, and it is in this form that the word appears in Césaire: "et le fouet disputa au bombillement des mouches la rosée sucrée de nos plaies."

Rimbaud's translators generally resort to a simple "buzz" to render the verb in English; Paul Schmidt, in his translation of "Voyelles," goes one step further and joins buzzing to bumbling: "A, black belt, hairy with bursting flies / Bumbling and buzzing over stinking cruelties." Etymologically the translation is successful, for "bumble" derives from the Middle English *bomben*, an onomatopoetic word signifying "boom" as well as "buzz." A similar derivation seems to have motivated Rimbaud's coining of *bombiner*: from the Latin *bombitire*, to resonate, to make noise.

A recent translation of Césaire resorts to a neologistic form in English: "and the whip argued with the bombilation of the flies over the sugary dew of our sores." [11] Césaire's context and the English translation both render a "bombardment" of flies that is at once auditory and gestural: the droning buzz of the flies that rivals the snap of the whip, produced by the onslaught or projectile-like attack of the insects, landing on the open wounds with all the force of a thousand tiny bombs. The French *bombarder*, certainly in the same lexical field, unites in its etymology the auditory and the gestural: a *machine de guerre* (1495), and, in earlier forms, a musical instrument.

When Louis Forestier approximates the meaning of the neologism in his notes as *voleter en bourdonnant*—this with a cryptic note adding that "progressively the word becomes an essential element of poetic creation"[12]—it is with an eye toward underlining this conjugation of the auditory and the gestural. Indeed, *bourdonner*, or buzzing, is one of Rimbaud's most frequently used words, so much so that the vague auditory atmosphere evoked by poems as varied as "Chanson de la plus haute tour" to "Enfance II" could be said to consist of a mild hum, the reverberation or murmur of a swarm of tiny wings. *Bourdon* etymologically is first of all a musical term, derived from the Provençal *bordos* or "verse," the Spanish *bordon*, a kind of refrain, rejoining the Old English *bourdon*: refrain. But it is also an insect in the bee family; the insect's name is the

same as the musical term. Since the Middle Ages the formation has been onomatopoetic in both meanings; it is impossible to determine whether one of the
two meanings is a figurative use of the other.

Insect-verse. Rimbaud's poetry is the music of the swarm: quick and repeated
agitation or vibration, a force field of unassigned frequencies ominous or lulling
depending upon the context, resounding, resonating:

> Des fleurs magiques bourdonnaient. Les talus le berçaient. Des bêtes
> d'une élégance fabuleuse circulaient. Les nuées s'amassaient sur la
> haute mer faite d'une éternité de chaude larmes.

> [Magic flowers hummed. The slopes cradled him. Animals of fabulous
> elegance wandered about. Clouds gathered on high seas made of an
> eternity of hot tears.]

("Enfance II")

The immediate effect of the verb is a crowd effect, the multiplication of voices.
Here the vague murmur of the flowers combines with the pluralization of all the
nouns, the accumulation of the clouds, the repetitive movements of rocking and
circulating, to culminate in the image of the high seas, whose waves, already
multiple, dense and moving, are further broken down into "an eternity of hot
tears." At each step the emphasis is on the multiple: each of the limitless number
of drops that make up the sea made palpable by its individual identity as a separate tear.

In an early poem Rimbaud devotes to the swarm, "Les Chercheuses de
poux," the child's body becomes the site of a crowd effect. It is worthwhile
examining this poem in its entirety. The opening stanza of "Les Chercheuses"
ties the experience of the swarm directly to dreaming, to the proliferation of fantasy:

> Quand le front de l'enfant, plein de rouges tourmentes,
> Implore l'essaim blanc des rêves indistincts,
> Il vient près de son lit deux grandes soeurs charmantes
> Avec de frêles doigts aux ongles argentins.

> [When the child's forehead, red and full of pain,
> Implores the white swarm of indistinct dreams,
> There come near his bed two charming sisters
> With delicate fingers and long silvery nails.]

The surface of the child's body, teeming with "red torments," is matched by an
interior swarm of vague dreams. In fact, it is only the arrival of the silver-tipped
fingers that will divide the child's body into an interior and an exterior — that will
make of the outer, physical swarm something distinct from the inner, mental one.

Elles assoient l'enfant devant une croisée
Grande ouverte où l'air bleu baigne un fouillis de fleurs,
Et dans ses lourds cheveux où tombe la rosée
Promènent leurs doigts fins, terribles et charmeurs.

Il écoute chanter leurs haleines craintives
Qui fleurent de longs miels végétaux et rosés,
Et qu'interrompt parfois un sifflement, salives
Reprises sur la lèvre ou désirs de baisers.

Il entend leurs cils noirs battant sous les silences
Parfumés; et leurs doigts électriques et doux
Font crépiter parmi ses grises indolences
Sous leurs ongles royaux la mort des petits poux.

Voilà que monte en lui le vin de la Paresse,
Soupir d'harmonica qui pourrait délirer;
L'enfant se sent, selon la lenteur des caresses,
Sourdre et mourir sans cesse un désir de pleurer.

[They take the child with them to an immense
Window, where blue air bathes a flowery grove,
And through his heavy hair, as the dew descends,
Their terrible, enchanting fingers probe.

He listens to their fearful slow breath vibrate,
Flowering with honey and the hue of roses,
Broken now and then with whispers, saliva
Licked back on their lips, a longing for kisses.

He hears their lashes beat the still, sweet air;
Their soft electric fingers never tire—
Through his grey swoon, a crackling in his hair—
Beneath their royal nails the little lice expire.

Within him then surges the wine of Idleness,
Like the sweet deluding harmonica's sigh;
And the child can feel, beneath their slow caresses,
Rising, falling, an endless desire to cry.]

The first four stanzas follow a similar movement: in each one, a vague, unde-
fined, nondifferentiated corporeal durée, like that of a slow-moving crowd, is
interrupted by a kind of acoustical or tactile aggression. Thus the "white swarm
of indistinct dreams" in the first stanza is interrupted when the silver-tipped fingers materialize. In the second stanza, the blue air bathes a tangle of flowers, a
pell-mell piling-up of flowers.[13] Into the heavy, liquid atmosphere, the bath of

blue air, the heavy hair, the drops of dew, comes the terrible staccato fineness of the fingers. In the next two stanzas, auditory interruptions occur: the vegetable, honey breath is broken by a *sifflement*, the intake of saliva; the "perfumed silences" are punctuated by the batting of eyelids, and the highly indistinct "grey indolences" are broken by a *crépitement*.

The poem's pervasive effect is one of a heavy and slow sensuous torpor, an erotic nondifferentiation or diffusion, a polymorphous expanse of erotic durée interrupted by specific acoustical or tactile aggression: the lunge of the fingers, fine and precise and described in quasi-military terms: metallic, silver-tipped, royal, electric, and terrible. The child's body is at one with the swarming liquid undulation borrowed from the lice; indolent, basking in the slow-moving caresses (for the fingers are also "charming") — all this broken up or punctuated by the metallic crackling, the staccato click of the individual deaths of the lice.

In the final stanza the waves and sighs of sensual torpor triumph in a lulling bath of sibilant repetition:

> Voilà que monte en lui le vin de la Paresse,
> Soupir d'harmonica qui pourrait délirer;
> L'enfant se sent, selon la lenteur des caresses,
> Sourdre et mourir sans cesse un désir de pleurer.

L'*en*fant, se s*ent*, selon la l*en*teur; car*esse*s, c*esse*, Par*esse*; the repeated *en* and *esse* contribute to the triumph of indolence in a material echo of the sigh of the harmonica, whose expansiveness and diffusion stand in direct contrast to the *sifflements*, *battements*, and *crépitements* of the two sisters. Yet if we recall that the two sisters are in some sense summoned forth out of the child's swarm of indistinct dreams, then we must recognize in the tapping, batting, and crackling, that is to say, in the military apparatus or *machine de guerre*, one pole of the adolescent body, while the harmonica's sigh, the musical instrument, serves as the other. Both movements, the diffuse and the punctual, the liquid and the solid, the musical and the military, the auditory and the gestural, belong to him: a "Chant de guerre parisien."

Read in this way the poem suggests the acoustical equivalent to the adolescent body's paradoxical relation to speed I described in Chapter 2: lethargy and torpor interrupted by a reptilian or metallic lunge. *Bourdonnement*, the indistinct buzzing noise of the swarm that is very close to silence — that immobile background reverberation may well, with a blast, burst into the space of sound. That burst, like the adolescent lunge, is not precisely sequential, but rather "virtual" or "potential" (*latent*) — and "virtual" or "potential" is not the opposite of real. (Similarly, the anonymous, blurry face in the crowd, the "man in the street," as we say, is always one step away from becoming "people in the streets": the crowd, the demonstration, the insurrection. The man in the street, the indistinct element in a swarm of people, stripped of any individual subjectivity, faceless, is always on the point of becoming "political man," always just at the limit of action.)

One of Rimbaud's favorite verbs, *bondir*, a verb that lies in a related lexical or semantic field to the neologism *bombiner* and the verb *bourdonner*, bears within it this dynamic of latency. *Bondir* was used in the Middle Ages to signify "resonate": to reverberate (which itself derives from the Latin *verberare*: to strike with a whip), to resound; its etymology shows it to derive from the popular Latin *bombitire*—hence its relation to Rimbaud's *bombiner*, as well as to words like *bombarder* or simply *bombe*. It was only in the fifteenth century that *bondir* took on its modern meaning of "to leap" or "to jump": to rise abruptly into the air with a leap, the sudden, upward lunge: "Et tandis que la bande en haut du tableau est formée de la rumeur tournante et bondissante des conques des mers et des nuits humaines." ("And while this band in the distance is made of the whirling, leaping sounds of conch shells and human nights"; "Mystique.") The murmur of the crowd and the sea partakes at once of the spectacular physics of the whirlwind (*tournante*) and the directiveness of the projectile (*bondissante*). Poetic activity is at least twice summed up by Rimbaud with the word *bondissement*.[14] In the Voyant letters, the poet's leap calls forth a crowd of other "horrible workers": "Qu'il crève dans son bondissement par les choses inouies et innomables: viendront d'autres horribles travailleurs." ("So what if he is destroyed in his ecstatic leap toward things unheard of, unnameable: other horrible workers will come.") And in the Commune poem whose very title calls attention to Rimbaud's fascination with the movement or migration of groups or populations, "Paris se repeuple," the poet's stanzas are weapons to be used against the return of the Versaillais to the streets of Paris: "Ses strophes bondiront: voila! voila! bandits!"

The frantic, busy immobility of latency resonates again in "Chanson de la plus haute tour," where the prairie, a collective unit that does not consist of men but that is still "felt" to be a swarm, has been consigned to oblivion, and thus freed or liberated for overgrowth, increase, uncultivated or uncontrolled expansion:

> Ainsi la Prairie
> A l'oubli livrée
> Grandie, et fleurie
> D'encens et d'ivraies
> Au bourdon farouche
> De cent sales mouches.
>
> [So the green field
> To oblivion freed
> Overgrown, flowering

With incense and weeds
And the wild noise
Of a hundred dirty flies.]

The flies preside over hypertrophic disorder; the words *sales* and *farouche*, which describe them, have connotations of savagery, barbarianism. Linked as it is to a landscape of excessive growth and teeming unproductive life—weeds and incense are not precisely useful—the *bourdon farouche* suggests a unit of collective, virtual, and similarly disorderly action.

The virtuality of the swarm can also be erotic in nature, as in "Vies,"[15] or in "Rêvé pour l'hiver": "Et tu te sentiras la joue égratignée / Un petit baiser comme une folle araignée / Te courra par le cou." ("Then you will feel something tickle your cheek / A little kiss like a crazy spider / Will run around your neck.") Elsewhere Rimbaud continues to identify the swarming sensation of vermin with the kiss:

> On se laisse griser.
> La sève est du champagne et vous monte à la tête . . .
> On divague. On se sent aux lèvres un baiser
> Qui palpite là, comme une petite bête.
>
> [You let yourself get drunk.
> The sap is champagne and goes straight to the head . . .
> You are wandering. You feel a kiss on your lips
> Which quivers there like something small and alive.]
>
> ("Roman")

Here the verb *divaguer*, the impersonality of the pronoun *on*, and the theme of drunkenness all contribute to a crowd effect; in fact, the sensation of wandering and the palpitation of the incipient (or remembered) kiss coincide with a transition in the poem from *vous* to *on*—a kind of desubjectivization or wavering of the self: impersonal individuation.

But the sensation of being covered with enormous swarms of tiny insects, of losing oneself in a hyperindividuated or cellular tingle, is not solely an erotic sensation in Rimbaud;[16] it contributes to the scatological grotesque of such satiric or invective-laden poems as "Le Juste," "Les Premières Communions," and "Accroupissements." In these poems the monstrous flux one is caught up in is suddenly and nightmarishly perceived to be made up of masses of tiny things—things that are alive: a grotesque hypertrophy of life, too much life: "Le cerveau du bonhomme est bourré de chiffons: / Il écoute les poils pousser dans sa peau moite." ("The old fellow's head is crammed with rags: He listens to the hairs growing in his moist skin"; "Accroupissements.") A microscopic or molecular attention to the concrete; the auditory phantasmagoria of individual hairs grow-

ing in a latrinal dankness becomes a horrific fascination with the body dissoci-
ated into its component cells, each cell alive and "growing." In "Les Premières
Communions," a similar sensation results from being slapped across the face by
a priest:

> L'enfant se doit surtout à la maison, famille
> Des soins naïfs, des bons travaux abrutissants;
> Ils sortent, oubliant que la peau leur fourmille
> Où le Prêtre du Christ plaqua ses doigts puissants . . .

> [The child's duty is first to his home, his family
> Whose cares are simple, whose work stupefying and honest;
> They leave, forgetting how their skin crawls
> Where the Priest of Christ has struck with his powerful fingers.]

Once again it is important to notice the impersonal, reflexive form: "la peau leur
fourmille"; "on se sent aux lèvres un baiser." Whether erotically or grotesquely
weighted, this awakening of colonies of the skin, this breaking down of the body
into the cells that make it up, goes hand in hand with a vacillation of the self
under the onslaught of the power of the swarm. The experience of "Je est un
autre" for Rimbaud is not, in other words, a metaphysical experiment. It is above
all corporeal, a lived sensation on both a micro- and a macrolevel, of the body
"getting away from you."

In the late 1860s and early 1870s, the expression *charmer les puces*, in working-class circles, meant to get drunk. In Rimbaud a rhetoric of intoxication often
serves to articulate the micro- and macrolevels of the "crowd effect": on the one
hand, the almost "delirium tremens" phenomenology, that focused and intense
sensation of "skin crawling," the trend toward the concrete and the small that
has some resemblance to a dissociation of the body into its component cells; on
the other, the contagious, euphoric element that sweeps through a crowd of
people increasing in number. Louis Barron, in his Commune memoirs, describes
this sensation well:

> Thus great and sublime movements begin by solemnities, festivals, and
> cheerful battles. Viable revolutions begin and continue this way. One
> comes down from the peak of intense excitement as if awakening from a
> dream. But a delicious memory remains of an instant of intoxication; it
> gives you the illusion of fraternity.[17]

One of the verbs most associated with crowd movement in Rimbaud and in nineteenth-century cliché, *fourmiller*, [18] carries with it both of these associations: to
grow to great numbers very quickly *and* to be the site of a sensation of prickling
as if one is buried alive in an anthill: the dispersion of the body's surface into a
thousand microsensations ("la peau leur fourmille"):

Il le prend par le bras, arrache le velours
Des rideaux, et lui montre en bas les larges cours
Où fourmille, où fourmille, où se lève la foule,
La foule épouvantable avec des bruits de houle,
Hurlant comme une chienne, hurlant comme une mer . . .
    "C'est la crapule,
Sire. Ça bave aux murs, ça monte, ça pullule . . ."

[He takes him by the arm, and tears the curtain
Back, and shows him the courtyard below
Where the mob swarms about, seething beneath them,
The awful mob that makes a roaring like the surf,
A howling like a bitch, a howling like the sea, . . .
    "That, Sire, is the Scum.

It drools round the walls, it rises, it seethes . . ."]
                                    ("Le Forgeron")

In "Chant de guerre parisien" Rimbaud uses a familiar cliché, the *fourmilière* or anthill, to designate the space of collective insurgency within Paris during the Commune; in the following passage, the *jaunes cabochons* are the bombs dropped on Paris by the Versaillais, and the Communards' activities, significantly, are designated by the verb *bambocher*—popularly, "to be on a drinking spree":

Plus que jamais nous bambochons
Quand viennent sur nos fourmilières
Crouler les jaunes cabochons
Dans des aubes particulières

[More than ever before we carouse
When onto our ant-heaps come
Tumbling the yellow heads
On those extraordinary dawns.]

Or consider, in the context of intoxication, the *vin de vigueur* of "Ma Bohème" and, once again, its dialectical partner, the *vin de la Paresse* of "Les Chercheuses de poux":

—Mes étoiles au ciel avaient un doux frou-frou
Et je les écoutais, assis au bord des routes,
Ces bons soirs de septembre où je sentais des gouttes
De rosée à mon front, comme un vin de vigueur . . .

[My stars above me rustled through the sky.
I listened to them, sitting on the road-sides

Those pleasant September evenings as I felt drops
Of dew on my forehead, like a vigorous wine . . .]
                                        ("Ma Bohème")

. . . et leurs doigts électriques et doux
Font crépiter parmi ses grises indolences
Sous leurs ongles royaux la mort des petits poux.

Voilà que monte en lui le vin de la Paresse,
Soupir d'harmonica qui pourrait délirer . . .

[Their soft electric fingers never tire—
Through his grey swoon, a crackling in his hair—
Beneath their royal nails the little lice expire.

Within him then surges the wine of Idleness,
Like the sweet deluding harmonica's sigh . . .]
                                        ("Les Chercheuses")

In "Ma Bohème" the stars produce a vaguely feminine crowd effect; the murmur is the rubbing or rustling of material against itself, the onomatopoetic *frou-frou*. The rustling of the stars transposes into hundreds of individual dew drops; or rather, the acoustical event "becomes" the sensation of droplets on the skin: feeling the skin divided into as many individual cells as there are dew drops, or as there are stars in the sky. (A similar move in "Les Poètes de sept ans" will link the swarming, rustling sound of the trees to the prickly sensation produced by ocular frottage: the swarming of thousands of pinpricks of light on the interior of the eyelids.)

The wine of vigor, like the surging wine of Idleness in "Les Chercheuses de poux," announces a virtual or potential energy, the desire to desire, linked in both poems to the surface of the child's body becoming the site of teeming, microscopic sensation. The wine of vigor ("O future vigueur!") and the wine of laziness are the same wine. This should not surprise us, knowing the positive ideological weight Rimbaud grants to laziness—*and* to intoxication. In fact, Walter Benjamin's provocative remark about the Surrealists, to the effect that "this loosening of the self by intoxication is, at the same time, precisely the fruitful, living experience that allowed these people to step outside the domain of intoxication,"[19] can be applied equally well to Rimbaud's construction of both laziness and intoxication as ideological resistance. Like laziness, intoxication is not a dulling, a numbness or impoverishment of sensation but rather an activity: too much sensation rather than too little.

Certainly the well-worn critical designation of Rimbaud as the poet of *Sensationnisme* is a way of generalizing a much more specific, and at the same time provocative, observation: Rimbaud's erotico-politics—for in Rimbaud there is little distance between political economy and libidinal economy—consists of the translation or effectuation of a crowd effect onto the body. What gets enacted in as early as the poem by that name, "Sensation" ("j'irai dans les sentiers, / Picoté par les blés" ["I shall go down the paths, / Getting pricked by the corn"]), is an almost molecularized, hypersensation of the body, at once fine and vast, as if the body itself were peopled by multiplicities, or as if each component cell had taken on a life of its own. Rimbaud's erotics, which we have already designated as affective rather than sentimental, are predicated on the effectuation of the power of the crowd, a power both destructive and generative. In the earliest "social illuminism" poems, the body affected is that of the earth, and the verb *frémir*, both a weak movement of oscillation that produces a light murmur, and the agitation that sweeps through a crowd under the effect of a shared emotion, is used to evoke the vibrato of universal harmony: "Le monde vibrera comme une immense lyre / Dans le frémissement d'un immense baiser" ("The world will resound like some vast lyre / That trembles in some endless vast embrace").[20] When this power rises up and expands, its effect is to make the self vacillate or to create a kind of "centrifugal" subjectivity; thus, the importance of reflexive verb forms and impersonal pronouns, the desubjectivization of these passages that signals a devaluation of individual subjectivity in favor of the construction of a (virtual) group subject. It is in this way, rather than according to any kind of intersubjective or identificatory structure, that we should understand the famous slogan "Je est un autre": something is happening that cannot be seized without letting go of the power to say "I."

Nowhere is the crowd effect as productive decomposition, both erotic and excremental, so elaborated, as in the long poem from 1871, "Les Poètes de sept ans." This poem, along with "Les Chercheuses de poux," provides what might be termed a microcosm of Rimbaud's swarm poesis. "Les Poètes de sept ans" is divided, like none of the other 1871 verse, into irregular verse-paragraphs rather than stanzas, as if to enact formally the opening toward spatial liberty or optimism that the poem celebrates. We can divide the poem thematically into three sections, each beginning with a scene of corporeal repression or spatial constraint of the child's body. In each section the child's fantasized liberation passes through an encounter with the swarm—in fact, a crowd effect, whether erotic or excremental in tone, becomes synonymous in the poem *with* the processes of fantasy, described from the child's point of view in the poem as "vision," "meditation," "dream," or "presentiment." These same processes are renamed by the repressive, all-seeing mother figure in the poem as *des tics noirs*, *répugnances*, or *pitiés immondes*.

> . . . Quand, lavé des odeurs du jour, le jardinet
> Derrière la maison, en hiver, s'illunait
> Gisant au pied d'un mur, enterré dans la marne

Et pour des visions écrasant son oeil darne,
Il écoutait grouiller les galeux espaliers.
Pitié! Ces enfants seuls étaient ses familiers
Qui, chétifs, fronts nus, oeil déteignant sur la joue,
Cachant de maigres doigts jaunes et noirs de boue
Sous des habits puant la foire et tout veillots,
Conversaient avec la douceur des idiots!
Et si, l'ayant surpris à des pitiés immondes,
Sa mère s'effrayait . . .

[Washed clean of the smells of the day, the garden
In winter, behind the house, filled with moonlight;
Stretched below a wall, buried in dirt,
Squeezing his eyes to make visions come,
He listened to the swarming sound of the mangy espaliers.
Pity! His only friends were puny kids
The ones with runny eyes that streaked their cheeks
Who hid thin yellow fingers black with mud,
Beneath old cast-off clothes that stank of shit;
They used to talk like gentle idiots!
And if she caught him at these filthy acts of pity,
His mother grew afraid . . .]

   In a parodic reversal of the bourgeois hygiene enforced by the mother, the child speaks of being "washed clean of the smells of the day." In a poem where colors have fixed social connotations and darkness is valued by the child, the realm of the day suggests the dominant bourgeois concerns of work, family, and commerce.[21] This symbolic lavage recalls the Drunken Boat's famous bath of purification and liberation ("Soaked the green water through my hull of pine, . . . washing me / Of the stains, the vomitings and the blue wine")—I will return to this association shortly. But the child is nonetheless spatially constrained by his position at the foot of the wall, "buried in dirt." The "visions" he produces by rubbing his eyes are composed of the microscopic prickly sensations of pressure against his eyelids (earlier in the poem he speaks of how he would "shut his eyes to see spots"); these visions are accompanied by the swarming sound of the mangy espaliers nearby, trees teeming with future life. *Grouiller*, a verb like *pulluler* or *fourmiller*, in and of itself awakens the agitation of a crowd: the murmur of many voices within a single voice. Immediately that sound is linked to an affect (*Pitié*) and to the appearance of numerous poor children, "black with mud," excremental, who are said to be "his familiars"—that is, a direct replacement or alternative to his own family, an alternative constellation to the oppressive mother-child dyad that dominates the poem. The mother's surveillance "surprises" him at these associations (*pitiés immondes*) and makes them,

by the very act of surprising him at it, masturbatory in nature. The mother's bourgeois hygiene, which is both sexual and social, emerges with her use of the word
immonde—from the Latin *mundus* or clean—*immonde* was one of the most commonly used adjectives in bourgeois anti-Commune rhetoric to describe the
Communards.[22]

In this first section then, liberating dreams are produced by ocular frottage, by
swarming sounds, by excremental associations with the poor children next door.
Such a conjugation between dreaming and the excremental is not unusual in
Rimbaud;[23] earlier in the same poem he speaks of "shutting himself up in the
cool latrine: / There he could think, be calm, and sniff the air."

In the second section spatial liberty is figured in more explicitly masturbatory
terms:

> A sept ans, il faisait des romans sur la vie
> Du grand désert, où luit la Liberté ravie,
> Forêts, soleils, rives, savanes!—Il s'aidait
> De journaux illustrés où, rouge, il regardait
> Des Espagnoles rire et des Italiennes.

> [Seven years old; he made up novels: life
> In the desert, Liberty in transports gleaming,
> Forests, suns, shores, swamps! Using
> Picture magazines: he looked, red-faced,
> At Spanish girls laughing and Italian girls.]

Conjuring up a Fenimore Cooper desert as dreamed landscape: the desert, like
the sea, is continually shifting and made up of innumerable particles. Its function
in this passage is similar to that of the teeming trees in the earlier one—not just
a forest or *a* savannah, but forests, shores, swamps, and, most strikingly, suns!—
more life, more activity.

In the final, most important section, all of the overwhelmingly oppressive
aspects of bourgeois private space descend with the simple mention of "Sundays
in December": the enclosure of bad weather heightened by that most claustro-
phobically familial day of enforced religious and leisurely activity:

> Il craignait les blafards dimanches de décembre,
> Où, pommadé, sur un guéridon d'acajou,
> Il lisait une Bible à la tranche vert-chou;
> Des rêves l'oppressaient chaque nuit dans l'alcôve.
> Il n'aimait pas Dieu; mais les hommes, qu'au soir fauve,
> Noirs, en blouse, il voyait rentrer dans le faubourg
> Où les crieurs, en trois roulements de tambour,
> Font autour des édits rire et gronder les foules.
> —Il rêvait la prairie amoureuse, où des houles

Lumineuses, parfums sains, pubescences d'or,
Font leur remuement calme et prennent leur essor!

[He hated pale December Sunday afternoons:
With plastered hair, on a mahogany couch,
He read the cabbage-colored pages of a Bible;
Dreams oppressed him every night in bed.
He hated God, but loved the men he saw
Returning home in dirty work clothes
Through the wild evening air to the edge of town,
Where criers, rolling drums before the edicts,
Made the crowds around them groan and laugh.
—He dreamed of prairies of love, pubescent stalks of gold
Swirled slowly around, and then rose up and flew.]

Sunday reading is not a liberating experience, and the child's dreams are oppressive in such a constrained atmosphere. The physical oppression of the child is associated directly with the oppression of workers—"les hommes qu'au soir fauve"—with this hypallage the adjective *fauve*, which the context leads us to expect would modify "men," instead refers to the evening, the potential of darkness. By now what would have seemed a bizarre or unusual juxtaposition—the transition from the laughter and grumbling of the crowd to the illuminated *prairie amoureuse*—is no longer a shock. The murmur of the crowd transforms into the *remuement calme* of the prairie, eroticized by *amoureuse* and *pubescence d'or* into an almost Fourierist vision of harmony. The polymorphous sexuality of the child attaches itself variously to the movement and noise of the crowds in the streets, to the ocular sensation of prickling eyelids, to the germinating pubescence of the prairie, to the dankness of latrines. The prairie takes flight, in the sense of an ascendance or *élan* that enables, in the poem's conclusion, the child's own flight, figured synecdochically by the vision of "sails" and accompanied by the swelling sounds of the *rumeur du quartier*:

Il lisait son roman sans cesse médité,
Plein de lourds ciels ocreux et de forêts noyées,
De fleurs de chairs aux bois sidérals déployées,
Vertige, écroulements, déroutes et pitié!
—Tandis que se faisait la rumeur du quartier,
En bas, — seul, et couché sur des pièces de toile
Ecrue, et pressentant violemment la voile!

[He read his novel—always on his mind—
Full of heavy ocher skies and drowning forests,
Flowers of flesh in starry woods uncurled,
Catastrophe, vertigo, pity and disaster!

—While the noises of the neighborhood swelled
Below—stretched out alone on unbleached
Canvas sheets, a turbulent vision of sails!]

The juxtaposition of city and nature serves to make of the fictional, natural catastrophe—the leaden, ocherish skies and the drowned forests—a figuration of social conflict that recalls the exploded earth, the geological enactment of social apocalypse that concluded "Soir historique," or the stormy night sky of "Larme," exploded into a melange of natural and urban elements: "Puis l'orage changea le ciel, jusqu'au soir. / Ce furent des pays noirs, des lacs, des perches, / des colonnades sous la nuit bleue, des gares." ("Then the storm changed the sky, until evening. / It was dark countries, lakes, poles of wood, / colonnades under the blue night, railway stations.")

It cannot be argued that such a montage of natural and urban elements amounts to a "naturalization" of history, a transformation of social movement into immutable, natural images. Rather the "rumor" or *bourdonnement* in Rimbaud, the distant drone resonating on the outskirts of one's sensibility, whether a *rumeur du quartier* or the "bourdon farouche / De cent sales mouches," is always the confused murmur of a large number of *human* voices: "The far sound of cities, in the evening, in sunlight, and always" ("Départ"); "the city, with its smoke and the noise of its trades" ("Ouvriers"); "the noise of insatiable movement that forms and ferments in the masses" ("Jeunesse"); "Voices reconstituted; a fraternal awakening of all choral and orchestral energies" ("Solde"); the chorus, or *choeur*:

Que le monde était plein de fleurs cet été! Les airs et les formes mourant . . .—Un choeur, pour calmer l'impuissance et l'absence! Un choeur de verres, de mélodies nocturnes.

[How the world this summer was full of flowers! Dying airs, dying shapes . . . A chorus to appease impotence and absence! A chorus of glasses of nocturnal melodies.]

("Jeunesse")

The word *choeur* in 1869 first takes on the figurative sense of a reunion of people who share an attitude or goal—here, the chorus is also one of verse (the homophone *vers*) and of glasses (*un choeur de verres*), combining the three key Rimbaldian elements of poetry, drunkenness, and the movement of the crowd.

In Rimbaud the perceived hum of a hot, buzzing summer evening ("l'herbe d'été puante et bourdonnante") deepens the solitude of the listener, to the point where the listener slowly perceives that solitude to be an extremely crowded one—one made up of the murmur of many voices. Included in the chorus at the same time are a former crowd—the voices of the dead ("the dead of '92 and '93")—and a crowd to come ("These poets will be!"). In Delahaye's description of a walk he took with Rimbaud through Paris in November 1871, both the ghosts of the recently crushed insurrection and the investment, beyond all hope, in a dream of future voices, can be heard:

> We took quite a long walk on the boulevard and around the Panthéon. He showed me the white holes in the columns: "From the bullets," he said. Everywhere, in fact, we saw the traces left on the houses by machine gun fire. I asked him where Paris was from the point of view of "ideas." In a weary voice he spoke a few brief words that revealed he had lost hope:
> "Annihilation, chaos . . . all the possible, and even probable *reactions.*"
> In this case could a new insurrection be foreseen? Did any Communards remain?
> "Yes, a few."
> He knew some determined ones . . . he would be with them . . . his ideal would be that result, he didn't see any other.[24]

The space appropriate to that future crowd, the space that will beckon to them, interpellate them, accommodate them, forms the bleak landscapes of Rimbaud's later poetry, particularly the prose poems: the tactile, haptic landscapes of desert, sea, and poles, more sonorous than visual, where crystal and fantastic cities rejoin ancient prefigurations of the end of the world in a triumphant victory of ice and snow: "And the Splendid Hotel was built amidst the glacial chaos and the polar nights" ("Après le Déluge"); "gray skies of crystal" ("Les Ponts"); "Chalets of crystal and of wood" ("Villes"); "this winter night, from promontory to promontory, from the tumultuous pole to the country house, from the crowds to the beach . . . beneath the tides and at the top of the deserts of snow" ("Génie"); "these regions of night . . . more violent than this polar chaos" ("Dévotion"). The motif of "crystal," of "polar chaos," serves to merge the fantastic cityscapes of the *Illuminations* with the landscapes of glacier and sea –these futuristic landscapes together, each granted a literal acceptance by Rimbaud, a status more important than that of the real, stand in opposition to cultivated nature: "the eternal Occident of forests and prodigious plantations" ("Villes"). The scenes or settings for glossolalia are those bleak and lonely places, seas, ice deserts, or futuristic, depopulated cities, that form the thread to a future people, to the joint and swift movement of a pack or horde: "Now plain and desert, horizon and field / Are still before the reddening storm's toilette . . . / See the thousand wolves" ("Michel et Christine").

It is in this way that we should understand the curious yet necessary dialectic of solitude and the swarm as it occurs in poems like "Les Poètes de sept ans" and "Le Bateau ivre." Both poems tell a similar story: emancipation (etymologically, "unhanding") as the transformation of a servile identity into a free identity. In the first poem the child is washed clean of the odors of the day; in the second the boat is stripped of all human vestiges and residues: wine stains, vomit, anchor, and rudder. Gone are the realms of commerce, family, work, and other principles of egoistic conservation. The ocean or the desert is established not only as a particular object of perception but as a perceptive system distinct from terrestrial perception, a more-than-human "language" different from the language of earth. The boat frees itself from the yoke of commerce, and the child also renounces links to the earth—the link of filiation—as if it is only through the most extreme solitude that one can arrive at a new solidarity among humans, a kind of floating population, apt to transform the circumstances of their lives but only on the condition that they first sever the cords that tie them to the earth. Sea and desert both necessitate a very different regime of movement from normal terrestrial movement (sand, continually shifting, forming waves, lies midway between liquid and solid). Terrestrial movement is always movement from one point to another, the two points designated and fixed. And, as Marx points out in the *Grundrisse*, it is precisely this movement *between* points that makes the object a commodity:

> This locational movement—the bringing of the product to the market, which is a necessary condition of its circulation, except when the point of production is itself a market—could more precisely be regarded as the transformation of the product *into a commodity*.[25]

Sea or desert movement, on the other hand, becomes confused with the displacement of the center of gravity; and the movement of the drunken boat is that of a subjectivity that has thrown off precisely that kind of harnessed, locational movement Marx describes:

> Then, delivered from my straining boatmen,
> From the trivial racket of trivial crews and from
> The freights of Flemish grain and English cotton.
> I made my own course down the passive rivers.

This new "emancipated" subjectivity that takes as its point of departure the radical atomization or isolation of the worker, and proceeds by *heightening* or exaggerating that atomization rather than masking it in myths of workers' community, runs the risk of being mistaken as a blueprint for individualist reform rather than for collective emancipation. But emancipation in Rimbaud is only as collective and political as it is individual and cultural.

In the end such landscapes, or nonitineraries, as we find in the "Drunken Boat" and whose existence we first saw alluded to in the early erotic wanderings of "Rêvé pour l'hiver" and "A la musique," are nothing without their promise of a distinctly other ("I have come to know the skies splitting with lightnings . . . I know the evening") state of perception, a more-than-human ("I have seen what men have imagined they saw!'') perception that no longer has solidity for its object or milieu—a perception that is at once cosmological and atomized, planetary and microscopic:

> Tu veux voir rutiler les bolides?
> Et debout, écouter bourdonner les flueurs
> D'astres lactés, et les essaims d'asteroids?

> [Do you want to see the meteors glow red?
> To stand and hear the hum of the influence
> Of milky stars, and the swarm of asteroids?]

> ("Le Juste")

Thus the importance of superlative, of hyperbole and plurals ("all murders and all battles"; "all snows"; "all the birds cry out at the same time in the trees")—the "more than," the wanting more of the Drunken Boat; "Eprouvons davantage," Rimbaud writes to Delahaye [we must feel more, experience more]. Or, in the poem of altered perception par excellence, "Matinée d'ivresse": "rassemblons fervemment cette promesse faite à notre corps et à notre âme créés: cette promesse, cette démence!" ("Let us re-create ourselves after that superhuman promise / Made to our souls and our bodies at their creation / That promise, that madness!") The violently transformed body of "Matinée d'ivresse," the more-than-human perception of the Drunken Boat, serve to indict the equally violent enforcement of existing limitations on human perception—and for Rimbaud those limitations are neither biological nor "ontological," but social, governed first and foremost by a marketing mentality engendered in modern capitalism that violently transforms people and limits them to the role of commodity: "carriers of Flemish wheat and English cotton." The disequilibrium of the boat, or the disfiguration of the *Voyant* ("But the problem is to make the soul into a monster . . . Think of a man grafting warts onto his face and growing them there"), is only a dialectical response, a fun-house mirror reflection of an *initial* disfiguration or mutilation inflicted under capitalism: the closure of fields of socially available perception, the reduction not only of the environment of freedom but also of the very desire for and memory of that environment. Familiarity with capitalist culture persuades us that this limitation—the specific way people, their bodies, and their physical perceptions are organized within capitalism—is not historical but natural and physical. Yet the scope and manner of the mind's attention, or of the body's capacity for sensation, are social facts—and it is precisely the blindness and dullness peculiar to social relations in market society that enable us to deny the social and allow it to be subsumed in the biological. To that blindness, that dullness that is the "human," that debasement of the body of the worker into a thing on the marketplace, Rimbaud responds with the more-than-human ("All the forms of love, of suffering, of madness"), the transformed utopian body of infinite sensation and libidinal possibility as figure for the perfected community, for associative or collective life ("For the first time, hurrah for the unheard-of work, / For the marvelous body!"): the Drunken Boat, the Drunken Morning.

Notes

1. Friedrich Nietzsche, *The Dawn*, in *The Portable Nietzsche*, trans. and ed. Walter Kaufmann (New York: Viking, 1954), 82.

2. Michael Bakunin, cited in Daniel Guérin, *Anarchism* (New York: Monthly Review Press, 1970), 33.

3. The most thorough discussion of the debates that transpired between Marx and Bakunin and the other libertarian anarchists during the 1870s can be found in Paul Thomas, *Karl Marx and the Anarchists* (London: Routledge & Kegan Paul, 1980).

4. Elisée Reclus, *L'Homme et la terre*, vol. 1 (Paris: Maspero, 1982), 71.

5. Michael Bakunin, "The Paris Commune and the Idea of the State," in *Bakunin on Anarchism*, ed. Sam Dolgoff (Montreal: Black Rose Books, 1980), 264.

6. Walter Benjamin, "Surrealism," in *Reflections*, ed. Peter Demetz, trans. Edmund Jephott (New York: Harcourt Brace Jovanovich, 1978), 187.

7. An interesting study remains to be written on the construction of a world-historical subject and on hyperbole as the trope of the antiautobiography in such texts as *Une Saison en enfer* and *Ecce Homo*: "failed" autobiographies that are minimally narrative, not in the least "objective," and lacking in anything resembling a coherent presentation of a "life story."

8. I refer the reader again to the analogous contemporary attempt being conducted by the French right to rewrite the libertarian aspects of the events of May 1968 so that they become merely the preparation for the "individualism" of the 1980s. See, in particular, Gilles Lipovetsky, *L'Ere du vide: Essai sur l'individualisme contemporain* (Paris: Gallimard, 1983), and Luc Ferry and Alain Renaut, *La Pensée 68: Essai sur l'anti-humanisme contemporain* (Paris: Gallimard, 1985). For an excellent refutation of this position, see Cornélius Castoriadis, "Les Mouvements des années soixante," in *Mai '68, Pouvoirs* 39 (1986): 107-16.

9. See Emile Zola, *Au bonheur des dames* (Paris: Gallimard, 1980). See also Michael B. Miller, *The Bon Marché, Bourgeois Culture and the Department Store, 1869-1920* (Princeton, N.J.: Princeton University Press, 1981); Richard Terdiman, *Discourse/Counter Discourse: The Theory and Practice of Symbolic Resistance in Nineteenth-Century France* (Ithaca, N.Y.: Cornell University Press, 1985); Rosalind H. Williams, *Dream Worlds: Mass Consumption in Late Nineteenth-Century France* (Berkeley: University of California Press, 1982).

10. Tzvetan Todorov, "A Complication of Text: The Illuminations," in Tzvetan Todorov (ed.), *French Literary Theory Today*, trans. R. Carter (Cambridge: Cambridge University Press, 1982), 229.

11. See Aimé Césaire, *The Collected Poetry*, trans. Clayton Eshleman and Annette Smith (Berkeley: University of California Press, 1983), 78. I thank Pat Cahill for drawing my attention to this reference.

12. Rimbaud, *Poésies*, ed. L. Forestier (Paris: Gallimard, 1973), 253-54. *Voleter*, a quick fluttering of wings, recalls the Fourierist verb *papilloner* used by Rimbaud in his early poem "Première soirée," a poem also frequented by a fly: "Je regardai, couleur de cire / Un petit rayon buissonier / Papilloner dans son sourire / Et sur son sein–mouche au rosier" ("The color of wax, I watched a little wild ray of light flutter on her smiling lips and on her breast—an insect on the rose-bush"). The verb *papilloner* in and of itself unites the insectile and the erotic in a manner we have begun to see as characteristic of Rimbaud.

13. *Fouillis* is a word used by Rimbaud in other poems to connote openness, plenty, proliferation: "Le buffet est ouvert, et verse dans son ombre / Comme un flot de vin vieux, des parfums engageants: / Tout plein, c'est un fouillis de vieilles vielleries" ("The cupboard is open, and gives off from its kindly shadows / Inviting aromas like a breath of old wine; / Full to overflowing, it's a jumble of quaint old things") "Le Buffet."

14. Georges Poulet, in *La Poésie éclatée* (Paris: PUF, 1980), discusses Rimbaud's poetry as a *bondissement* from a phenomenological perspective. See especially 127-28 and 149-50.

15. In "Vies," the prairie or plain is the site of an erotic encounter whose memory is associated with the thundering wings of a flock of scarlet pigeons: "Je me souviens des heures d'argent et de soleil vers les fleuves, la main de la campagne sur mon épaule, et de nos caresses debout dans les plaines poivrées. — Un envol de pigeons écarlates tonne autour de ma pensée." ("I remember hours of silver and sun near rivers, the hand of the countryside upon my shoulder, and I remember our embraces, standing in the scented plain. A flight of scarlet pigeons thunders about my thoughts.")

16. "Les serpents géants dévorés de punaises" ("Giant reptiles pullulant with lice") "Le Bateau ivre"; "O ton front qui fourmille de lentes" ("O your forehead, swarming with nits!") "Le Juste."

17. Louis Barron, *Sous le drapeau rouge* (Paris: Albert Savine, 1889), 112.

18. See the fragmentary line "Pourquoi les astres d'or fourmillant comme un sable?" ("Why the golden stars swarming like the sands?") or, from "Les Premières Communions": "Et mon coeur et ma chair par ta chair embrassée / Fourmillent du baiser putride de Jésus!" ("My heart and my flesh which your flesh has embraced / Seethe with the rotten kisses of Jesus!")

19. Walter Benjamin, "Surrealism," 179.

20. Or, from "Les Réparties de Nina":

> De chaque branche, gouttes vertes,
> Des bougeons clairs,
> On sent dans les choses ouvertes
> Frémir des chairs.

> [From each branch; clear drops tremble,
> Bright buds glow,
> Everything opens and vibrates;
> All things grow.]

21. See Steve Murphy's excellent, but brief, reading of this poem in "Le Regard de Rimbaud," *Revue des sciences humaines* 1 (1984): 57-62.

22. See Paul Lidsky, *Les Ecrivains contre la Commune* (Paris: Maspero, 1982), 151.

23. See "Oraison du soir" where one of Rimbaud's extremely rare figures of comparison concerns just such a conjunction: "Tels que les excréments chauds d'un vieux colombier / Mille rêves en moi font de douces brulures." ("Like steaming dung within an old dovecote / A thousand Dreams within me softly burn.")

24. Ernest Delahaye, cited in Rimbaud, *Oeuvres complètes*, ed. Rolland de Renéville and Jules Mouquet (Paris: Gallimard, 1967), 745.

25. Karl Marx, *Grundrisse: Foundations of the Critique of Political Economy*, trans. Martin Nicolaus (London: New Left Review, 1973), 534. Italics in the original.

Chapter 5
Metaphors and Slogans

If "mature" class consciousness partakes of the serial logic of groupings like the party or the state, then the movement of Rimbaud's swarm is much more that of the *informe* ("if it has no form he gives it no form"): the spontaneous, fermenting element of the group. By underlining the unformed, virtual, or "gathering" nature of Rimbaud's swarm poesis, I am not then qualifying it as "immature," but rather questioning the theoretical dominance of dicta like "maturity" and "immaturity" as conceptually formative in standard Marxist critiques of class consciousness. Liberty or emancipation is the prerequisite condition for acquiring the "maturity" for liberty — not some reward to be granted when maturity is achieved. It would certainly be as misguided to apply a developmental model to Rimbaud's utopian erotico-scatological version of the crowd as it would be to await the discovery of Rimbaud's "mature" poetic manuscripts in a hut in Ethiopia.

A class is defined by its interests, and interests operate on the level of the preconscious. A class presents well-defined figures, well-identified roles and *métiers*, figurative image-models. The swarm, however, is activated by unconscious desire, or by an intensified desire to desire ("O million d'oiseaux d'or, O futur vigueur!"), and desire presents *non*figurative indications: people given way to flows, part-objects that are not synecdoches for some missing totality—the curve of a shoulder, postures and gestures. If we renounce the evolutionary vision of the swarm as a rudimentary and less well organized social form, as something formless, utopian, primitive, or otherwise incompatible with the realities of a complex society, we can begin to see it as that which escapes from any of those paranoid or colonial formations—what Nietzsche calls "formations of sovereignty"—such as the armies whose discourse Rimbaud parodies in "Démocratie":[1]

> "Aux centres nous alimenterons la plus cynique prostitution. Nous massacrerons les révoltes logiques.
> Aux pays poivrés et détrempés!—au service des plus monstrueuses exploitations industrielles ou militaires."

["In the metropolis we will feed the most cynical whoring. We will destroy all logical revolt.
On to the languid scented lands! In the service of the most monstrous industrial or military exploitations."]

It is these latter "molar" groupings, to borrow the valuable distinction Deleuze and Guattari make between molar and molecular, that promote the crowd's organization into a statistical accumulation and a spatiotemporal grid: the "vision of numbers," the square in Charleville, the hegemony of bourgeois rationalism. Rimbaud's swarm suggests an alternative vision of numbers, of pluralization or the crowd—not the interests of a particular class, but a half-real, half-fantastic libidinal geography of migrants displaced at the limits of class: classes that are fractured, in flight.

For this reason Rimbaud's swarm constitutes a genuine *lieu mixte*. His verse takes from the realm of high art formal elements such as the alexandrine or the sonnet form, and mixes them with Ardennais slang, scatological invective, and political diatribe. We cannot conclude from this, however, that Rimbaud's poetry exists as "countercultural"—in opposition to the philosophy, art, or poetry of the dominant high culture of his time. Such a rigid system of cultural purification rituals or artistic stratification was characteristic, as we have seen, *of* that high culture—of Leconte de Lisle and others of the most conservative representatives of the Parnassian school. Rimbaud's work resonates instead with all the anxieties of the real and imaginary displacements authorized by a cultural space that enables passages, meeting places, contagion *between* one class and another, or even between one species and another:

> Chinois, Hottentots, bohémiens, niais, hyènes, Molochs, vieilles démences, démons sinistres, ils mêlent les tours populaires, maternels, avec les poses et les tendresses bestiales.

> [Chinese, Hottentots, gypsies, simpletons, hyenas, Molochs, old insanities, sinister demons, they mingle popular, homespun turns with bestial poses and caresses.]

("Parade")

> J'aimais les peintures idiotes, dessus de portes, décors, toiles de saltimbanques, enseignes, enluminures populaires; la littérature

démodée, latin d'église, livres érotiques sans orthographe, romans de
nos aïeules, contes de fées, petits livres d'enfance, opéras vieux,
refrains niais, rhythmes naïfs.

[I liked absurd paintings, pictures over doorways, stage sets, carnival
backdrops, billboards, colored prints, old-fashioned literature, Church
Latin, erotic books badly spelled, the kind of novels our grandmothers
read, fairy tales, little children's books, old operas, silly refrains, naïve
rhythms.]

(''Alchimie du verbe'')

The point to emphasize about this famous heap is not so much the collective or
popular ''authorship'' of most of its elements, but rather the latent political effect
of the juxtaposition of badly spelled erotic books with Church Latin — all under
the affirmation (''J'aimais'') that renders each at once specific and equivalent. In
Rimbaud there is no isolation of the popular into a regional preserve, into some
ritualized carnivalesque space of pure *dépense*.[2] He is not a regionalist—his practice, rather, involves promoting the danger and utopian fantasy that both result
from contagion. The disorder of his poetry, in other words, lies less in his creation of a specifically rebellious, adolescent, or Communard countercultural
product than in his particular perspective *on* the dominant, shared culture. His is
less a savage, adolescent, or Communard culture than a savage, adolescent or
Communard relationship *to* culture. In his own flight from poetry (a flight that
began not in 1875 with his ''silence'' but rather in 1869 when he wrote his first
poem), from the customs or discourse of the poetic salon, from the formal and
lexical restrictions on what constituted verse, Rimbaud becomes subversive to
dominant culture. To the extent that he can no longer stand to be *l'être poète*, he
produces a culture in disorder, one that is equally distanced from the received
images of culture *and* counterculture.

I

Rimbaud's flight from *l'être poète* can best be charted in terms of his flight from,
or at lease his deep ambivalence to, the poet's characteristic tool of metaphor.
Interesting problems have assailed those critics who attempt to approach Rimbaud according to a metaphor/metonymy axis; those problems are instructive and
worth reviewing. Sartre, one of Rimbaud's best but elliptic readers, in a brief
passage in *Saint Genet*, sets up a bipolar opposition between what he stops just
short of calling a ''leftist'' turn of the imagination and a ''rightist'' one. The first
is represented by Rimbaud's ''centrifugal,'' ''generous,'' and ''explosive'' metaphor; the second, by the ''miserly,'' ''retractile'' metaphor of Mallarmé, Baudelaire, or Genet:

There are two types of unification in modern poetry, one expansive, the other retractile. . . . the first tendency—which is that of Rimbaud— forcibly compels natural diversity to symbolize *an explosive unity*. . . . To see the dawn as a "people of doves" is to blow up the morning as if it were a powder keg.[3]

Baudelaire and Mallarmé assume an (ontotheological) order among objects that actually have none; they condense and assimilate scattered elements. Rimbaud's only dynamic unity is one of combustion: his metaphor explodes and scatters in all directions. We can rephrase Sartre's distinction in terms of our own reading of Rimbaud's swarm—particularly since the example Sartre chooses from "Le Bateau ivre," "l'Aube exaltée ainsi qu'un peuplement de colombes," ("Dawn exalted like a swarm of doves") is in fact a "swarm" example. The difference he is underlining lies, on the one hand, in conceiving unity in an extrinsic or molar manner, as a unity of assemblage, a grouping or assimilation of juxtaposed parts, and, on the other, in conceiving of a kind of unity of production: a cell that produces its own parts by continual differentiation and division—both compression and explosion. Understood this way, Sartre's description of the two tendencies, and of Rimbaud as exemplary of the second tendency, is convincing; the problem, however, lies with his principal category. If the constitutive property of metaphor is its condensatory and assimilative movement, then does a "metaphor" that performs the opposite function still deserve to be called a metaphor?

In order to account for the specificity of Rimbaud's metaphor, other critics have felt called upon to revise altogether the definition of metaphor, or to announce an entirely new category within metaphor that emerges full blown in Rimbaud's work. Hugo Friedrich, for example, has coined the phrase "absolute metaphor" in conjunction with Rimbaud, and quotes Hugo von Hofmannsthal's comment about Novalis to approximate what he means: "The most wonderful poetic sentences are those that describe with great physical precision and clarity something that is physically impossible."[4] He describes Rimbaud's practice as that of combining into word clusters component parts that each have a vivid, sensory quality: the combination, however, creates an unreal structure such as the physical eye would never encounter. Rimbaud's metaphors "go far beyond the license that has always been permitted by the metaphorical forces inherent in language." Like Sartre, Friedrich is forced to define Rimbaud's metaphor as precisely that which "goes beyond" metaphor.

Linguist Harald Weinrich chooses to focus on a number of Rimbaud's uses of color to show that Rimbaud redefines that which, since Aristotle, has been thought of as the "bold" or "audacious" metaphor. His examples are *vin bleu* from "Le Bateau ivre" and *lèvres vertes* from "Métropolitain."[5] The truly audacious metaphor, Weinrich argues, is not, as has been traditionally asserted, made of combining elements from widely distinct or distant semantic fields. "Sad milk,'' for example, joins two distant semantic fields by ascribing an emotion to a food. Such a metaphor is not as bold as one that departs *only a little* from our own sense perceptions: ''blue wine'' does not transport us into another sphere, but only moves us across the color wheel. Unlike ''sad milk,'' in other words, ''blue wine'' does not ascribe to wine a characteristic that it does not have—it merely distorts that characteristic. Our attention is focused on the ''contradiction'' inherent in a metaphor like ''blue wine''; ''sad milk,'' while contradictory in the way that all metaphors are ''contradictory,'' is a contradiction we find easy to accept because it challenges neither our sense perceptions nor our notion of what milk *is*. We accept the ''contradiction'' (and therefore do not notice it). ''Blue wine,'' on the other hand, we notice. Rimbaud's metaphors, Weinrich concludes, function as contradictory predication.[6]

Friedrich and Weinrich both emphasize that the ''bold'' or ''absolute'' metaphor, the metaphor as contradictory predication, rivets the reader's attention on the language or ''surface'' of the text by, so to speak, blocking the representational function. ''We are now in a world whose reality exists in language alone'' (Friedrich, 57). Tzvetan Todorov arrives at a very similar conclusion, but via a more radical route. Rimbaud, he argues, has, quite simply, no use for metaphor—or, for that matter, for tropes in general! ''Rimbaud's writing is not governed by the principle of resemblance. . . . Metaphor, Baudelaire's master trope, is all but absent here'';[7] ''I would say rather that the language of the *Illuminations* is essentially literal and does not require, or even admit, transposition by means of tropes.''[8]

We are left then with a truly contradictory predication: Rimbaud's language is literal and yet not representational, or rather literal (nonfigurative) and yet bearing no discernible relationship to any referential function—cut off from any extralinguistic reality.

How can this be the case? Let's return to the examples of audacious metaphors cited by Weinrich, the ''blue wine'' and the ''green lips'' from a slightly different angle. *Vin bleu*, according to Delvau's *Dictionnaire de la langue verte*, was a widespread popular slang expression in the late 1860s for a *vin de barrière*; the term derived from people having noticed that the cheap wine served in cabarets in the zone when spilled made bluish stains on the tablecloths. Near the end of his 1913 partisan account of the exile experience of Communards in Switzerland, Lucien Descaves recounts attending a memorial dinner of *anciens combattants*, Communards celebrating the anniversary of March 18, 1871. In the course of the evening, many popular songs from the old days were sung, including this one:

> Jarni! Versez-moi du vin bleu!
> J'aime son goût de pierre à feu
>   Et cordieu!
> Sitôt qu'il me monte à la tête,

> Je suis heureux,
> Je suis joyeux,
> Je crois à la vertu d'Jeanette!

[I swear! Pour me some cheap wine!
I love its taste of flint
    And Body of Christ!
As soon as it goes to my head,
    I'm happy,
    I'm gay,
I believe in the virtue of Jeanette.][9]

Lèvres vertes was a popular mid- and late nineteenth-century cliché often found in passages like the following describing prostitutes (absinthe drinkers?) in the wee hours of the morning: "des femmes échevelées, crottées, déchirées, au regard hebeté de la fatigue du vice, aux lèvres vertes, aux seins froissées . . ." ("dishevelled, dirty, broken women with the dazed look of the fatigue of vice, with green lips, with bruised breasts").[10] "Green lips" in this context connotes the ill health of a vice-ridden life. Vermersch, in his 1871 Commune poem "Les Incendiaires," eliminates the connotation of vice usually found in bourgeois descriptions of the poor and the working class; instead, the "green lips" of the corpses of Communards assassinated by the Versaillais become the source of a future insurrectionary call to arms:

> Aujourd'hui, dans Paris, sous les pavés des rues,
> Ils foulent nos morts à leurs pieds;
> Les pères mitraillés, les mères disparues,
> Dans leurs berceaux de sang souillés
> Les orphelins, levant leurs mains, demandent grâce
> A ces assassins triomphants!
> Ce que pour l'avenir contiennent de menace
> Les mains de ces petits enfants,
> Ce que plus tard diront avec leurs bouches vertes
> Les cadavres ensanglantées . . . [11]

[Today, in Paris, beneath the paving stones
They trample our dead underfoot;
The fathers machine-gunned, the mothers disappeared,
In their blood-stained cradles
Orphans, reaching out their hands, ask for mercy
From the triumphant assassins!
For the future what menace lies contained
In the hands of those little children,

In the future what words will come from the green lips
Of those bloodied corpses . . .]

Such contextual revelations about Rimbaud's language usage are not meant to
suggest that the *Elle* of the closing moments of "Métropolitain" is either a prostitute or a dead Communard, or that the Drunken Boat doubles as a working-class
cabaret—though it is, of course, significant that both examples, as well as others
that could be cited, are drawn by Rimbaud from the *lieu mixte* of *barrière*/caba-
ret/working-class slang. They do, however, support my argument that Rimbaud's
language is firmly anchored in society, and that even the most difficult or hermetic texts, the *Illuminations*, are concerned with posing the problem of that
society and especially that society's future. (In fact, the very hermetic quality of
the *Illuminations* should be taken as symptomatic: the loneliness of these texts, or
of lyric expression itself, is latent in the atomization of late nineteenth-century
culture. The general, binding validity of such texts, their link to society, derives
from the density of their individuation. The *Illuminations*, to the extent that they
foreground an imperative discourse, a collective agency of enunciation rather
than refer back to a single determinable subject or landscape, bear a stronger
relation to nonlinguistic reality, to the outside of language, than do Rimbaud's
early realist or representational texts like "A la Musique.")

The examples of "blue wine" and of the *Illuminations* taken in their entirety
show that what we have been trained (by formalist readings) to view as the most
nonreferential moments in a text or in an oeuvre—Rimbaud at his most "surre-
alistic"—in fact represent a higher degree of referential truth. Formalist readings
construct a "sociolect" that has to be transcended in order to arrive at "poetry,"
defined as such as a break with representation. But it is only by repressing social
context that we can read "blue wine" as an exceptional poetic transcendence of
some background referential sociolect. Rimbaud's text gives the lie to readings
that would construct the poetic and the sociolect as contradictory or warring
terms.

Formalist readings will often go so far as to situate a poetic work within the
diachronics of a homogeneously conceived, literary history. But in order fully to
grasp poetry as the product of a *historical* imagination, is it not necessary to read
the work synchronically in conjunction with discourses and especially with *language* that is not distinctly literary? Rimbaud's tropology (or antitropology, as the
case may be) is historically conditioned; it cannot be examined without considering the rhetorical function of the work within the wider cultural system, within
the whole set of socially and historically specific discourses and representations
in which it participates.

Tzvetan Todorov's remarks about the *Illuminations* provide a telling example
of the insights and limitations of formalism. Todorov cites Rimbaud's line "here,
anywhere," from "Démocratie" as an example of Rimbaud's fondness for asser-

tions that are nakedly contradictory. Here is the context of the citation from "Démocratie":

> "Aux centres nous alimenterons la plus cynique prostitution. Nous massacrerons les révoltes logiques.
>
> Aux pays poivrés et détrempés!—au service des plus monstrueuses exploitations industrielles ou militaires.
>
> Au revoir *ici, n'importe où*. Conscrits du bon vouloir, nous aurons la philosophie féroce; ignorants pour la science, roués pour le confort; la crevaison pour le monde qui va. C'est la vraie march. En avant, route!"

> ["In the metropolis we will feed the most cynical whoring. We will destroy all logical revolt.
>
> On to the languid, scented lands! In the service of the most monstrous industrial or military exploitations.
>
> Farewell *here, anywhere*. Conscripts of good intention, we will have savage philosophy; knowing nothing of science, depraved in our pleasures, to hell with the world around us . . . This is the real advance! Forward . . . March!"]

"Rimbaud," writes Todorov, "sometimes proposes two very different terms, as if he did not know which was more appropriate, or as if the choice were unimportant."[12] But is not the point, precisely, in any systematic reading of "Démocratie," that the choice (here, anywhere) *is* unimportant? Not because Rimbaud favors contradictory assertions, but because for an expanding, mobile, and imperialistic bourgeois class, here *is* the same as anywhere. By failing to recognize the spatial equivalence or leveling of cultural difference, the bourgeois spatial hegemony evoked by a line like "Au revoir ici, n'importe où," read in context, Todorov is forced to deny any diachronic reading of Rimbaud's poetry whatsoever.

Todorov is, I think, correct when he concludes that Rimbaud has no use for metaphors or for tropes in general. He is right in virtually eliminating a tropological reading of Rimbaud, and in so doing, he intuits an important political analysis. But he uses his intuition instead to support the formalist position that literature is an extrasocial phenomenon—that while social forces or events might and do sometimes, even drastically, affect literature from the outside, the real, the intrinsic nature of literature and literary language remains immune and true to itself alone. Is not the problem rather one of *historicizing* Rimbaud's resistance to metaphor? How is such an ambivalence to figuration culturally and historically determined? Why, at this particular moment, would Rimbaud produce a materialist poetry made up of language that is "essentially literal"?

We cannot begin to answer these questions by lingering on the metaphor/metonymy axis; instead we must look at the way figuration is thwarted or undermined in the *Illuminations*. Part objects in the prose poems, for example, as

Todorov notes, do not refer back to any whole—they are literal parts. The "green lips" of "Métropolitain" are not lips in search of some lost owner. Rimbaud, in other words, sabotages synecdoche. But how are we to account for such a sabotage? Can we locate the desire behind the sabotage and consider it, as well as any other linguistic technique, as inseparable from a pragmatics, a wish? In the case of the sabotaged synecdoche, we might consider the following. Whole objects and persons are not the preferred objects of wish production, and Rimbaud's "montage" technique in the *Illuminations* closely resembles the process of mechanical wish production. If we recall the montage or *bricolage* technique we saw operative in barricade construction and street warfare during the Commune ("find flowers which are chairs!"), we find a clue: use familiar parts to invent new functions. The previous "whole" (social context, dominant organization of space, of bodies) must be sabotaged to allow for new functions, pieces put back together again: thus in the *Illuminations*, the importance of conjugations, the "and . . . and . . . and"; conjugation rather than metaphor.

In the *Illuminations*, two principal strategies are at work. The first is to omit, to lose, to get rid of. The following linguistic and grammatical elements are eliminated: conjunctions expressing logical relations, causal links, a great deal of verbs, syntactic transitions, subordinating clauses. The poems, in other words, are organized paratactically, an organization which, somewhat like the military organization adopted by the Communards—that "fantasia of war" in the words of Louis Barron—sometimes doubles for disorder:

> And what organization can be attempted in the full storm of anarchy
> and civil war, when the best compasses are defective, and when
> everything drifts and goes astray? O illusion! Not to see that the
> insurgents are already logically organized, and that we would change
> nothing about that organization, even if it is found derisive and called
> disorder and confusion, for disorder and confusion are of the very
> essence of voluntary troops under leaders who are freely elected—that is
> to say, subordinated to their subordinates.[13]

Parataxis, originally, derives from the Greek word meaning to arrange in order to do battle—to dispose in rows, side by side. Clauses lie "in association with" each other, but that association is not formed into a hierarchy. Thus, for example, the repeated "There is . . . There is . . . There is . . ." of "Enfance III," or the equally repetitive format of "Solde": "For sale . . . For sale . . . For sale . . ."; or this passage, from "Promontoire":

> Des fanums qu'éclaire la rentrée des théories; d'immenses vues de la
> défense des côtes modernes; des dunes illustrées de chaudes fleurs et de
> bacchanales; de grands canaux de Carthage et des embankments d'une
> Venise louche; de molles éruptions d'Etnas et des crevasses de fleurs et
> d'eaux des glaciers . . .

[Shrines that glow with the return of theories; vast views of modern coastal fortifications; dunes patterned with burning flowers and bacchanales; the great canals of Carthage and embankments of a sinister Venice; soft eruptions of Etnas, crevasses of flowers and melting glaciers . . .]

None of these clauses bears a dependent relation on any that surround it. One need only look to Mallarmé to find an opposing organizational tendency, that of *hypotaxis*: the principle of syntactic subordination and dependence. (Valéry was aware of this contrast when he spoke of Mallarmé's "symbolic calculations" versus Rimbaud's "unknown radiations.")

The second strategy is to overload or surcharge—Rimbaud's use of punctuation best illustrates this practice. Consider the role played by exclamation and direct affective statement: "O world! and the clear song of new sadnesses!"; "His body!"—in fact, the whole parade of exclamation points in "Génie" or "Solde"; the frenetic use of the dash in "Barbare" and elsewhere; exaggeration ("the hundred thousand altars of the cathedral"), and the importance of number in general; the "wanting more" of hyperbole; the sheer semantic acceleration of certain passages that creates in the reader the anxiety that the poem might never end. This anxiety is, of course, very close to that produced by crowds, and Rimbaud's prose poems in fact follow the same four rules Canetti applies to crowd formations.[14] Like the crowd in Canetti's first rule, the prose poem has no natural boundaries: it wants to grow (see, especially, "Villes" or "Promontoire"). Second, within the crowd, there is equality; the elements of a crowd, like the clauses in "Phrases," are organized paratactically. Third, the crowd, according to Canetti, loves density, and the densest crowds grow the fastest. Similarly, it is those very dense passages in the *Illuminations* where the sheer accumulation and speed of the clauses seem almost to take on a dizzying life of their own:

> Les brasiers, pleuvant aux rafales de
> givre, —Douceurs!—les feux à la pluie du
> vent de diamants jetée par le coeur terrestre
> éternellement carbonisé pour nous. —O monde!—

> [Bright fires, raining in squalls of
> sleet—Delight!—Fires in the rain of a
> diamond windthrown by this terrestrial core
> charred forever for us—O World!—]

> ("Barbare")

> L'ardeur de l'été fut confiée à des oiseaux
> muets et l'indolence requise à une barque de
> deuils sans prix par des anses d'amours morts
> et de parfums affaissés.

[The passion of summer is left to the
tongueless birds and the necessary indolence
to a rich funeral barge by the eddying calm
of dead loves and fading perfumes.]

("Fairy")

And finally, the crowd is moving somewhere; it has a goal—and here we could assemble a list of the downward abrupt movement and stark simplicity of Rimbaud's concluding sentences, the lapidary, bomblike closure of many of the prose poems: "It can only be the end of the world advancing" ("Enfance IV"); "Now is the time of the Assassins" ("Matinée d'ivresse"); "A blast of air blows away the limits of homes" ("Nocturne vulgaire"); "And finally, when you are hungry and thirsty, there is someone who chases you away" ("Enfance III").

If, as John Ashbery has commented, Rimbaud is the only poet to have "gotten beyond the *lucidity* of the French language,"[15] he has done so, it seems, by operating simultaneously *above* and *below* the French language—by "impoverishing" it syntactically at the same time that he overloads it with local variation and urgent exclamation. Rimbaud's language, then, intervenes into French; it bears a contestatory relation to the formal constants of the French language.

If Rimbaud's poetry thwarts a tropological analysis, it does so to the extent that we can begin to understand it as made up of a whole swarm of linguistic forms that demonstrate language threatening to move beyond language: invective, slogans, exclamations, satire, manifestos. Rimbaud's poetry lends itself to an analysis that focuses on those discursive forms in which acts are linked to enunciation by a social or collective obligation. And to understand those forms we will have to consider them as inseparable from the social obligations, the social collectivities or milieux that formed Rimbaud's discursive field and that inscribed on him particular ideological effects.

II

The first such collectivity is a negative one. Rimbaud's reaction formation to the petit bourgeois provincialism of Charleville rings out loud and clear in the satire and sarcasm that color his early, nightmarish caricatures of small-town life ("A la Musique," "Les Assis," "Les Pauvres à l'église"). In these poems the original sense of the Greek *sarkasmos*—to bite the flesh of the conquered adversary—is all too apparent. We have already noted instances of oral aggression (the literal and figurative biting) in early poems like "Les Déserts de l'Amour," "A la Musique," and "Les Poètes de sept ans"; in one of the Voyant letters from that period, Rimbaud sums up something of a policy statement: "Tout ce que je puis inventer de bête, de sale, de mauvais, en action et en paroles, je le leur livre"

("Anything I can invent that is stupid, dirty, or bad, in actions or in words, I throw it up to them").

Satire is a genre of contamination, a genre less elevated than that of lyric poetry whose commitment to a rhetoric of originality is of primary importance. Originality matters far less in satire; instead, one makes direct contact with the discourse of the enemy, often citing it directly or mimicking it, all the while marking the extreme point of one's own ideological divergence from it. Satire is an example of what Vološinov would call "speech within speech, utterance within utterance, and, at the same time, . . . speech about speech and utterance about utterance."[16] Rimbaud's Charleville poems are characterized by this social and regional multiaccentuality—even a nonsatiric, essentially sympathetic poem like "La Maline" depends on a reading that gives full weight to the regional and class specificity of the servant girl's closing remark. The rhetoric of contempt that emanates from poems like "Les Assis" underlines Rimbaud's ideological divergence from petit bourgeois aspirations; that contempt slices through the monolithic nature of petit bourgeois discourse and severs everything that would attach it to a universal or "molar" logic.

The same ideological function is served in Rimbaud's letters from the period in which we can see him putting his talent for neologism in the service of invective: "Je n'ai rien de plus à te dire, la contemplostate [contemplation = stasis] de la Nature m'absorculant [*absorber* + *enculer*] tout entier."[17] And it emerges most clearly in his productive association with a second group or collectivity, the poetic group whose very name proclaims their characteristically contestatory verbal posture: the *Zutistes*.

The Cercle du Zutisme, a loosely knit group of mostly poets and artists whose existence is alluded to in various contemporary publications (mostly small student journals), apparently met regularly in the Hotel des Etrangers, 2 rue Racine, Paris, from 1871 until perhaps as late as 1875. The group took shape in the wake of a serious political split within the ranks of the Parnassians. Anti-Communard poets like Leconte de Lisle, who had received a monthly salary from Napoléon III, and who had been named Chevalier de la Légion d'Honneur during the last years of the Second Empire, were increasingly ostracized and set up as targets for derision by Verlaine, Rimbaud, engraver André Gill, and the brothers Cros—the latter directly responsible for the founding of the Zutistes.

The *Album zutique*, which was illustrated in a fantastic style by Rimbaud's friend Germain Nouveau and contained a sketched portrait of Rimbaud by André Gill, surfaced for the first time in an auction in 1936. A fragmented compilation of insult, provocation, obscenity, and pastiche, the album bore witness to the production of a group whose affairs—secret languages, banquets, reunions—foreshadowed many of the activities of the Dadaists and Surrealists. The Zutistes practiced joint authorship; their preferred activity was to create obscene versions of poems written in the manner of the author selected for derision (François

Coppée and Louis Belmontet, poets who sang the glories of the Second Empire, were their favorite victims). This kind of formal satire staged a dialogue on the level of signatures, since the Zutistes signed their pieces with the name of the caricatured author, and underneath that name their own names or initials—thus, A.R. and P.V. signed a piece entitled "Sonnet du trou du cul" designed to parody a volume of poetry by Merat entitled *L'Idole* where the individual elements of a woman's beauty are serialized: "Sonnet du front," "Sonnet des yeux," and so on. This dialogue of signatures created interesting confusion in the *Album*'s readers about who were actually members of the Zutistes: Verlaine, for example, is both a parodist and a victim; and for many years it was thought that several of the "victims" had actually authored the texts parodying their own work.

Rimbaud's association with the Cercle du Zutisme and the texts he coproduced from that period have been all but uniformly ignored by Rimbaud critics intent on charting the artistic formation of the solitary genius. Such satiric and buffoonish verse, such adolescent posturing and clowning around have been viewed as having little importance for Rimbaud's poetic development. In a similar fashion, Rimbaud's homosexuality has been both trivialized and mythologized into a series of somewhat lurid anecdotes surrounding events in his relationship with Verlaine. In fact, the existence of a whole homosexual subculture—our third collectivity—can be traced through the amazing quantity and semantic richness of the jargon, false names, the playful names, the aliases that proliferated among Rimbaud and his more intimate friends, Verlaine, Delahaye, and Nouveau. In the epistolary *manie* of Rimbaud and his associates, slang and *patois* usages—what Verlaine referred to as a "parisiano-ardennais" accent—and monstrous, vulgar deformations of the most simple vocabulary become an obsession. This "accent" serves to render the identification of people, places, and things in the letters a bit uneasy: something close to a private language, both in verbal form and in the elaborate caricatures and drawings they exchanged between themselves, was gradually developed.[18] Verlaine and Delahaye, for example, characteristically refer to Rimbaud in their correspondence as *Chose* or *l'Oestre* (gadfly): a large fly whose larvae live parasitically under the skin of certain mammals. *L'oestre* is included in the vocabulary of sexuality as well: *oestre vénérien* means an ardent or immoderate desire for the pleasures of love, while the Greek *oestrus* signifies a prophetic or poetic delirium. Delahaye's other names for Rimbaud include various "colonial" designations: *le Senegalais*, *le Cafre*, *le Hottentot* (from the Dutch meaning "stutterer"). Delahaye is in turn called by an impressive variety of deformations of his proper name (Delamorue, Delatrichine, Delatronche, Delahuppe, Delahuppette, etc.), all of which evoke unconventional forms of sexuality as well as pejorative terms for women. Recent studies analyzing the derivations of these (im)proper names point to a practice of homosexual self-designation: the affirmation of and participation in homosexual subculture by way of a private language.[19]

Secret languages, code names, jargon, slang peculiar to various small groups: these linguistic phenomena are less about rhetorical figures than they are about introducing and maintaining variation in the common, standardized element of a public language—operating a subversive state of variation within the common element of language. The surcharge of naming among Rimbaud and his intimates should not be read as a rhetorical figure but rather as a phenomenon indicating the presence of a collective agencing ("Je est un autre"; "on me pense") at the heart of every enunciation.[20] When Rimbaud invents himself an alternative name to sign his poem "Ce qu'on dit au poète à propos de fleurs," he chooses "Alcide Bava," a surname whose literal meaning of foaming at the mouth, and whose figurative connotations of stinging or venomous words affirm all the excessive linguistic and nonlinguistic practices Rimbaud cultivated. But behind "Bava" also lurks *bavarder*—gossip, the language of the crowd: speech that is neither uniquely private nor officially standardized in an impersonal public form. In the collective experience of gossip we can detect the two elements of the language of the swarm rejoined: the repetitive, droning buzz (the refrain, the *bourdon*) and the unique, eventful variation (the lyrical leap, the *élan*, the potential "sting"). Gossip is repetition with a difference: the same transmitted again and again with each variation that contributes to it taking on its own unique value.

III

The satire provoked by small-town provincialism, the invective and contestatory pastiche of the Zutistes as collective author, the secret language of a homosexual subculture—I have left until now the most important of the group "identifications" that marked Rimbaud, namely, the Commune. To some extent I mean "Commune" in this instance as shorthand for a number of linguistic practices— working-class slang, revolutionary discourse, caricature, invective—that while considerably more visible and prominent during the Commune, were certainly in existence before the end of the Empire. The culture and the language of the Commune cannot be abstracted from the working-class movement and cultural forms that preceded it. (Nor can it be isolated from its own interaction with the bourgeois culture with which it is constantly in dialogue.) But while we should beware of granting a lyrical or nostalgic privilege to the Commune as exceptional moment, it is nevertheless possible to ascertain aspects of the verbal and visual forms of the Commune that are both striking and particular.

The first of these has to do with sheer quantity. Social and political conflict are expressed in these months by an astounding abundance of newspapers, pamphlets, tracts, propaganda brochures, professions of faith, declarations of intention, manifestos:

Under the Commune, naturally, an infinite number of journals have sprung up. Try to count, if you absolutely must, the leaves in a forest, the grains of sand on the shores, the stars in the sky, but don't even try in a dream to enumerate the *gazettes* that have seen the light since that blessed day of March 18.[21]

In fact, some seventy new journals and periodicals were introduced during the two months of the Commune.[22] Mendès, whose irony in the preceding quote is apparent, is forced to admit that "at this time the press is queen. A deposed queen, a degraded [*encanaillée*] queen, but queen nevertheless."[23] The liberated press takes on an extraordinary vigor, and readership, by all accounts, is high:

> Voices pierce the ear, crying out the *Mot d'ordre*, the *Vengeur*, the *Cri du peuple*, the *Père Duchêne*, and we buy them, we read them, some of them out loud, the *Mot d'ordre* for the amusing article by Rochefort; the *Vengeur* for the tirades by Félix Pyat; the *Cri du peuple* for the word "people"; the *Père Duchêne* for his "great anger" that no one, not even him, feels, and for those *bougres* and *foutres*, simulated vulgarities, that make us laugh.[24]

Through this literature of persuasion and *rapportage*, an often new and newly affective vocabulary is disseminated into diverse social classes. The Commune policy of providing "instant information" to a population that included many illiterates, and many who could not afford to buy a newspaper, resulted in a staggering quantity of *murailles* as well: announcements and denouncements, political posters, proclamations that were often read aloud as people gathered in the streets. *Affiches* of all colors and formats covered the walls of Paris for the first time; Edmond de Goncourt, writing in his journal on April 17, 1871, complains: "Posters, more posters, and still more posters!"[25] A letter from Rimbaud to Demeny dated the same day is considerably more celebratory in its description of the proliferation of verbal and visual material in the streets of Paris:

> Causons Paris . . . On s'arrêtait aux gravures de A. Marie, les *Vengeurs*, les *Faucheurs de la mort*; surtout aux dessins comiques de Draner et de Faustin. . . . Les choses du jour étaient le *Mot d'ordre* et les fantaisies, admirables, de Vallès et de Vermersch au *Cri du Peuple*.
> Telle était la littérature — du 25 février au 10 mars.

> [Let's talk Paris . . . We stopped in front of engravings by A. Marie, the *Vengeurs*, the *Faucheurs de la mort* ; and especially the cartoons by Draner and Faustin. . . . The items for the day were the *Mot d'ordre* (Rochefort's journal which appeared from February 1 to May 20, 1871) and the admirable fantasies by Vallès and Vermersch in the *Cri du Peuple*.
> Such was literature — from February 25 to March 10.]

"Such was literature": Rimbaud expands the boundaries of literature to include propaganda, political "fantasies," engravings, and caricature—ephemeral, satirical genres afloat in a complex set of social discourses and representations. The function of literature is less to signify than to point to an entirely revolutionary situation; far from providing a décor for the "real" social conflict taking place, the small revolutionary periodicals, the cartoons and wall art in fact serve to *articulate* that conflict. Literature is affiliated with the *mot d'ordre*, the slogan, rather than with the metaphor.

Partial liberalization of the press laws had occurred under the Second Empire in 1868, but the progressive collapse of censorship from September 1870 to June 1871, as Adrian Rifkin's work has shown, marked this period as one of unparalleled experimentation in political imagery in France. Caricatures that appeared in popular newspapers like *La Charge*, to which Rimbaud sent his poem "Trois baisers," or *Le Hanneton*, whose editor, Vermersch, played such an important role in Commune culture, were most often printed on separate sheets, colored by hand, sold by street vendors, and stuck up on walls and fences:

> During this time the walls burst out laughing. *Paris-gavroche*, *Paris-voyou*, *Paris-catin* are all convulsed in front of the caricatures that ingenious merchants hang with pins on their front doors. . . . Who is drawing these strange images, devilishly colored, vulgar, rarely pleasant, often obscene? They are signed with unknown names, pseudonyms undoubtedly; their probable authors—among whom it's said that we should have to count talented artists—make one think of upper-class libertine women who have gotten mixed up in some orgy and who are seen naked, but masked; or of satyrs who wear a fig leaf that covers only their faces. (Mendès, 159-60)

In his description of the caricatures and their anonymous authors, Mendès allows a slippage to take place from the work to its composer: obscene caricatures have obscene authors; libertine women or satyrs. By using these analogies Mendès denounces what he takes to be talented (middle-class) artists "slumming" in debased representations, using their talents in the service of the insurrection, becoming, like Mendès's *bête noire*, Courbet, *encanaillé*. And in so doing Mendès himself can be seen manipulating what are perhaps the two most distinctive aspects of Commune cultural forms, namely, overtly erotic representations and defamatory invective and gesture. The insult, perhaps the most characteristic and the richest stylistic form of the Commune, did not limit itself to ephemeral social groupuscules, but was instead widely integrated into social, political, and everyday speech. And while the political cartoonists and sloganeers of the Commune go plundering somewhat indiscriminately in the stockpile of revolutionary images and representations, a close examination of these caricatures and verbal forms as a group compared to those of the decade preceding the Commune shows a decisive "liberation" of form and theme in the direction of overtly erotic representations. Particularly widespread—on both the left and the right—was the practice of manipulating erotic imagery in the service of political denunciation: precisely Mendès's tactic in labeling pro-Commune artists and cartoonists "satyrs" or in accusing them of debased sexual slumming.

Rimbaud launches what he calls his "contemporary psalm," the "Chant de guerre parisien," directly into this fray of debated and disputed sexual/political forms. Written in May of 1871, the "Chant de guerre" is undoubtedly Rimbaud's most successful attempt to breach the barrier between high art and *reportage*:

> Le printemps est évident, car
> Du coeur des Propriétés vertes,
> Le vol de Thiers et de Picard
> Tient ses splendeurs grandes ouvertes!
>
> O Mai! Quels délirants culs nus!
> Sèvres, Meudon, Bagneux, Asnières,
> Ecoutez donc les bienvenus
> Semer les choses printanières!
>
> Ils ont schako, sabre et tam-tam,
> Non la vieille boîte à bougies;
> Et des yoles qui n'ont jam . . . jam . . .
> Fendent le lac aux eaux rougies!
>
> Plus que jamais nous bambochons
> Quand viennent sur nos fourmilières
> Crouler les jaunes cabochons
> Dans des aubes particulières:
>
> Thiers et Picard sont des Eros
> Des enleveurs d'héliotropes,
> Au pétrole ils font des Corots:
> Voici hannetonner leurs tropes . . .
>
> Ils sont familiers du Grand Truc! . . .
> Et couché dans les glaïeuls, Favre
> Fait son cillement aqueduc,
> Et ses reniflements à poivre!
>
> La grand'ville a le pavé chaud
> Malgré vos douches de pétrole,
> Et décidément, il nous faut
> Vous secouer dans votre rôle . . .
>
> Et les Ruraux qui se prélassent
> Dans de longs accroupissements,

Entendront des rameaux qui cassent
Parmi les rouges froissements.

[Spring is evidently here
For from the heart of the green Estates
The flight of Thiers and Picard
Lays its splendors wide open!

O May! What delirious bare asses!
Sèvres, Meudon, Bagneux, Asnières,
Listen to the welcome arrivals
Sowing springtime joys!

They have shakos, sabres, and tom-toms,
Not the old candle-box;
And boats that have nev . . . nev . . .
Cut through the lake of bloodied waters!

More than ever we carouse
As onto our ant-hills come
Tumbling the yellow heads
On those extraordinary dawns:

Thiers and Picard are Cupids
And ravishers of heliotropes too;
They paint Corots with petrol
Here their tropes buzz about . . .

They are all great friends of the Grand Turc!
And Favre, lying in his gladiolas
Blinks and weeps his crocodile tears
And sniffs his peppery sniff!

The Big City has hot cobblestones
Despite your showers of petrol;
And decidedly we have to
Shake you up in the roles you play

And the Rustics who loll about
In long squattings
Will hear boughs breaking
Among the red rustlings.]

The formal structure of the poem, with its octosyllabic verse, shows traces of the
conventional Provençal song, the *canso* or *chanson*; and indeed, at first glance,
the traditional elements of a pastoral love song have all been assembled: May,
Eros, flowers, sowing, dawn, even landscapes (Corots)—all the "springtime

joys'' (*choses printanières*). But the spring dawn is in fact the false sun of Versaillais incendiary bombing over Paris and its suburbs, the flowering is the flowering of artillery bombardment, and the peaceful Corot landscape is the city aflame.

Set adrift as it is in a sea of disputed contemporary political ''semes'' and representations, the poem has presented notorious difficulties for its modern readers. I would like to point to aspects of the poem that are exemplary of the difficulty sometimes encountered in charting the movement of particular terminology as it is appropriated in turn by left and right. This ideological slippage or ''borrowing'' is not, however, the source of all the ambiguities of the poem. The opening stanza, for instance, in which Thiers and Picard take flight, is ''straightforwardly'' ambiguous in its wordplay: the *vol* of Thiers and his minister of the Interior is at once an ascent to the green estates (*Propriétés*) of Versailles; a theft—the words *propriété* and *vol* in such close proximity can only be an echo of the famous slogan of Proudhon (whose work Rimbaud, according to his biographers, read avidly), ''Property is theft''; and a rape (*viol*). The idea of rape is reinforced within the poem by the term ''ravishers'' (*enleveurs*); Thiers and Picard have violated the true flowers of spring, the sun-loving heliotropes, metonyms for the insurgents who are turned toward the true light of the revolution.[26] (The Versaillais flower, by contrast, is the gladiola, whose connotations as a flower of death and war—''little swords''—reappear in the ''Dormeur du Val'': the dead soldier lies with his feet in the gladiolas.) The rape by the Versaillais that opens the poem announces a general theme of obscenity (the ''delirious bare asses,'' the ''wide open splendors''), which bears some comment, particularly in relation to Rimbaud's use of scatological references elsewhere in his poetry. In some of his other early verse—poems like ''Vénus Anadyomène'' or ''Accroupissements,'' for example—or in his collaboration with the Zutistes, Rimbaud's production of scatological imagery can be read as a defiant but vague cultural gesture directed against the overwhelmingly strict censorship of a political regime intent on enforcing strict moral norms while itself disregarding those norms. In this poem the target is explicitly the hypocrisy and vulgarity of the Versaillais; as such, the poem participates in a whole system of working-class or popular puritanism whereby sexual perversion or depravity comes to function as a metonym for the entire structure of social inequality. In this system, erotic perversity stands in for the general luxury, waste, and parasitic behavior of the privileged classes. While such imagery was prevalent during the Commune, it can certainly be found in material from the last years of the Empire—in disparaging references to the sexual habits of the emperor and his family, for example. This construction of sexual depravity as the activity of the privileged can be found in Rimbaud's two other most overtly Commune poems, ''L'Orgie parisienne ou Paris se repeuple,'' and ''Les Mains de Jeanne-Marie.''

Figure 5. Moloch, *Tentative de viol*. Thiers assaulting the Republic. Courtesy Bibliothèque Nationale.

And in the caricature, *Tentative de viol*, for instance, Thiers, labeled with a *fleur-de-lis*, is shown assaulting the Republic, while Favre, the minister of foreign affairs under Thiers, holds a candle. (Many such representations of the Republic fending off sexual assault can be found.)[27] Its artist, Moloch (a pseudonym for Alphonse Hector Colomb), is precisely the kind of artist who would qualify for an accusation from Mendès of sexual depravity (another artist "servicing" the Commune . . .); in Rimbaud's poem, however, depravity is clearly the property of the Versaillais.

"Thiers and Picard are Cupids [*des Eros*]": by now in the poem, "Eros" has only nonneutral (i.e., obscene) connotations. Favre appears in the next line adopting the characteristic pose he shows in all the revolutionary caricatures of the period: weeping crocodile tears after having negotiated France's capitulation to the Prussians. With Favre, the three Versaillais leaders fall into place as the *Trois Grâces*, shown here in a popular anonymous cartoon depicting the three as nude political prostitutes cavorting for the favors of imperialist regimes, and particularly for the king of Prussia. "They are great friends of the *Grand Truc*": original versions of the poem show *Grand Turc* instead of *Grand Truc*; editors have opted, wrongly I think, for the latter. For *Grand Turc*, according to Delvau,

LA COMÉDIE POLITIQUE.

En Scène.   Derrière le Rideau.

Figure 6. La Comédie politique. En scène. Derrière le rideau (signed E.D.). Courtesy Bibliothèque Nationale.

was a working-class designation for the king of Prussia; and in the Coppée poem that undoubtedly forms an intertext with "Chant de guerre parisien," a poem entitled "Chant de guerre circassien," the widows of warriors are invited to sell themselves to Turkish merchants.

But the Versaillais trio is also, and in a real sense, a trio of zeros (*des Eros*) and not heros: zeros, or what Delvau's dictionary lists as popular slang for men without value, energy, consistency, or anything. This signification is obviously at work in the Derville caricature, undated, but probably from the end of the

Figure 7. Les Trois Grâces (Musée de Versailles). Anonymous. Picard, Thiers, and Favre. Courtesy Bibliothèque Nationale.

Empire, entitled *Triomphe des Zeros*. Rife with anticlerical iconography, the caricature shows an empty banquet table; one thermometer hanging on the wall

TRIOMPHE DES ZÉROS.

Figure 8. Triomphe des Zéros (signed E. Derville). Courtesy Bibliothèque Nationale.

behind the table registers the government as midway between a dictatorship and a monarchy, while another thermometer registering "talent, courage, and ability," reads zero.

The true difficulty of the poem comes in the fifth stanza, specifically in its last, virtually untranslatable line, "Voici hannetonner leurs tropes," and even more specifically, in the word *hannetonner*. The word *hanneton* (mayfly) radiates with a wealth of connotations. Some of its ambiguities are suggested in this passage from Gustave Lefrançais's Commune memoirs where the insects are at once the insurgents (who have literally "replaced" them that spring) and the whirring hum of the Versaillais bombardment:

> The bombardment, announced only the day before by the official
> Versaillais journal [*l'Officiel*], has in fact been going on since April 3
> throughout the area, but it is now more violent than ever before.
>   We have all, for some time now, gotten used to the whirring noise of
> the shells, which the Communards compare very accurately, I think, to
> the hum [*bourdonnement*] of mayflies [*hannetons*]—insects that, by the

Figure 9. Delahaye. *Le Nouveau Juif errant.* Photo by Kristin Ross, from Carré, *Autour de Verlaine et de Rimbaud.*

way, frightened no doubt by our gunfire, show no sign of life this year.[28]

A *hanneton* is first of all a mayfly or cockchafer; *Le Hanneton* was the title of a republican journal and satirical review suppressed under the imperial censor and revived and edited by Vermersch under the Commune. The word thus has full revolutionary connotations, to which Flaubert seems to allude in the entry under this word in his *Dictionnaire des idées recues*: "Children of spring. A good subject for a pamphlet. Their destruction is the dream of every prefect."[29] In addition, the term plays a part in the personal, insectile vocabulary developed by Rimbaud and his intimates; like *l'oestre* (gadfly), the term seems to designate Rimbaud himself. A drawing by Delahaye illustrating Rimbaud's return on foot from Austria in 1875 shows him crossing the Black Forest with a single stride under the wings of a *hanneton colossale*, a huge mayfly. Such associations link the swarms of mayflies to the revolutionary insurgents, themselves "children of May," who have already been compared in the preceding stanza by means of *fourmilières* (anthills) with insects. In this case the line reads relatively straightforwardly: "Voici hannetonner leurs tropes" refers to the Versaillais troops (as well as to their rhetoric, in the more evident sense of *tropes*) wiping out (demayflying) the swarm of insurgents. But *hannetonner* as a verb, Delvau informs us, was a popular slang expression meaning to act like a child, to con-

duct oneself foolishly—this meaning most likely derived from the slang significance of *hanneton* as a mania, a fixed idea (thus the manic, satiric dimension of
the journal *Le Hanneton*). Hence the Versaillais troops (and tropes) behave child-
ishly; indeed, the Versaillais are associated elsewhere in the poem with childish
elements (the boat that nev . . . nev . . .: a popular nineteenth-century children's
song, a sort of "Little Engine That Couldn't"; the tom-tom, both a toy and, once
again, inflated rhetoric or tropes). Read in this way, as Steve Murphy maintains,
the *hannetons* are the Versaillais whom the Communards, at the end of the poem,
are seen shaking out of the trees. Aimé Césaire provides an interesting intertext
that supports this reading. His poem about the revolutionary Haitian poet René
Depestre includes a stanza where the *hannetons* are the outdated poetic forms
that are choking the life energy out of the springtime revolution:

> j'aime mieux regarder le printemps. Justement
> c'est la révolution
>   et les formes qui s'attardent
> à nos oreilles bourdonnant
> ce sont mangeant le neuf qui lève
> mangeant les pousses
> de gras hannetons hannetonnant le printemps.

> [I'd rather look at the spring. Precisely
> it is the revolution
>   and the forms which linger
> humming in our ears
> are, eating the new which sprouts
> eating the shoots
>   fat cockchafers cockchafing the spring.][30]

Once again the insect or parasite (the one who does not work) functions ambig-
uously: either as the Versaillais, the ruling class of parasites, or as the swarm of
insurgents who have put down their tools for arms and who carouse (*bambochons*).

If sexual depravity is the mark of the Versaillais, then carousing is the activity
of the insurgents. A *bambocheur*, according to Delvau, was, in working-class
circles, an idler, a drunk, or generally, a *débauché*: in short, a *sublime*. Again in
this poem Rimbaud attributes positive value to intoxication; in so doing he reap-
propriates and manipulates to his own end one of the leading weapons of bourgeois antiworker racism. In a host of nineteenth-century writings on workers
from Zola to Denis Poulot, a fatal, quasi-racial propensity to drunkenness (as
well as to laziness) becomes the crucial quality or "vice" in the construction of
the "type" of the "bad worker."[31] Bosses and managers in fact had nothing
against alcohol per se; they tended rather to evaluate "vice" and "immorality"

as exactly proportional to the time that workers were not occupied by paid work or by minimal family upkeep. To draw the best profit from the work force, employers must monopolize the expenditure of energy of the workers—they must prevent them from mobilizing their energy elsewhere.

The bourgeois equation of intoxication and the crowd was of course particularly prevalent in right-wing histories of the Commune. Edmond de Goncourt's questions are typical: "How much is wine responsible for whetting patriotic, liberal, Communard feelings in this uprising? What strange statistics might be gathered about all the wine drunk during this period and the part it plays in national heroism?"[32] However, the association of drunkenness and the crowd appears even in the etymology of the invective used by the upper classes throughout the century to designate "the masses." During the Commune, monarchist journals refer to the crowd either as *la vile multitude* (a phrase originally attributed to Thiers), *la crapule*, or *la canaille*, and hearken back, in an almost incantatory way, to "la canaille de 1789, de 1830, de 1848."[33] *Crapule* is derived directly from the Latin *crapula* (drunkenness); in this light we might reconsider Rimbaud's verb choice when he writes to Izambard in May 1871: "Now I'm depraving myself [*je m'encrapule*] as much as I can." (He goes on to establish the activity of *s'encrapuler* as a virtual synonym for the "calculated disordering of the senses.") *Canaille*, from the Latin *cane* (dog), carries with it associations of debauchery, and specifically drunkenness. In a characteristic move of appropriating invective and making it his own, the blacksmith in the closing moments of Rimbaud's "Le Forgeron" will proclaim his membership in the vile multitude: "Oh! The air is full of the smell of battle! What was I saying? I'm part of the rabble!" ("Je suis de la canaille.") Rimbaud's blacksmith here echoes proclamations like the one by Vermersch in *Le Père Duchêne* (December 1869): "We belong to the rabble [*la canaille*]!"[34] Or the one that thousands attending a *fête populaire* in the Tuileries in April 1871 heard and joined in as they listened to popular singer La Bordas perform Darcier's 1865 song, "La Canaille":

> "La Canaille" is the revolutionary hymn of the new era; an apology, a glorification of the wronged worker. Just as the insurgents in sixteenth-century Holland donned the title of scoundrel [*gueux*] that the Spanish branded them with, so the insurgents at the end of the Empire, the terrorized vanquished of the June days of 1848, the workers, sworn to hatred of these foppish Royalists of 1869, embrace the word *canaille* that is thrown in their faces as the supreme insult. . . . All the verses of that poor rhapsody resound and ring out from her mouth like swords, and the profound refrain:

> > C'est d'la Canaille!
> > Eh bien! . . . j'en suis!

[It's the rabble!
And yes . . . I'm one of them!]

clacks beneath her tongue like the red scarf used to enflame the furor of the bull.[35]

What is invective or denigration when spoken by some, is reappropriated and refashioned by others into a rallying cry, a slogan, an expression of solidarity. Thus the adjectives Rimbaud uses most consistently in his manifesto (the Voyant letters) to describe poetic activity—adjectives like *hideux, immonde, monstrueux, difforme*—are exactly those adjectives used in anti-Communard literature to describe the Communards and their activities.[36] This is not really surprising, since all of these adjectives in some sense connote disorder, and the semantic opposition between "order" and "disorder" during the Second Empire was not at all politically neutral. "Order" becomes the symbol of a triumphant bourgeoisie—which refers to itself as "the party of order"—as well as its ideal. Even the proliferation in the Voyant letters of the prefix "in-," Rimbaud's favorite prefix ("il s'agit d'arriver à l'*in*connu . . . *in*effable torture . . . les choses *in*ouies et *in*nomables . . . si c'est *in*forme il donne de l'*in*forme . . . la femme arrivera à l'*in*connu," etc.), can be read politically, since prefixes essentially translate relations.[37]

Anti-Communard rhetoric like that of Daudet, who called the Commune "Paris au pouvoir des nègres," or like that of Gautier, who described the Communards as "savages, a ring through their noses, tattooed in red, dancing a scalp dance on the smoking debris of society,"[38] aimed at establishing a massive racially constituted category that would include in one breath animals, workers (particularly working-class women), barbarians, savages, and thieves. Much of Rimbaud's strategy consists of reappropriating and *affirming*, as he does in the letters and elsewhere, anti-Communard invective. While anti-Communard literature sought to establish a *racial* connection between "savages" and workers, Rimbaud, particularly in poems like "Mauvais Sang" and "Démocratie," instead reaffirms the *political* connection that indeed exists between oppressed workers in European capitals and the colonial *outre-mer* oppressed. In this context we might also consider Rimbaud's own embracing of or construction of himself as *voyou*: the worst possible "type" in anti-Communard diatribe.[39] The *voyou* first appears in 1830, as a term systematically used by the bourgeoisie; Flaubert uses it in *L'Education sentimentale* to refer to the insurgents of 1848. The *voyou* is something like the limit case of laziness as ideological refusal, for the bad worker, though lazy, works, if only ineffectually; the *voyou* refuses all work.

The term "assassins," another favorite of Rimbaud's ("Now is the hour of the assassins!"), was another prevalent anti-Communard insult, especially between March and May of 1871. The government at Versailles and its press stigmatized the "crimes" of the Commune, such as the execution of the hostages, by calling the insurgents "assassins." Gautier, for instance, calls the Communards "d'atroces scélerats, des assassins, des incendiaires." (The Communards reply in turn with *bombardeurs*, referring to the Versaillais bombings of the western and southwestern *quartiers* of Paris that took many victims.) "Assassins" was used interchangeably by the Versaillais with *barbares* (cf. Rimbaud's poem by that title) and *sauvages*, even *Peaux-Rouges*—this last usage sheds new light on the liberationary trio of the boat, the child, and the *Peaux-rouges* in the opening stanzas of "Le Bateau ivre."

V. N. Vološinov has written about this particular volatility of the sign in revolutionary periods, the way in which a given ideological sign's embeddedness, its overdetermination, is shaken like a loose tooth as the sign becomes disputed, appropriated, and *intended* for a chosen usage:

> Each living ideological sign has two faces, like Janus. Any current
> curse word can become a word of praise, any current truth must
> inevitably sound to many other people as the greatest lie. This inner
> dialectical quality of the sign comes out fully in the open only during
> times of social crisis or revolutionary changes. In the ordinary
> conditions of life, the contradiction embedded in every ideological sign
> cannot fully emerge because the ideological sign in an established,
> dominant ideology is always somewhat reactionary and tries, as it were,
> to stabilize the preceding factor in the dialectical flux of the social
> generative process, so accentuating yesterday's truth as to make it
> appear today's.[40]

The term "Commune" itself is an interesting case in point. As one scholar of the Commune puts it, "The Commune was at once the thing and the rallying cry, the reality and the sign, the fact and the ideology."[41] That is, the term corresponded both to a state of affairs, a form of social relations that had already been realized during the siege of Paris, and to the hope for a radical political transformation involving universal (male) suffrage, and the transmission of power to elected, revocable deputies. The slogan "Vive la Commune!" which was already ending workers' meetings in the last months of 1870, helped recall the battle cry of the Commune of 1793; as a slogan, the term "Commune" had come to embody a host of working-class hopes and a swarm of bourgeois fears. Why did it cause such panic? Because, as one observer noted, "There's blood on that word."[42]

In both cases the affective charge of the word had gained precedence over its semantic content. As with all slogans, affectivity destabilizes semantic content; what is transmitted is not a precise meaning but rather the desires that mobilized a particular situation, and that have survived, in a compressed or frozen, lapidary form, only to be reawakened and reanimated decades later.

In the late 1860s the very practice of sloganeering underwent a mutation. The word "slogan," which had always designated a rallying cry—the word derives from the Celtic meaning "battle cry of the dead"—acquired, for the first time, an additional meaning: that of the brief, striking phrase used in advertising or commercial promotion. A 1929 Russian film about the Commune entitled *La Nouvelle Babylone* (with subtitle, appropriately, the Commune slogan "A l'assaut du ciel!") illustrates this dialectics-at-a-standstill perfectly.[43] The film collapses Marx's writings on the Commune into Zola's great department store novel, *Au bonheur des dames*; in one particularly memorable scene, grand pianos are pushed out of department store windows to be used for building barricades. Rimbaud was particularly attuned to the contemporary use of sloganeering in the 1870s—the one available only after a certain stage of commodity production and distribution had been reached. In the *Album zutique* he published a sonnet entitled "Paris" composed entirely of advertising pitches lifted from neighborhood storefronts. And in what is perhaps his most moving prose poem, "Solde," a poem structured as one long advertising spiel, revolutionary euphoria becomes as marketable a commodity as anything else. In an atmosphere made up of equally magic and modern installations, the revolutionary cry and the advertising slogan are indistinguishable from each other in an onslaught of consumer goods and services:

A vendre les corps sans prix, hors de toute race, de tout monde, de toute sexe, de toute descendance! Les richesses jaillissant à chaque démarche! Solde de diamants sans contrôle!
A vendre l'anarchie pour les masses; la satisfaction irrépressible pour les amateurs supérieurs; la mort atroce pour les fidèles et les amants!
A vendre les habitations et les migrations, sports, féeries et conforts parfaits, et le bruit, le mouvement et l'avenir qu'ils font!

[For sale—
Priceless bodies, beyond race or world or sex or lineage! Riches in ubiquitous flood! Unrestricted sale of diamonds!
For sale—
Anarchy for the masses; wild satisfaction for knowing amateurs; Atrocious death for the faithful and for lovers!
For sale—
Homesteads and migrations, sports, enchantment and perfect comfort, and the noise, the movement and the future they entail.]

To the extent that Rimbaud is *not* remembered for his metaphors, he is remembered instead in the form of slogans. Rimbaud has been transmitted culturally to us *as* a series of slogans. "Changer la vie." "L'amour est à réinventer." "Je est un autre." "Il faut être absolument moderne." (By contrast, the names of Baudelaire and Mallarmé do not evoke a single slogan.) The fact that Rimbaud comes to us in the particular form of the slogan bears some relationship to the peculiar future of his text, his ascendencies and declines, the moments and geography of the diffusion or neglect of his work. Rimbaud's verse orchestrates the battle cry of the dead: the dead of 1892 and 1893, the "ever-growing crowd of somber ghosts," the "thousands, on the fields of France . . . of yesterday's dead"—a past and passing crowd of fellow travelers. But the goal of such an orchestration is to call forth or beckon to a future crowd ("These poets will be!"). This interpellation *across* generations, a kind of diachronic constellation or latent community, does much to undermine the classically generative or Oedipal model of poetic lineage and transmission—but it does, nevertheless, raise the question of transmission, of continuity. How is a contestatory text transmitted?

A slogan might, in Alice Kaplan's words, offer a particular condensed accounting for history, and "if the suggestion it offers is sufficiently powerful in the *social* sense of the term, it will be, as it were, 'present' for the interpretation of the next historical event even *as it happens.*"[44] In this way, she continues, "Interpretive form actually carries its effect into the real: history is telling and making at once." Rimbaud's "presence" in May 1968, as libidinal precursor, as slogan ("Changer la vie"), his "presence," before that, for the Surrealists, a group whose writings, as Walter Benjamin pointed out, are not "literature" but something else—"demonstrations, watchwords, bluffs, forgeries";[45] his "presence" for a Caribbean poet like Aimé Césaire who chooses to create a distinctly similar poetics of interjection and parataxis—this presence is not so much the inheritance of a "thing" or an artistic monument as the embracing of a situation, a posture in the world: the conditions for community, the invention or dream of new social relations. What is transmitted is not a solitary, reified literary monument but rather the often prescient strategies that constructed and mobilized it and, what is more, *prevented* its own monumentalization. The process, in other words, is one of historical relays and not an architectonic problem of the model or monument. It suggests a powerful notion of repetition quite close to Kierkegaard's where repetition, instead of being repetition of the same, is experienced in terms of a "breaking forth," a "passage beyond." And the future of a text, its "future vigor," the strategies it will help form, its displacement across generations, is, in the case of Rimbaud, the most vital part of its history and its contribution to history. For the force of an idea lies primarily in its ability to be displaced.

Notes

1. The term *démocratie* undergoes a profound modification during the Second Empire when it is appropriated by the imperial regime in opposition to the bourgeois regime—the emperor claiming to have given back to the people its sovereignty. See Dubois, *Le Vocabulaire politique et social en France de 1869 à 1872* (Paris: Larousse, 1962), 109-110. Republicans and Socialists hesitated to use such a tainted word; Blanqui, for example, in 1852, writes, "Qu'est-ce que donc qu'un démocrate,

je vous prie? C'est là un mot vague, banal, sans acception précise, un mot en caoutchouc.'' (''What is a democrat, I ask you? This is a vague and banal word, one without any precise meaning, a rubber word.'') Rimbaud plays with the ideological slippage of the term when he entitles his parody of colonial discourse, ''Democracy.''

2. ''There is a zoo of pleasures to Rabelais. To Rimbaud . . . It would be wrong to say the zoo was a jungle, but the animals did not seem to have cages.'' Jack Spicer, ''A Fake Novel about the Life of Arthur Rimbaud,'' in *The Collected Books* (Los Angeles: Black Sparrow Press, 1975), 154.

3. Jean-Paul Sartre, *Saint Genet: Actor and Martyr*, trans. Bernard Frechtman (New York: Braziller, 1963), 463-68. Sartre's emphasis.

4. Hugo Friedrich, *Structure of Modern Poetry*, trans. Joachim Neugroschel (Evanston, Ill.: Northwestern University Press, 1974), 56.

5. ''L'eau verte pénétra ma coque de sapin / Et des taches de vins bleus et des vomissures / Me lava, dispersant gouvernail et grappin'' (''Soaked the green water through my hull of pine, / Scattering helm and grappling and washing me / Of the stains, the vomitings and blue wine''); ''Le Bateau ivre''; ''Le matin où, avec Elle, vous vous débattîtes parmi les éclats de neige, les lèvres vertes, les glaces, les drapeaux noirs et les rayons bleus, et les parfums pourpres du soleil des pôles, — ta force.'' (''The morning when, with Her, you struggled in the glaring snow, the green lips, ice, the black banners, the blue rays of light, and the purple perfumes of the polar sun — your strength.'') ''Métropolitain.''

6. See Harald Weinrich, *Metafora e menzogna: la serenita dell'arte* (Bologna: Il Molina, 1976), 55-114. My thanks to Franco Moretti for alerting me to this text.

7. Tzvetan Todorov, ''Poetry without Verse,'' in Mary Ann Caws and Hermine Riffaterre (eds.), *The Prose Poem in France* (New York: Columbia University Press, 1983), 70.

8. Todorov, ''A Complication of Text: The Illuminations,'' in Todorov (ed.), *French Literary Theory Today*, trans. R. Carter (Cambridge: Cambridge University Press, 1982), 233.

9. Lucien Descaves, *Philémon: Vieux de la vieille* (Paris: Albin Michel, 1913), 170.

10. B. Gastineau, *Le Carnaval* (Paris, 1854), cited in Jacques Rancière, ''Le Bon Temps ou la barrière des plaisirs,'' in *Révoltes logiques* 7 (1978): 45.

11. Eugène Vermersch, ''Les Incendiaires'' in Jean Varloot (ed.), *Les Poètes de la Commune* (Paris: Les éditeurs français réunis, 1951). Rimbaud, in ''Les Mains de Jeanne-Marie,'' his Commune poem celebrating the role women played in the insurrection, makes a pun on the term *incendiaire*:

> Une tache de populace
> Les brunit comme *un sein d'hier*;
> Le dos de ces Mains est la place
> Qu'en baisa tout Révolté fier!

> [A stain of the mob
> Browns them like the breasts of yesteryear;
> The backs of these Hands are the place
> Where every proud Rebel has kissed them!]

12. Todorov, ''A Complication of Text,'' 232.

13. Barron, *Sous le drapeau rouge* (Paris: Albert Savine, 1889), 40-41.

14. See Elias Canetti, *Crowds and Power*, trans. Carol Stewart (New York: Farrar, Straus & Giroux, 1962), 29.

15. John Ashbery, ''An Interview with John Ashbery,'' *San Francisco Review of Books* 3 (November 1977): 9. Ashbery's emphasis.

16. V. N. Vološinov, *Marxism and the Philosophy of Language*, trans. Ladislav Matejka and I. R. Titunik (Cambridge, Mass.: Harvard University Press, 1986), 115.

17. Rimbaud, letter to Delahaye, May 1873, *Oeuvres complètes*, 288. See also his letter to Izambard, August 25, 1870: "Ma ville natale est supérieurement idiote entre les petites villes de province. Sur cela, voyez-vous, je n'ai plus d'illusions. Parce qu'elle est à côté de Mézières, — une ville qu'on ne trouve pas, — parce qu'elle voit pérégriner dans ses rues deux ou trois cents de pioupious, cette benoîte population gesticule, prud'hommesquement spadassine, bien autrement que les assiégés de Metz et de Strasbourg! C'est effrayant, les épiciers retraités qui revêtent l'uniforme! C'est épatant comme ça a du chien, les notaires, les vitriers, les percepteurs, les menuisiers et tous les ventres, qui, chassepot au coeur, font du patrouillotisme aux portes de Mézières! ma patrie se lève! . . . Moi, j'aime mieux la voir assise." *Ventre* is popular working-class slang for the propertied class; with *patrouillotism* Rimbaud combines *patriotisme* with *patroller* and with *trouille*: a slang term meaning to be afraid (with connotations, dating from the fifteenth century, of excrement, i.e., to shit in one's pants from fear). Rimbaud's earliest schoolboy writings consist of experiments with curses and obscenities strung together: "Ah! saperlipotte de saperlipopette! sapristi! saperlipopettouille! . . . saperlipouille!" Here, he combines *peter* (to fart) with *pouilles*, from *pouiller* (to insult, taken originally from *s'epouiller*, to look for fleas; *pouillerie* were people ridden with fleas and other vermin).

18. For a collection of the sketches and drawings exchanged between Verlaine, Rimbaud, Delahaye, and Nouveau, see Jean-Marie Carré, *Autour de Verlaine et de Rimbaud* (Paris: Université de Paris, 1949).

19. See Jean-Pierre Chambon, "Les Sobriquets de Delahaye (Notes pour l'analyse de l'onomastique privée du groupe Rimbaud/Verlaine/Nouveau/Delahaye)," *Parade Sauvage*, Bulletin no. 2 (January 1986): 69-81.

20. See Gilles Deleuze and Félix Guattari, *Mille Plateaux* (Paris: Minuit, 1980), 123.

21. Catulle Mendès, *Les 73 journées de la Commune* (Paris: E. Lachaud, 1871), 230-31.

22. Susan Lambert, "The Caricatures," in [Victoria and Albert Museum], *The Franco-Prussian War and the Commune in Caricature* (London: Thanet, 1971), 5.

23. Mendès, *Les 73 journées*, 112.

24. Barron, *Drapeau rouge*, 70-71.

25. George Becker (ed. and trans.), *Paris under Siege 1870-1871: From the Goncourt Journal* (Ithaca, N.Y.: Cornell University Press, 1969), 259.

26. See Steve Murphy's reading of this poem in "Le Regard de Rimbaud," *Revue des sciences humaines* 1 (1984), 57-62.

27. I am indebted to Adrian Rifkin's discussion of Commune caricature in "No Particular Thing to Mean," *Block* 8 (1983): 43-44.

28. Gustave Lefrançais, *Souvenirs d'un révolutionnaire* (1886; reprint, Paris: Société Encyclopédique Française and Edition de la Têtes de Feuilles, 1972), 407.

29. Gustave Flaubert, *Dictionnaire des idées recues* (Paris: Aubier, 1978), 88.

30. Aimé Césaire, "Le Verbe marronner / à René Depestre, poète haitien," in *The Collected Poetry*, trans. Clayton Eshleman and Annette Smith (Berkeley: University of California Press, 1983), 370.

31. See, in particular, Alain Cottereau's introduction to Denis Poulot, *Le Sublime, ou le travailleur comme il est en 1870, et ce qu'il peut être* (Paris: Maspero, 1980), esp. 17-24.

32. Becker (ed. and trans.), *Goncourt Journal*, 266.

33. Dubois, *Vocabulaire politique*, 94.

34. *Le Père Duchêne*, December 7, 1869. Recent readings of "Le Forgeron" have shown the explicit target of the crowd's invective, Louis XVI, to be in fact an oblique representation of Napoléon III. A bourgeois revolution is replaced anachronistically with a proletarian revolution synchronic with Rimbaud's own situation in 1870. See Marc Ascione, "Le Forgeron, ou 'dans la langue

d'Esope,''' *Parade Sauvage* 2 (April 1985): 12-20, and Steve Murphy, ''La Figure du forgeron,'' *Parade Sauvage*, Bulletin 2 (January 1986): 15-23.

35. Barron, *Drapeau rouge*, 123-24.

36. See Lidsky, *Les Ecrivains contre la Commune* (Paris: Maspero, 1982), 151.

37. Around the time of the Commune, ''in-'' is part of the prefixal system of political vocabulary designating opposition; it would be replaced progressively in subsequent decades by the political lexicon of ''non-.'' See Chapter V of Dubois, *Vocabulaire politique*.

38. Théophile Gautier, letter to his daughter, cited in E. Tersen, *Vive la Commune!* (Paris: Editions Sociales, 1951), 25.

39. See Lidsky, *Ecrivains contre*, 108-11.

40. Vološinov, *Marxism and the Philosophy of Language*, 23-24.

41. Maurice Dommanget, *Hommes et choses de la Commune*, cited in Lefebvre, *La Proclamation de la Commune* (Paris: Gallimard, 1965), 139.

42. J. Le Berquier, quoted in Dubois, *Vocabulaire politique*, 113.

43. For a French translation of the film scenario, see Grigori Kozintsev and Léonid Trauberg, *La Nouvelle Babylone*, in *L'Avant-scène du cinéma*, December 1, 1978, 3-56.

44. Alice Kaplan, *Reproductions of Banality: Fascism, Literature, and French Intellectual Life* (Minneapolis: University of Minnesota Press, 1986), 67-68.

45. Walter Benjamin, ''Surrealism,'' in Peter Demetz (ed.), *Reflections*, trans. Edmund Jephott (New York: Harcourt Brace Jovanovich, 1978), 179.

Bibliography

Bibliography

Angenot, Mark. *La Parole pamphlétaire: Contribution à la typologie des discours modernes*. Paris: Payot, 1982.

Ascione, Marc. "Le Forgeron, ou 'dans la langue d'Esope'." *Parade Sauvage* 2 (April 1985): 12-20.

Ashbery, John. "An Interview with John Ashbery." *San Francisco Review of Books* 3 (November 1977): 8-13.

Bakunin, Michael. *Bakunin on Anarchism*. Ed. Sam Dolgoff. Montreal: Black Rose Books, 1980.

Barron, Louis. *Sous le drapeau rouge*. Paris: Albert Savine, 1889.

Barthes, Roland. "Nautilus et Bateau ivre." In *Mythologies*, pp. 90-92. Paris: Seuil, 1957.

Baudry, Jean-Louis. "Le Texte de Rimbaud." *Tel Quel*, no. 35 (Autumn 1968): 47-63; no. 36 (Winter 1969): 34-53.

Becker, George, ed. and trans. *Paris under Siege 1870-1871: From the Goncourt Journal*. Ithaca, N.Y.: Cornell University Press, 1969.

Beckett, Samuel, trans. "Drunken Boat." In *Collected Poems in English and French*, pp. 92-105. New York: Grove, 1977.

Benjamin, Walter. "Surrealism." In *Reflections*, ed. Peter Demetz, trans. Edmund Jephott, pp. 177-92. New York: Harcourt Brace Jovanovich, 1978.

Benjamin, Walter. *Understanding Brecht*. Trans. Anya Bostock. London: New Left Books, 1973.

Berque, Jacques, ed. *Nomades et vagabonds*. Paris: 10/18, 1975.

Bersani, Leo. "Rimbaud's Simplicity." In *A Future for Astyanax: Character and Desire in Literature*, pp. 230-58. Boston: Little, Brown, 1976.

Blanchot, Maurice. *The Gaze of Orpheus*. Trans. Lydia Davis. Barrytown, N.Y.: Station Hill Press, 1981.

Blanqui, Auguste. *Instructions pour un prise d'armes*. [1868] Paris: Editions de la Tête de Feuilles, 1972.

Borail, Jean, ed. *Les Sauvages dans la cité*. Paris: Champ Vallon, 1985.

Boudry, Robert. "Courbet et la Fédération des artistes." *Europe*, April-May 1951, 35-47.

Brecht, Bertolt. "Against George Lukács." Trans. Stuart Hood. In *Aesthetics and Politics*, pp. 68-85. London: New Left Books, 1977.

Brecht, Bertolt. "The Days of the Commune." Trans. Leonard Lehrman. In *Revolution and Reaction: The Paris Commune 1871*, ed. John Hicks and Robert Tucker, pp. 193-232. Amherst: University of Massachusetts Press, 1973.

Broc, Numa. "L'Etablissement de la géographie en France: diffusion, institutions, projets (1870-1890)." *Annales de la géographie* 83 (September-October 1974): 545-68.

Brown, Bruce. *Marx, Freud, and the Critique of Everyday Life: Toward a Permanent Cultural Revolution*. New York: Monthly Review Press, 1973.

Canetti, Elias. *Crowds and Power*. Trans. Carol Stewart. New York: Farrar, Straus & Giroux, 1962.

Carré, Jean-Marie. *Autour de Verlaine et de Rimbaud*. Paris: Université de Paris, 1949.

Castells, Manuel. *City and the Grassroots*. Berkeley: University of California Press, 1983.

Castoriadis, Cornélius. "Les Mouvements des années soixantes." In *Mai '68, Pouvoirs* 39 (1986): 107-16.

Césaire, Aimé. *The Collected Poetry*. Trans. Clayton Eshleman and Annette Smith. Berkeley: University of California Press, 1983.

Césaire, Aimé. *Discours sur le colonialisme*. Paris: Présence Africaine, 1955.

Chambon, Jean-Pierre. "Les Sobriquets de Delahaye (Notes pour l'analyse de l'onomastique privée du groupe Rimbaud/Verlaine/Nouveau/Delahaye)." *Parade Sauvage*, Bulletin no. 2 (January 1986): 69-81.

Choury, Maurice, ed. *Les Poètes de la Commune*. Paris: Segher, 1970.

Clastres, Pierre. *Society against the State*. Trans. Robert Hurley. New York: Urizen Press, 1977.

Clément, Jean-Baptiste. *1871: La Revanche des Communeux*. Vol I. Paris: Jean Marie, 1886-87.

Cluseret, Gustave-Paul. *Mémoires du général Cluseret*. 3 vols. Paris: Jules Levy, 1887-88.

Coetzee, John M. "Anthropology and the Hottentots." *Semiotica* 54 (1985): 87-95.

Cottereau, Alain. "Vie quotidienne et résistance ouvrière à Paris en 1870." Introduction to Denis Poulot, *Le Sublime, ou le travailleur comme il est en 1870, et ce qu'il peut être*, pp. 7-102. Paris: Maspero, 1980.

Dalotel, Alain, Alain Faure and Jean-Claude Freiermuth. *Aux origines de la Commune: Le Mouvement des réunions publiques à Paris 1868-1870*. Paris: Maspero, 1980.

Decaunes, Luc, ed. *La Poésie parnassienne de Gautier à Rimbaud*. Paris: Seghers, 1977.

Delahaye, Ernest. *Rimbaud: L'Artiste et l'être moral*. Paris: Albert Messein, 1923.

de Koninck, Rodolphe. "La géographie critique." In *Les Concepts de la géographie humaine*, ed. A. Bailly, pp. 121-32. Paris: Masson, 1984.

Deleuze, Gilles. *Nietzsche and Philosophy*. Trans. Hugh Tomlinson. New York: Columbia University Press, 1983.

Deleuze, Gilles, and Félix Guattari. *Mille Plateaux*. Paris: Editions de Minuit, 1980.

Delvau, Alfred. *Dictionnaire de la langue verte*. [1865-66] Paris: Marpon & Flammarion, 1883.

Depping, Guillaume. "Le Mouvement géographique." *Journal officiel de la République française*, October 23, 1881, 1-2.

Descaves, Lucien. *Philémon: Vieux de la vieille*. Paris: Albin Michel, 1913.

Dommanget, Maurice. *L'Enseignement, l'enfance et la culture sous la Commune*. Paris: Editions Librairie de l'Etoile, 1964.

Drapeyron, Ludovic. "Le But, la méthode et l'oeuvre de la *Revue de géographie*." *Revue de géographie* 9 (1881): 1-8.

Dubois, Jean. *Le Vocabulaire politique et social en France de 1869 à 1872*. Paris: Larousse, 1962.

Du Camp, Maxime. *Les Convulsions de Paris*. 4 vols. Paris: Hachette, 1878-79.

Dunbar, Gary. "Elisée Reclus, Geographer and Anarchist." *Antipode*, 10/11 (1979): 16-21.

Edwards, Stewart, ed. *The Communards of Paris, 1871*. Ithaca, N.Y.: Cornell University Press, 1973.

Edwards, Stewart. *The Paris Commune 1871*. Devon: Newton Abbot, 1972.

Eisensweig, Uri. *Territoires occupés de l'imaginaire juif*. Paris: Christian Bourgois, 1980.

Engels, Friedrich, and Paul Lafargue and Laura Lafargue. *Correspondance*. Vol. 1. Paris: Editions sociales, 1956.

Enzensberger, Hans. "Une théorie du tourisme." In *Culture ou mise en condition?* Trans. Bernard Lortholary, pp. 79-92. Paris: Juillard, 1965.

Febvre, Lucien. *La Terre et l'evolution humaine: Introduction géographique à l'histoire*. Paris: Renaissance du livre, 1922.

Fénéon, Félix. "Arthur Rimbaud: *Les Illuminations*." In *Le symboliste* (October 7, 1887); rpt. in *Oeuvres plus que complètes*, ed. Joan Halperin, vol. II, pp. 572-75. Geneva: Massot, 1970.

Ferry, Luc, and Alain Renaut. *La Pensée '68. Essai sur l'anti-humanisme contemporain*. Paris: Gallimard, 1985.

Flaubert, Gustave. *Dictionnaire des idées recues*. Paris: Aubier, 1978.

Friedrich, Hugo. *The Structure of Modern Poetry*. Trans. Joachim Neugroschel. Evanston, Ill.: Northwestern University Press, 1974.

Gascar, Pierre. *Rimbaud et la Commune*. Paris: Gallimard, 1971.

Gauny, Louis Gabriel. *Le Philosophe plébien*. Ed. Jacques Rancière. Paris: La Découverte, 1983.

Giblin, Béatrice. "Le Paysage, le terrain et les géographes." *Hérodote* 9 (1978): 74-89.

Glissant, Edouard. *L'Intention poétique*. Paris: Seuil, 1969.

Gorz, André, ed. *Critique de la division du travail*. Paris: Seuil, 1973.

Gros, Jules. "La Mer Saharienne et le Capitaine Roudaire." *L'Exploration: Journal des conquêtes de la civilisation sur tous les points du globe* 1 (1876): 220-24.

Guérin, Daniel. *Anarchism*. Intro. Noam Chomsky. New York: Monthly Review Press, 1970.

Hérisson, le Comte d'. *Nouveau journal d'un Officier d'ordonnance: La Commune*. Paris: Ollendorf, 1889.

Homberg, Théodore. *Etudes sur le vagabondage*. Paris: Forestier, 1880.

Hudson, Brian. "The New Geography and the New Imperialism: 1870-1918." *Antipode* 9 (September 1977): 12-19.

L'Internationale situationniste 1958-69. Paris: Champ-Libre, 1975; English version, ed. and trans. Ken Knabb, *Situationist International Anthology*. Berkeley: Bureau of Public Secrets, 1981.

Jameson, Fredric. *The Political Unconscious. Narrative as a Socially Symbolic Act*. Ithaca, N.Y.: Cornell University Press, 1981.

Jameson, Fredric. "Rimbaud and the Spatial Text." In *Re-writing Literary History*, ed. Tak-Wai Wong and M. A. Abbas, pp. 66-93. Hong Kong: Hong Kong University Press, 1984.

Juin, Hubert. "La Commune et les écrivains de son temps." *Magazine littéraire*, no. 50 (March 1971): 9-17.

Kaplan, Alice. *Reproductions of Banality: Fascism, Literature, and French Intellectual Life*. Minneapolis: University of Minnesota Press, 1986.

Kaplan, Alice, and Kristin Ross. "Introduction." *Everyday Life. Yale French Studies* 73 (Fall 1987): 1-4.

Kozintsev, Grigori, and Léonid Trauberg. *La Nouvelle Babylone*. Screenplay. In *L'Avant-scène du cinéma*. December 1, 1978, 3-56.

Lacoste, Yves. "A bas Vidal . . . Viva Vidal!" *Hérodote* 16 (1979): 68-81.

Lacoste, Yves. *La Géographie, ça sert d'abord à faire la guerre*. Paris: Maspero, 1982.

Lafargue, Paul. *Le Droit à la paresse*. [1880]; rpt. ed. Maurice Dommanget. Paris: Maspero, 1965.

Lafargue, Paul. *Idéalisme et matérialisme dans la conception de l'histoire*. Paris: de Lille, 1901.

Lautréamont, le Comte de (Isidore Ducasse). *Oeuvres complètes* Ed. Maurice Saillet. Paris: Livre de poche, 1963.

Leconte de Lisle, C. M. *Oeuvres diverses*. 4 vols. Paris: Société d'édition, 1978.

Lefebvre, Henri. *Critique de la vie quotidienne*. 3 vols. Paris: L'Arche, 1958-81.

Lefebvre, Henri. *Le Droit à la ville*. Paris: Anthropos, 1968.

Lefebvre, Henri. *La Proclamation de la Commune*. Paris: Gallimard, 1965.

Lefebvre, Henri. *La Production de l'espace*. Paris: Anthropos, 1974.

Lefebvre, Henri. *La Révolution urbaine*. Paris: Gallimard, 1970.

Lefebvre, Henri. *La Vie quotidienne dans le monde moderne*. Paris: Gallimard, 1968.

Lefrançais, Gustave. *Etude sur le mouvement communaliste à Paris en 1871*. Neuchatel: Guillaume fils, 1871.

Lefrançais, Gustave. *Souvenirs d'un révolutionnaire*. [1886]; rpt. Paris: Société Encyclopédique Française and Editions de la Téte de Feuilles, 1972.

Le Play, Frédéric. *Les Ouvriers Européens*. [1864] Tours: A. Maine, 1877-79.

Le Play, Frédéric. *La Réforme sociale en France, déduite de l'observation comparée des peuples Européens*. Paris: H. Plon, 1864.

Levasseur, Emile. "L'Etude et l'enseignement de la géographie." *Séances et travaux de l'Académie des sciences morales et politiques* 46 (1871): 418-30.

Lidsky, Paul. *Les Ecrivains contre la Commune*. Paris: Maspero, 1982.

Lipovetsky, Gilles. *L'Ere du vide. Essai sur l'individualisme contemporain*. Paris: Gallimard, 1983.

Lissagaray, Prosper-Oliver. *L'Histoire de la Commune de 1871*. [1876]; rpt. Paris: Maspero, 1967.

Lukács, Georg. *The Theory of the Novel*. Trans. Anya Bostock. Cambridge, Mass.: MIT Press, 1971.

McKay, Donald Vernon. "Colonialism in the French Geographical Movement 1871-1881." *Geographical Review* 33 (April 1943): 214-32.

Mallarmé, Stéphane. *Oeuvres complètes*. Ed. Henri Mondor and G. Jean-Aubry. Paris: Gallimard, 1945.

Malon, Benoit. *La Troisième défaite du prolétariat français*. Neuchatel: Guillaume fils, 1871.

Maran, René. *Batouala*. Paris: Albin Michel, 1965.

Marx, Karl. *Capital*. Vol. 1. Harmondsworth: Penguin, 1979.

Marx, Karl. *Early Writings*. Trans. Rodney Livingstone and Gregor Benton. Intro. Lucio Colletti. New York: Vintage, 1975.

Marx, Karl. *Grundrisse: Foundations of the Critique of Political Economy*. Trans. Martin Nicolaus. London: New Left Review, 1973.

Marx, Karl, and Friedrich Engels. *The Communist Manifesto*. Ed. D. Ryazanoff. New York: Russell & Russell, 1963.

Marx, Karl, and Friedrich Engels. *Writings on the Paris Commune*. Ed. H. Draper. New York: Monthly Review Press, 1971.

Marx, Karl, and V. I. Lenin. *The Civil War in France: The Paris Commune*. Intro. Friedrich Engels. New York: International Publishers, 1940.

Matarasso, Henri, and Pierre Petitfils. *Vie d'Arthur Rimbaud*. Paris: Hachette, 1962.

Meier, Olga, ed. *The Daughters of Karl Marx: Family Correspondence 1866-1898*. Trans. Faith Evans. Intro. Sheila Rowbotham. New York: Harcourt Brace Jovanovich, 1982.

Mendès, Catulle. *Les 73 journées de la Commune*. Paris: E. Lachaud, 1871.

Mesnard, Jules. *Les Merveilles de l'Exposition de 1867*. Paris: Imp. de L'ahure, 1867.

Michel, Louise. *La Commune*. Paris: Editions Stock, 1898.

Miller, Michael. *The Bon Marché, Bourgeois Culture and the Department Store, 1869-1920*. Princeton, N.J.: Princeton University Press, 1981.

Moretti, Franco. *Signs Taken for Wonders. Essays in the Sociology of Literary Forms*. Trans. Susan Fischer, David Forgacs, and David Miller. London: Verso, 1983.

Moretti, Franco. *The Way of the World*. London: Verso, 1987.

Murphy, Agnes. *The Ideology of French Imperialism, 1871-1881*. Washington, D.C.: Catholic University of America Press, 1948.

Murphy, Steve. "La Figure du forgeron." *Parade Sauvage*, Bulletin 2 (January 1986): 15-23.

Murphy, Steve. "Le Regard de Rimbaud." *Revue de sciences humaines* 1 (1984): 57-62.

Murphy, Steve. "Rimbaud et la Commune?" In *Rimbaud multiple. Colloque de Cérisy*, pp. 50-65. Ed. Alain Borer. Gourdon: Bedou & Touzot, 1985.

Nietzsche, Friedrich. *Ecce Homo. How One Becomes What One Is.* Trans. R. J. Hollingdale. Hammondsworth: Penguin, 1979.

Nietzsche, Friedrich. *The Portable Nietzsche.* Trans. and ed. Walter Kaufmann. New York: Viking, 1954.

Nodier, Charles. "De l'utilité morale de l'instruction pour le peuple." In *Rêveries*, pp. 173-89. Paris: Plasma, 1979.

Paris sous la Commune, par un témoin fidèle: La Photographie. Paris, 1871(?).

Le Père Duchêne, December 7, 1869.

Petitfils, Pierre. *Rimbaud.* Paris: Juillard, 1982.

Picard, Ernest. "Préface." *Révue de géographie* 1 (January-June 1877): 1-3.

Portales, Charles. *Des Mendiantes et des vagabonds.* Nimes: Baldy & Roger, 1854.

Porter, Carolyn. "Are We Being Historical Yet?" Proceedings of the "States of Theory" conference, University of California at Irvine, April 1987.

Poulet, Georges. *La Poésie éclatée.* Paris: PUF, 1980.

Poulot, Denis. *Le Sublime, ou le travailleur comme il est en 1870, et ce qu'il peut être.* Paris: Maspero, 1980.

Rancière, Jacques. "Le Bon temps ou la barrière des plaisirs." *Révoltes logiques* 7 (1978): 25-66.

Rancière, Jacques. *La Nuit des prolétaires.* Paris: Fayard, 1981.

Rancière, Jacques. *Le Philosophe et ses pauvres.* Paris: Fayard, 1983.

Rancière, Jacques. "La Représentation de l'ouvrier ou la classe impossible." In *Le retrait de la politique*, pp. 99-112. Ed. Phillipe Lacoue-Labarthe and Jean-Luc Nancy. Paris: Galilée, 1983.

Rancière, Jacques. "Ronds de fumée: (Les poètes ouvriers dans la France de Louis-Philippe)." *Revue des sciences humaines*, no. 190 (1983): 31-47.

Reclus, Elie. *La Commune de Paris: au jour le jour; 19 mars-28 mai, 1871.* Paris: Schleicher frères, 1908.

Reclus, Elisée. *An Anarchist on Anarchy.* London: Tochatti, 1897.

Reclus, Elisée. *Correspondance.* Vols. I and II. Paris: Schleicher, 1911.

Reclus, Elisée. *L'Homme et la terre.* [1905-8]; rpt. ed. Béatrice Giblin, Paris: Maspero, 1982.

Reclus, Elisée. "Preface." F. Domela Nieuwenhuis. *Le Socialisme en danger.* Paris: Stock, 1897.

Reclus, Paul. *Les Frères Elie et Elisée Reclus.* Paris: Les Amis d'Elisée Reclus, 1964.

Rifkin, Adrian. "Cultural Movement and the Paris Commune." *Art History* 2 (June 1979): 201-20.

Rifkin, Adrian. "No Particular Thing to Mean." *Block* 8 (1983): 36-45.

Rifkin, Adrian. "Well-formed Phrases: Some Limits of Meaning in Political Print at the End of the Second Empire." *Oxford Art Journal* 8 (1985): 20-28.

Rimbaud, Arthur. *Complete Works.* Trans. Paul Schmidt. New York: Harper & Row, 1976.

Rimbaud, Arthur. *Illuminations.* Trans. Louise Varèse. New York: New Directions, 1957.

Rimbaud, Arthur. *Oeuvres complètes.* Intro. Tristan Tzara. Lausanne: Henri Kaeser, 1948.

Rimbaud, Arthur. *Oeuvres complètes.* Ed. Rolland de Renéville and Jules Mouquet. Paris: Gallimard, 1967.

Rimbaud, Arthur. *Poésies.* Ed. Louis Forestier. Paris: Gallimard, 1973.

Rimbaud, Arthur. *A Season in Hell and The Drunken Boat.* Trans. Louise Varèse. New York: New Directions, 1961.

Rivière, Louis. *Un Siècle de lutte contre le vagabondage.* Paris: Bureaux de la revue politique et parlémentaire, 1899.

Rollet, C. *Enfance abandonnée, vicieux, insoumis, vagabonds.* Clermont-Ferrand: Mont-Louis, 1899.

Ross, Kristin. "Artaud and Van Gogh: Reading in the Imaginary." *Enclitic* 7 (Fall 1984): 116-25.

Rossel, Louis. *Mémoires, procès et correspondance.* Paris: J. J. Pauvert, 1960.

Rougerie, Jacques. *Procès des Communards.* Paris: Gallimard, 1978.

Sahlins, Marshall. *Stone Age Economic.* Chicago: Aldine Atherton, 1972.

Santos, Milton. *Pour une géographie nouvelle*. Paris: Publisud, 1984.

Sarrazin, Hélène. *Elisée Reclus ou la passion du monde*. Paris: Découverte, 1985.

Sartre, Jean-Paul. *What Is Literature?* Trans. Bernard Frechtman. New York: Harper & Row, 1965.

Sartre, Jean-Paul. *Saint-Genet: Actor and Martyr*. Trans. Bernard Frechtman. New York: Braziller, 1963.

Schulkind, Eugène. "La Commune de 1871 à travers sa littérature." *La Pensée*, nos. 35 and 36 (March-April 1951, May-June 1951): 29-82.

Shanin, Teodor, ed. *Late Marx and the Russian Road: Marx and the "Peripheries of Capitalism."* New York: Monthly Review Press, 1983.

Spicer, Jack. "A Fake Novel about the Life of Arthur Rimbaud." In *The Collected Books*, pp. 149-167. Los Angeles: Black Sparrow Press, 1975.

Taussig, Michael. *The Devil and Commodity Fetishism in South America*. Chapel Hill: University of North Carolina Press, 1980.

Tchernoff, J. *Le Parti républicaine au coup d'état et sous le Second Empire*. Paris: Pedone, 1901.

Terdiman, Richard. *Discourse/Counter-Discourse: The Theory and Practice of Symbolic Resistance in Nineteenth-Century France*. Ithaca, N.Y.: Cornell University Press, 1985.

Tersen, Emile. *Vive la Commune!* Paris: Editions Sociales, 1951.

Thomas, Edith. *Les "Pétroleuses."* Paris: Gallimard, 1963.

Thomas, Paul. *Karl Marx and the Anarchists*. London: Routledge & Kegan Paul, 1980.

Todorov, Tzvetan. "A Complication of Text: The *Illuminations*." In *French Literary Theory Today*, pp. 223-37. Ed. Tzvetan Todorov, trans. R. Carter. Cambridge: Cambridge University Press, 1982.

Todorov, Tzvetan. "Poetry without Verse." In *The Prose Poem in France*, pp. 60-78. Ed. Mary Ann Caws and Hermine Riffaterre. New York: Columbia University Press, 1983.

Vallès, Jules. *L'Insurgé*. Paris: Garnier, 1970.

Varloot, Jean, ed. *Les Poètes de la Commune*. Paris: Les éditeurs français réunis, 1951.

Verlaine, Paul. *Poèmes érotiques*. Paris: Editions Jean-Claude Lattès, 1979.

Verlaine, Paul. *Rimbaud raconté par Paul Verlaine*. Ed. Jules Mouquet. Paris: Mercure de France, 1934.

Vermersch, Eugène. *Les Hommes du jour*. Paris: Towne, 187? [n.d.].

[Victoria and Albert Museum.] *The Franco-Prussian War and the Commune in Caricature 1870-1871*. Intro. Susan Lambert. London: Thanet Press, 1971.

Vidal de la Blache, Paul. *Tableau de la géographie de la France*. Introduction to Ernest Lavisse, *Histoire de France*. Volume I. Paris: Hachette, 1903.

Vološinov, V. N. *Marxism and the Philosophy of Language*. Trans. Ladislav Matejka and I. R. Titunik. Cambridge, Mass.: Harvard University Press, 1986.

Weber, Max. *The Protestant Ethic and the Spirit of Capitalism*. Trans. Talcott Parsons. New York: Scribners, 1958.

Weinrich, Harald. *Metafora e menzogna: la serenita dell'arte*. Bologna: Il Molina, 1976.

Williams, Rosalind. *Dream Worlds: Mass Consumption in Late Nineteenth-Century France*. Berkeley: University of California Press, 1982.

Wolman, Gil J. *Résumé des chapitres précédents*. Paris: Editions Spiess, 1981.

Wright, Gordon. *France in Modern Times*. New York: Norton, 1981.

Zeldin, Theodore. *France 1848-1945: Taste and Corruption*. Oxford: Oxford University Press, 1980.

Zola, Emile. *Au bonheur des dames*. Paris: Gallimard, 1980.

Zola, Emile. *La Débacle*. Paris: Livre de poche, 1979.

Index

Index

Theory and History of Literature

Since 1981, **Kristin Ross** has been teaching literature at the University of California, Santa Cruz. She received her Ph.D. in French and comparative literature from Yale University, where she was granted the Kanzer Fellowship for Psychoanalytic Studies in the Humanities. She is the author of essays on Proust, Artaud, Prévost, and Blanchot, and co-editor, with Alice Kaplan, of an edition of *Yale French Studies* entitled *Everyday Life* (fall 1987).

Terry Eagleton is a fellow and tutor in English at Wadham College, Oxford. His books include *The Rape of Clarissa*, *Literary Theory: An Introduction* (both published by Minnesota), *Walter Benjamin, Criticism and Ideology*, *The Function of Criticism*, *William Shakespeare*, and *Against the Grain*.